# GUNS, GOLD & CARAVANS

# Guns, Gold

# Caravans

The Extraordinary Life and Times of Fred Meyer Schroder,
Frontiersman and Soldier of Fortune, in California,
Mexico, Alaska and China, including his Discovery
of the Mysterious Pyramids of Shensi and
Rescue of the Boy Emperor.

ROBERT EASTON

CAPRA PRESS • 1978
Santa Barbara

*For Cleaver and Andy,*
*and Jane who makes it possible*

Jacket design by Margaret Dodds.
Layout and map by Marcia Burtt.
Editorial assistance, Ann Koepfli.
Typesetting by Graham Mackintosh.
Camerawork by Santa Barbara Photoengraving.
Printed by R. R. Donnelley & Sons.
First edition published May 1978.

**Library of Congress Cataloging in Publication Data**

Easton, Robert Olney.
   Guns, gold, and caravans.

    1. Schroder, Fred.  2. Pioneers—United States
—Biography.  3. Soliders of fortune—Biography.
4. China—Description and travel—1901-1948.
I. Title.
CT275.S3455E2     909.81'092'4   [B]    77-25022
ISBN  0-88496-122-2

CAPRA PRESS
631 State Street
Santa Barbara, California 93101

# CONTENTS

## AUTHOR'S NOTE

*On assignment from a national magazine I rang the doorbell of a modest brown-shingled cottage on a quiet side street in Oakland, California. An editor was sending me to interview a man he described euphorically as "the last of those veteran frontiersmen, explorers, prospectors, soldiers of fortune" who roamed the earth when it was considerably younger than it is now. I half expected to find a white haired colossus. The man who opened the door was short and compact. He didn't seem old. Greeting me, his voice was firm, his movements vigorous. He smiled readily but I noticed a don't-meddle-with-me expression about his blue eyes and hawk's nose. At ninety-two he was not going gently into any good-nights.*

*Fred Meyer Schroder's reluctance to talk about himself proved a barrier at first but gradually I elicited material which seemed fascinating. As I got to know him, looked through his scrapbooks and photograph albums, met his friends, discovered the fabric of his life, I felt like an explorer of lost worlds. With him I pursued horse thieves along the Mexican border of the 1870s, prospected for gold in Alaska and the Yukon before, during, and after the Klondike Rush, met Mother Woods— the first female sourdough in the Far North—and Molly Dexter, another Arctic heroine, caravanned in Mongolia and Tibet, collected animal specimens for the Smithsonian Museum in Manchuria and Siberia, saw huge flat-topped pyramids in China.*

*Sometimes I doubted his credibility. I read everything I could lay hands on dealing with the events and places he described, talked to his old companions, scholarly experts, eyewitnesses. They corroborated Schroder. I began to realize that here was a common man of most uncommon dimensions. In his person Far West became Far North and Far East. Busy living the strenuous life, unaware of doing anything particularly momentous, he closed the gap whereby western culture encircled the globe.*

*Sometimes I thought him harsh and cruel. I reminded myself that experience is often harsh and cruel. And if, paradoxically considering his exceptional characteristics, he had an ordinary man's interest in the big bang, the big buck, the big drink, the big killing, it was typically fitting and proper. His "we" was unconditional. It included Homo sapiens regardless of circumstance.*

*What consistently impressed me was his earthy good humor. Relax, brother, it seemed to say. Don't take anything too seriously including yourself. Learn to accept that universal thump Herman Melville talks about—laugh at it and with it. It won't kill you. Or if it does the loss won't matter much in the long course of the world's history.*

*This is his story as he told it to me. He was a natural storyteller— representative of that oral age epitomized by Homer, refreshed in our memory by Alex Haley's* Roots, *the age which still exists in less developed countries and in isolated regions of our own, where communication is primarily by word of mouth and speaking and word-feel are often elevated to a fine art.*

*Sometimes when talking to him I realized I was conversing with another age, across an abyss of time, so near and yet so far away—those plains with ten thousand antelope and gazelle, those skies dark with ducks, those trees uncut, those streams unpolluted, man still in the minority, not oppressing nature but surviving among other creatures who share her habitats, taking according to his needs—indeed powerless to take much more. By listening carefully could I divine that secret truth, that answer, which seems always to lurk just behind or just ahead of us and which will explain once and for all where we have been, where we are going and why we are here?*

*The dozen or so articles Schroder and I published together barely touched the surface of his experience. I decided that someday I would deal with it fully—in his own voice and idiom because they are in many ways the best measure of a man and his time.*

*That is how Fred Meyer Schroder became the "I" of what follows. Appropriately his story begins at its beginning: with a boy, a dog, and the life of a border stock ranch a hundred years ago. I've added notes where they seemed appropriate.*

—R. E.

# I

# GUNS ON THE MEXICAN BORDER:
## 1877 - 1894

# 1.  A Gift From a Chief

Mother died the summer I was nine. That fall the Indians came as usual to gather acorns and piñon nuts in our valley and as usual one of the chiefs came to the house to ask permission of the Old Man, my bachelor uncle and guardian, Mother's brother.

The request was merely a formality since the Old Man rented much of their reservation for pasturage for a rental of two steers a year—"two barbecues a year"—and things were understood, but this morning the Chief had something to add. He was wearing the red flannel shirt and loose fitting Levi overalls of the 1870s, and as he came slowly up the walk between the rosebushes, he pulled a brindle puppy from his hip pocket and handed her to me. It was his way of saying he and his people—waiting down the lane with their burros, blankets, and huge cone-shaped carrying baskets—had heard of Mother's death and were sorry. They were the Capitán Grandes, our good friends. As I glimpsed them, framed behind him under the oaks, their sympathy came up to me like something out of the earth itself.

"Ugh, lap dog, eh?" the Old Man scoffed. The minute I'd taken her in my arms she'd begun to wriggle and lick at me.

We had plenty of dogs around the place, mainly Southern foxhounds to which the Old Man was partial, but no pets. He didn't believe in pets so I'd never had a dog of my own. Yet now he couldn't very well offend the Chief by ordering me to refuse a gift, and still he hated to see his rule against pets broken.

While he fumed I thanked the Captain—speaking Spanish as most of our Indians did—and set the pup down. She scampered away among the rosebushes and tried to make friends with a mother hen and chicks, got soundly pecked on the nose and came scampering back, tail between her legs, kie-yie-ing.

The Old Man snorted. "See there? She hasn't got enough gumption to bite her own fleas!"

For the first time in my life I stood up to him. I wanted that dog. She represented something precious I might have and something precious I'd just lost.

"She's a *good* dog," I retorted. "Look at that short head and strong jaw! She's got bull in her!"

He glared down at me over his chin whiskers. "Bull? Indian mongrel is what she's got. But no bull!"

"She has too got bull!" I wrapped my arms about her protectively. "She'll catch wild cattle for us some day—won't you, Jip? I'll call her Jip!"

The Chief had begun to smile. It became necessary for the Old Man to assert himself. "I know what she'll catch and you too, young mister, if you're both not careful! A boy's bad enough! A boy with a dog I can imagine! We'll give her a try, see? If she makes good, she stays. If not, she goes!"

The Old Man seldom failed to make himself clear. He'd studied to be a surgeon at the University of Heidelberg in the days before the War Between the States and was accurate with words as with most other things. He owned dozens of books which he read far into the night, seated in his easy chair at the fireside, a pitcher of red mission wine at his elbow, the elbow bending more and more freely as the night wore on. He smoked a big hook-shape meerschaum pipe he'd brought from Germany and they told me he gave me puffs of it when I was a baby, saying tobacco was better than milk to grow up on. He used to take me hunting while I was still very small. We'd be riding along. "Get me that squirrel!" he'd command. Maybe I hadn't even seen the squirrel, one of the blue-gray variety that jump around through our California oaks. No matter. I'd have to get off my horse and go look for it. By that time maybe it had ducked into its hole. "Well, why didn't you shoot it before it ducked?" And if I hit it in the body instead of the head, I got criticized for that too. I was never good enough. I suggested I might do better if he bought me one of the new Winchester repeating rifles which had just come onto the market but he snorted and kept me using the old muzzle-loader dating from Andrew Jackson's time. It nearly knocked me flat every time I fired it.

The Old Man—his real name was Frederick David Conrad Meyer*—had come west from South Carolina with Mother and Father following the war. They'd owned property in Kansas City, then in Starr County, Texas, grown restless, moved on. The spot they finally chose to settle was our valley and oak grove on the southern slopes of six-thousand-foot-high Cuyamaca Mountain, not far from the Mexican border, looking down toward San Diego and the sea. My father was killed a few months after their arrival in a fight with horse thieves in Horse Thief Canyon, a cleft in the wilderness that ran south into Mexico. Later the Old Man was ambushed there, too, and received a load of buckshot in his back. By that time I was old enough to remember how they'd carried him into the house and dug the buckshot out of him, using his own surgical instruments, no anesthetic but whiskey, he yelling at them not to be afraid but to dig deeper and get it all out. For months afterward he couldn't ride a horse but drove around in a buckboard, his rifle under the seat.

Being left in his custody was like being left alone with a bear. He was cantankerous, short, thick-set and had a tuft of chin whiskers like a grizzly's.

"Keep both eyes open!" he'd yell, seeing me aim with one eye, and I did learn to keep them both open and to shoot a slow-flying bird like a meadowlark out of the air.

He relented enough that first night, however, to let Jip sleep in a box on the front porch. "But don't go near her if she cries!" he warned. "There's no quicker way to spoil a pup!"

Well, of course she cried. She was away from home and mother for the first time. Why shouldn't she cry?

He bellowed back at her like a wild bull from his bed in the room next mine. After he'd grown quiet I slipped out from under the covers and across the floor.

I had to go through his room to reach the porch. I could see his whiskers protruding over the counterpane and his six-shooter

*At the end of the text readers will find additional information concerning persons, places and events dealt with on this and subsequent pages.

hanging in its holster from the bedpost. He kept it handy because horse thieves still visited us by the light of the moon, or a bobcat might get after the chickens and peacocks who roosted in the oaks of the grove. I shivered as I tiptoed across the floor, trying to plant my bare feet on the lion and deer skins wherever possible. I was afraid that if he waked suddenly he might shoot me by mistake!

At last I reached the safety of the porch. The minute I took Jip in my arms she quieted. Her little wet nose and warm tongue went all over me in the dark. Holding her close I crept back to bed.

Next morning when the Old Man shouted at me that it was five o'clock, I delayed finishing dressing until he was dressed and gone. Then I slipped Jip out from under the covers and out of doors.

Night after night my stratagem was repeated. Not till long afterward did I discover he was awake and watching me most of the time.

# 2.  To Be a Man

I was taught that Charleston, South Carolina, was our home, that my people had amounted to something there, that we were Rebels and proud of it, that we had not lost the war by being outfought but by being too few, and that Mr. Lincoln's name was never to be mentioned in our house and Robert E. Lee's birthday observed with solemnity. Later I learned that unlike the Old Man my parents were of the postwar generation. Reaching maturity young, they wanted something new and different. Risking all they owned, they'd embarked with him on a venture into that great unknown, the Far West.

Since Jip was my only playmate except for the children of the Indians and Spanish-speaking vaqueros who lived on the ranch, we spent many happy hours together whenever the Old Man wasn't around. Sometimes we hunted the bumblebees who lived in holes in the meadow below the house where the Sweetwater River ran cold and clear from Cuyamaca Peak and the wild grass grew to my waist. The first bee to emerge from its hole was mine—I swatting it with a wooden paddle made for the occasion. The next was Jip's—she swatting it with her paw. When all the bees had been accounted for, we dug up their comb and shared it. You've never tasted honey till you've tasted bumblebee honey. It's twice as sweet as ordinary honey.

We had fun, too, Sundays hunting wood rats with the Indians. The rats lived in large piles of sticks and leaves heaped up as high as four feet above the ground. They were more like squirrels than rats, their meat clean and delicious, and the Indians prized it highly for stews. The bucks would climb on top of their nests and jab with long poles until the rats ran out. Then the squaws, kids, dogs, and Jip and I went into action with sticks, clubs, bows and arrows.

[15]

Our arrows had brushwood points hardened in fire and forced into the ends of hollow reeds. We feathered them with hawk or chicken feathers bound in place with sinew from a deer's back, twisting the feathers slightly to give the arrow a revolving motion in flight. The rifling in a rifle barrel does much the same thing for a bullet. Our bows were willow and our bowstrings babiche trimmed to an even thickness by eye. The eye was an everyday tool and we learned to depend on it.

I grew quite accurate with bow and arrow and could kill birds or rats at fifteen yards, but I worried lest Jip fail to discover what her teeth were for. She seemed to think wood rats were made for her to play with and was bitten around the nose and mouth repeatedly before she learned to bite back. And the Old Man would inevitably be watching and turn away in disgust.

The day came, as I knew it would, when he took her with him and the grown dogs to hunt on the Peak. It was her trial. I could have gone, I was too nervous to. I lay all of that still warm October morning in the barrel-stave hammock strung between two oaks in the grove, listening to the cry of the hounds, now strong, now faint. I wondered if they were singing Jip's praises or disgrace. Toward noon I knew the worst. I saw her slink home alone and go to the kitchen door with the cats.

The Old Man rode in not far behind, the pack trailing after. "Cottontail rabbit thumped the ground a time or two and she was gone!" he stormed. "I'd have put a bullet through her if I could have caught her!"

"You can't shoot her!" I flared up. "She's my dog!" And then with sudden inspiration I added: "Besides, she's all I've got!"

I saw him hesitate. Maybe it wasn't fair to use my orphan's state against him, but I was desperate. He'd adored my mother, his only sister, the only woman he ever loved, really, and, until her death, the only link between him and their old life. She was a tiny mite of a thing, feisty and full of fun whenever she wasn't ill. The year before she died she'd taken me back to Charleston and exhibited me to our relatives there, the Bischoffs, Krackes, Meyers, Schroders, and I'd met the cousin who reportedly delighted the city three weeks after Appomattox by riding into town on the horse of a Union general, and I met Uncle Kracke, a noted rascal, who'd cornered the rice market during the Union blockade of the port and made a fortune when two of his ships from New Orleans slipped through the Federal fleet. We stayed with my aunt in a large frame house next the Old German Artillery Hall. Wearing Little Lord Fauntleroy white collar and knee britches, I distinguished myself there by tying an inflated pig's bladder containing some dried peas to the cat's tail and watching the cat sail around the room and out the window. On another occasion I made slippers for the cat out of walnut shells and watched her go skating across the polished floor. We left soon. I was glad. I hated wearing suits. And young as I was I could sense it was all over in Charleston: here a leg missing, there an arm, and all the talk and laughter covering a deep and bitter gloom.

Back in our new land, trundling up the fifty miles of winding dusty road from San Diego in the Old Man's surrey, smelling the pungent odors of the chaparral and seeing the big raw sandstone rocks and pines ahead, I had that feeling of anticipation I was destined to have all my life on leaving civilization and entering wild country.

"All right," the Old Man said now, after thinking about it a minute, "we'll give Jip another chance."

This time it was a wild sow. Wild pigs—in reality domestic ones gone wild—had run upon the Peak since Spanish times. They were big, black and mean. The boars weighed up to four hundred pounds and could rip your horse's belly open with one slash of their tusks. Even a medium-sized sow like this one could snap a dog's leg with one bite.

The old hounds got sensible holds on her ears but Jip, being a pup, walked trustingly up to her face. The sow landed on her with everything she had. I was present this time and wanted to interfere but the Old Man wouldn't let me.

"Let her make her own way!" he growled.

In the end I was grateful. Little by little Jip realized that pig wasn't doing right by her. Growl by growl the bulldog in her began to come out. Long after the Old Man had put a bullet through the sow's head, she was still chewing one hairy black ear.

"Mighty hard on 'em after they're dead!" he scoffed. I didn't care. I knew I had the best and bravest dog in the world, riding home on my saddle in front of me, bruised and bloodied but not beaten. I doctored her with some of the salves and ointments from the Old Man's medicine cabinet. He didn't practice medicine regularly but occasionally helped neighbors in distress and kept a supply of potassium permanganate and carbolic acid handy along with scalpel and forceps.

"Any dog can handle a pig," he observed that night at supper while Mary served us steaming hot biscuits with gravy and pig's liver. "Just wait till she meets a cat!"

Indian Mary, patient and kind, had been Mother's house-keeper and to a degree my mammy Southern style. She was dignity, maternity, stability all rolled into one. In the Indian way she never raised her voice to me, never scolded, tolerated all my pranks and foolishness, so I loved her deeply. She imparted to me some of her stoic acceptance of life, a quality she expressed in the way she moved and spoke and in the beautiful baskets she wove out of coiled grass, creating designs and patterns from her imagination and tribal tradition. With Cap Hulburd and Justin Robinson, the Old Man's cronies and perpetual guests, Mary constituted our family now. She was paid no money. Her salary was our home and its life and whatever she needed to eat or wear and a gold piece now and then.

A week or so after the pig episode the dogs treed a big tufted-ear lynx up the canyon above the house. The Old Man shot his legs out from under him with his .44 Colt and down he came, crippled but with plenty of fight left. That was the way we trained our dogs.

As the pack jumped him he caught Jip with his teeth through the skin of her upper lip. Imagine a lynx's teeth through the skin of your upper lip. She cried and cried. She begged him to let her go. But he wouldn't. That was the making of her. She had to stay and take it. After a while she got tired of taking it. Despite the way he had her, she squirmed and sank her teeth into him. Tooth to tooth, eye to eye, they chewed it out. Long after he was dead she was still chewing.

The bulldog in her came out that day and never went back. Cats became her special hate. Every time she saw one, she re-membered what that lynx had done to her.

I was coming along too. I could shoot nearly on a par with the Old Man now, pistol (old-fashioned .32 percussion cap) or rifle, left hand or right. Double insurance, he called it. There was not much pity in him. He seldom mentioned my father or mother. And he used to quote the Parthian maxim: "Teach a boy to ride and tell the truth."

So matters stood when one day he said to me: "Go up onto the Mesa and get us a mess of quail for supper!" By "mess" he didn't mean fifteen or twenty but half a sack. I got our double-barreled 12-gauge hammer gun and some of the brass shot shells we loaded at home, saddled Guatay, my bay pony, tied a gunny sack behind the saddle, called to Jip and Hec, her boyfriend, a black-and-white foxhound, and started up the steep trail toward the Mesa. It was early February, clear and warm, the grass greening after the rains, the wild lilac blooming so thickly in places its fragrance almost made me sick.

On top of the Mesa we found the quail feeding in openings in the chaparral. Jip pointed them for me in her usual way—she looked not at them but at me. She'd watch me till she saw that I saw the quail.

We'd collected nearly half a sack and Hec was off somewhere scouting around when all of a sudden we heard a deep *boe-woe*, which meant he'd found a trail. After a minute his voice rose sharply. That meant the trail was hot. Jip went to join him. Her nose wasn't much good so she left cold trails to the hounds, but when they struck a hot one she could tell by their voices and was gone to join the fun.

I threw the sack of quail across the back of my saddle and galloped after her. Hec's voice had reached frenzy pitch by this time. When I stopped to get a bearing on it, I heard Jip's shrill war cry too. "They're really onto something!" I thought. The brush held me back but finally I located them in a watercut in dense growth about a hundred yards off the trail. Tying Guatay to a limb, I crept up along the edge of the cut, gun in hand, until I was opposite the place where the din came from. There, very carefully, I peeked over.

Thirty feet below me, hemmed against my side of the bank by the dogs, was a big male mountain lion. He was crouched facing them, his back to me, his right forepaw cocked like a boxer's hand, tail switching angrily from side to side. The sight of him took my breath away.

Next to horse thieves, lions were our greatest menace. They preyed voraciously on our colts, and since horses were our chief crop—we raised them by the score for stagecoach companies as well as for saddle and carriage stock—the lions' depredations were a serious matter. I'd seen the ripped-open carcasses of colts they'd killed, and the ground torn up for half an acre where they'd fought with our jennies. We ran jennies with our mares and colts as protection against lions because a burro's senses are much keener than a horse's and a jenny will give warning of the approach of a lion and will fight him to the death to protect her mares and colts. I'd seen the bloody condition of a jenny after these battles and wondered how the lion looked. Nevertheless, like most boys in our part of the world I had a powerful ambition to kill a lion and achieve a status amounting to manhood.

Jip came too close. He belted her with his paw. She flew through the air and landed on some rocks ten feet away. I thought her killed or badly crippled but back she came game as ever. It encouraged me. Instead of departing for home and help as I'd been thinking of doing, I emptied both barrels of the 12-gauge into his backside.

I never stopped to think that I was using only quail shot. The result was much the same as if I'd shot him in the rear with hot pepper. He went straight in the air clawing and squalling like a cat with firecrackers tied to his tail, came down, bowled the dogs over, and departed for Old Mexico with Jip and Hec hot behind.

"Guess I'll have to get me a gun that will kill something!" I said aloud gruffly, the way one does to buck one's self up.

I jumped on Guatay and galloped for home. The farther I got from the lion, the braver I felt. By the time I'd reached the kitchen door and pitched my sack of quail at Cap Hulburd, who happened to be standing there, I felt like killing lions. The Old Man was nowhere to be seen. That suited me. I wanted to handle this matter myself. Without a word to Cap, I hurried to the bunkhouse, grabbed my Winchester carbine, a repeater and a recent present from the Old Man, and charged back up the trail to the Mesa as fast as Guatay could go.

Nearing the top, I found myself hoping the dogs had lost him.

He'd looked awfully big when he'd shot up in the air. But when I got on top I heard them in the distance. They'd stayed with him. I'd have to.

I raced through the brush at full speed. Sometimes just plain velocity helps in cases like that. It was thorny and dusty. It scratched and choked me and again the odor of the lilacs nearly suffocated me but on I went, and finally, in one of the thickest, thorniest patches of brush and lilac, centered around a big bushy liveoak, I found them.

I couldn't see the lion but could hear him. He was up in that oak and he left no doubt how he was feeling. He was *mad*. The dogs were making a continuous racket around the trunk and all together there was a good deal of noise and confusion.

I thought how nice it would be to shoot him from the saddle where I sat safe. But there was no chance of that. If I wanted him, I'd have to get off and go get him. I started to get off and remembered I was only twelve, a long way from home, and there was a wounded lion up in that tree; and then I started to get off again and again I remembered. Finally I got off.

Clutching my rifle tightly with both hands, I slipped forward nervously through the lilacs. They were like trees ten or twelve feet high. I kept peering up through them, trying to locate him, not wanting to walk right underneath a wounded lion, but he was nearly overhead when I saw him. I realized instantly what my quail shot had done. It had inflated him. He looked twice as big as before. Of course I was looking *up* at him now, not down, and that makes a difference.

I aimed for his neck. It was a shot I'd made successfully dozens of times on rabbits and deer. I squeezed the trigger, knew I'd hit him. Next, a body came hurtling toward me but it wasn't a dead body. Whether by accident or design, he jumped almost on top of me, crashing down through oak leaves and lilac branches like the whole sky falling, and I was trying to get out from under, and getting caught in the brush, and trying to lever another shell into the chamber, when he landed six feet from me.

I saw his wild yellow eyes. I saw the blood on his neck where my bullet had hit. Unable to move, I could only watch, and I saw that for a fraction of a second he was bewildered by his wound, his fall, and the sight of me. Then he would come and kill me.

In that fraction of a second Jip appeared behind him. I saw her clamp her teeth on his long skinny tail. I saw him debate which to go for, her or me. Finally he chose her, and there was just room enough among the lilacs for him to whirl and hit her with all his might.

She flew through the air. She'd be going yet, I think, but a lilac trunk stopped her. It knocked a *yow* out of her which told me she was still alive. Before he could turn back to me, Hec was on him. Then Jip flew at him again, streaming blood, voicing her outrage. I managed to get another cartridge into the chamber and put a bullet through his head. After which the world began to spin. I saw stars and sat down hard.

My faintness lasted only a moment. When I came to, Jip was licking my face. "Why get upset now?" she seemed to say. "It's all over!" I could see the lion's muscles twitching under his hide, and all around was the warm fetid odor of blood and death.

Half an hour later I was riding proudly down the trail, hoping to find the Old Man and say offhand, "Killed me a lion up on the Mesa. Got time to come help me skin him?"

I met him coming toward me at a trot, his sorrel in a sweat, his vest tails flapping. "What's all this rifle shooting?" he demanded. Rifle shooting could mean trouble. I saw the butt of his own Winchester protruding from its saddle scabbard.

"Just killed me a—" I started to say, but before I finished he broke in.

"What's the matter? Couldn't you skin him yourself?"

Burning with chagrin, I followed him to where the lion lay. Then I saw with satisfaction that a serious look crossed his face.

He got down and made the official examination. Most of my quail shot had lodged between the lion's outer hide and his thin inner skin and had been eating into him like acid. My first bullet had penetrated his neck between the jugular and the bone, missing his spine by a fraction.

"What's the matter, couldn't you break his neck?" the Old Man demanded sarcastically.

I said nothing. Life had gone sour.

"Next time make that first shot count, you hear?"

"Yes, sir."

"You might not have a chance for a second."

"Yes, sir."

"But for Jip, you might not be here!"

"Yes, sir."

He gave her a pat on the head for congratulations and a chuck under the chin for her wounds. Then softly he began to laugh. It was a sound he made only when truly amused. Starting deep down, it rose until his whole body shook. In the voice of one man speaking to another, he said, "I can't get over your warming his ass with that quail shot! That really was rare!"

# 3.  Yaqui Tom

My upbringing wasn't all saddle leather and gun smoke. In addition to the dozens of books in our library, there were the many bound volumes of *Harper's* and *The Century*, regarded as nearly as sacred as the Bible and there was Justin Robinson, the Old Man's crony and perpetual guest, to teach me my three "R's." Gentle and effeminate, Jus had been a concert singer in Europe and the Old Man had first known him there. Poor Jus was a hermaphrodite, or so the story went that I heard later, and was said to have fallen in love with a man in Madrid while on a concert tour in Spain and to have had a child by him. Broken by misfortune in later years, he came to mend his body and spirit in our mountain air, and the Old Man drove him up in a wagon from San Diego, Jus prostrate and almost too weak to move, and he became the central or female figure of a strange trio whose other members were the Old Man and Cap Hulburd. Those two crusty old scamps could be as harsh as grindstones with each other and with me but never with Jus. Sometimes Jus would sing to them in his melodious contralto voice. Sometimes he'd wear women's clothes. I thought they were merely part of his operatic get-up. Sometimes he read aloud dramatically from the German philosophers and poets Hegel and Schiller, whom the Old Man much admired.

Jus was always kind and patient with me but I couldn't be a scholar. Numbers came easily and I could remember everything I was told, but I couldn't become interested in *David Copperfield* no matter how often Jus insisted it was a classic and should be read. Dickens used too many words, in my opinion, and had a predilection for orphans which I didn't share.

Yaqui Tom was another matter. Tom came to us one October

[24]

afternoon stark naked or nearly so, trotting at the heels of the Old Man's horse, the Old Man and his sorrel dusty from the long ride out of Sonora where he'd been on a cattle-buying trip, and Tom dusty, too, and wearing nothing but his yellow yucca-fibered g-string. I'd seen naked or nearly naked Indians before, Yumas and Cocopahs from the Colorado River country east of our mountains, but never one trotting at the Old Man's heels this way—up the lane between the houses, people staring, dogs running out to bark, the Old Man clearly enjoying the sensation he and Tom were creating, on through the oak grove and over to the barn where I was standing.

Without a word the old scoundrel got down and led his horse inside. Tom stopped within a few feet of me, never having been in a barn and not knowing what to make of one. He was the finest looking Indian I'd ever seen. Backbone straight. Cheekbones and forehead high. Eyes wide apart. Black hair cut off at the shoulder. His manner dignified despite his being thrust suddenly into strange surroundings.

"Do you speak Spanish?" I asked him in Spanish. He flashed me a smile. "*Si!*"

"Quit jawing with that Redskin!" the Old Man yelled from inside.

I winked at Tom. He grinned back. I knew I'd made a friend.

We took him to the kitchen and let Mary fill him up. She treated him like a wild prince but Tom was shy and hardly looked up from his plate. Then the Old Man pitched some clothes at him and showed him a cabin under the oaks where he could sleep. Next morning when we emerged from the bunkhouse, there was Tom crouched on the top step naked as before.

The Old Man claimed he bought Tom from some Mexican soldiers who were about to shoot him. The Mexicans were in fact trying to exterminate the Yaquis, who'd long refused to submit to their rule, and they kept trying for years with varying degrees of success but in this instance, as was not uncommon, they allowed cash to prevail over official policy. The Old Man claimed he gave thirty dollars for Tom and that was why Tom dogged his heels so closely. Whatever the fact of the matter, Tom learned to wear clothes but he never became what you would call civilized.

He hated sleeping between four walls, so the Old Man let him build a grass shack on the rocky point overlooking the grove and ranch buildings, and there he lived as a free American citizen.

I suppose few boys have had such a mentor as Tom and none will again. He taught me trailing, how to walk, how to trot, how to look for things, how to be still. I never became the master he was but I learned the rudiments. He taught me how to sit down when attacked by dogs, a trick as old as Homer; how to tell from the angle of a bent grass blade, rising slowly back to meet the sun, how many minutes had elapsed since the deer stepped on it; how to bake the *amole* root; how to drink from a barrel cactus. Together we roamed one of the most inhospitable stretches of landscape on earth, the Colorado Desert, and I acquired knowledge that stood me in good stead later in Alaska and Mongolia.

We ate the eighteen-inch-long chuckwalla lizards that have tasty white meat, shot wild sheep in the cliffs overlooking what is now Imperial Valley—and was then called the Overflow Desert—and camped with the Indians at a place where palm trees grew and warm water ran, a place since famous as Palm Springs.

For sport we lassoed gila monsters with loops of grass from among the reeds of the Colorado River overflows and put them in a sandy hole with a rattlesnake and watched who won. Each killed the other as a rule.

Yet when it came to shooting I could show Tom a trick or two. He didn't know much about guns. The Yaqais were using mostly lances and bows and arrows against the muskets and rifles of the Mexican Army. I showed him how to "bark" a squirrel by hitting the trunk in front of its throat and stunning it so that after it fell out of the tree you could pick it up alive and say that you'd caught it, or charmed it down with your singing; and I taught him how to aim with both eyes open and to shoot low on a downhill target.

As for work, in the fall we sowed grain, Tom driving, I sowing from the back of the wagon, arms moving rhythmically from side to side, the flying grain covering a semicircle of about fifteen feet and doing the job as well or better than a machine drill did later.

In winter we helped Joe Lopez, our foreman, and Juan Marron, our top rider, pull cattle out of bog holes, or repaired fences (rock, brush, or log fences, no barbed wire yet), watched for lions, fixed harness and saddle gear. In spring we rounded up stray cattle, helped with branding, "fought" calves that developed blackleg. No vaccination existed for blackleg, an often fatal disease caused by eating too much green grass. Every spring a number of calves died of it. They would lie down and not get up unless we "fought" them to their feet and kept them fighting mad by twisting their tails, punching their ribs, batting them over the head with our hats. Most that we treated that way lived and it taught me a lesson: when you get mad enough, you usually survive.

In summer we helped with the threshing. Loose hay was piled high around the solid cedar snubbing post in the center of the round corral. With pitchforks fashioned from oak limbs we distributed hay from the central stack until the hard-packed earth of the corral was covered to a depth of about six inches. Then we turned small bands of horses into the corral in relays and kept them running around and around while their feet threshed out the grain. From time to time we distributed more hay from the central stack. By the end of the day there would be a foot or two of loose straw covering the floor of the corral, the grain having settled to the bottom near the ground. Next day our squaws winnowed the grain by tossing it up across the wind with wood shovels. Then the process would be repeated until all the grain was threshed.

A break in routine occurred at midsummer, usually around the Fourth of July. A priest would come up from San Diego to marry the young couples and bless all our houses with incense and prayers and we would hold a fiesta. The neighbors would come, a dance floor would be set up under the oaks of the grove, an American flag unfurled on a staff, and there would be music and dancing—square dances, schottishes, waltzes, and even the stately gavotte; plus a grand exchange of news and views. There would also be horse and foot races and always the traditional Spanish *carrera del gallo* or rooster race. A dozen live roosters were buried in two parallel rows five or six feet apart—just their heads and necks showing above ground—and we galloped between the rows, leaning now to this side, now to that, snatching at their bobbing heads. He who pulled the most roosters out of the ground won the Old Man's ten-dollar gold piece.

Horses were, as I've said, our chief product. At one time we owned more than 500 head. They ran wild from the slopes of Cuyamaca Peak to the San Diego River and were never shod, sheltered, or fed. Consequently they were tough and self-reliant. Our Arabs, mostly grays, would weigh 850 to 900 and were sold as saddle stock. Our Morgans, usually bays, weighed about 1,000 and sold as riding or carriage horses. The deep-brown Orloffs, weighing up to 1200 were used almost entirely in carriage work.

The stagecoach companies bought many of our Morgans for their San Diego-Yuma and San Diego-Los Angeles and San Bernardino runs. At purchase time, each animal was lassoed by us, thrown, and examined for soundness by a veterinary and a company buyer. It gave us a chance to practice with our braided rawhide lariats made by Old Mienda, the ranch saddlemaker and leather worker, in his shop near the barn. Mienda, our "artist," wore a calfskin vest with the red hair still on it and was treated with great respect. Otherwise he might not make you the saddle, belt, or hatband you wanted. Mienda's saddletrees, incidentally, were made of wood seasoned for two years in the manure pile near the barn—alder if you wanted a light saddle, oak if a heavy one. They were always fitted individually to your horse's back as a tailor fits a suit of clothes to a man, and he decorated their skirts with designs of his own creation, roses, baskets, and a variety of curlicues.

Mienda's reatas were sixty feet long (in Spanish times they'd reached nearly twice that length—imagine a lariat 110 feet long!) and were cut entirely from the hide of one or two steers, preferably a solid-colored animal, and preferably red, because Mienda believed that red animals had the toughest hides and that where two colors of hair met there was always a weakness. Tom and I helped him flesh the hides with oaken gougers and cure them with ashes. Before braiding, we tested the strips he cut from them with a good stout pull against a tree with a workhorse.

At the direction of the stagecoach company representatives, we burned serial numbers into the left front hooves of the horses being purchased, after the veterinarian had given them his okay. Along with our secret "C" brand no larger than a twenty-five-cent piece concealed in the long hair under their jaws, the foot brand helped identify and recover them if they strayed or were stolen.

Horse stealing was of course widespread. It was the organized crime of those days and some of its practitioners were astonishingly expert. One afternoon, for instance, we brought sixteen head down from the Mountain and put them in the pasture by the house. Among them was a beautiful cream-colored woods colt. Today we would call him a palomino. He was to be mine. I slept little that night, thinking about him. Next morning my colt and all the others we'd put in the pasture were gone. We followed their tracks down Horse Thief Canyon into Mexico and on through the chaparral breaks and rocky gorges nearly as far as San Quintin on the coast before we lost them.

During these pursuits we sometimes got near enough to exchange shots with our visitors and recover some of the stolen stock but usually they escaped scot free with all their loot, channeling it into the thieves' underground that ran down through Baja and across, by boat, to the Mexican mainland.

Cattle were much less valuable than horses until the early 1880s and we sold ours at three or four dollars a head, chiefly for their hides and tallow as in mission days. But then the populations of San Diego and Los Angeles began to grow and there began to be a market for beef. All our cattle were Mexican longhorns, multicolored, not as big as Texas longhorns but horny enough and, on occasion, as fleet as deer. They led us on many a breakneck chase, and here again Jip proved her worth. She learned to fasten to the noses of the wild ones, the *broncos*, and hang there no matter what her punishment, slowing them, sometimes stopping them completely, until we could catch up with our lassoes.

Sometimes I imagined what my life might be like when I reached the glorious age of twenty-one and inherited my share of the ranch. I didn't care for the idea of living with the Old Man. Perhaps I would renovate the Rancho Viejo, the crumbling adobe hacienda in the next valley, which had been the home of the Lopez family, our predecessors. Overgrown with grapevines and honeysuckle, surrounded by olive trees dating back nearly a hundred years, it was a familiar haunt of mine. I used to go there alone and dream. Sometimes I dreamed I would become a rancher like my father and own hundreds of horses and cattle. Or should I become a gold miner? The rich strike at Julian on the other side of the Mountain was at its height, filling the countryside with prospectors and claim stakers, eventually yielding millions in quartz gold.

Everybody in California was going to be rich some day. That belief was in the air we breathed, the ground we walked on, the thoughts we thought, and came straight to us from Gold Rush times which weren't so very far away.

When work was slack, Tom took me with him up to the rancheria of the Lagunas near the top of the Coast Range. It was the remotest, the wildest, its people the most energetic. As we arrived the dogs would bark and the kids begin to yell. We'd get off, shake hands with the men, squat with them and roll a smoke, ask how the acorns were coming, how the piñon nuts were doing, if the tribe would visit the ranch in the fall as usual and if they'd seen any wild sheep. Then there might be a horse or foot race, and I developed speed of foot that proved useful later. Their houses consisted of one room and were made of reeds and thatch, watertight, with sides not more than four feet high and roofs sloping to a low peak. Blankets or sheepskins were piled in corners on the dirt floor and there was usually a shelf where the women kept their combs—old combs of bone with teeth sawed in them with saws—and maybe a precious bit of looking glass and a bead or two.

At sundown the women, wearing their Mother Hubbards, would dish out supper from the common stewpot, which contained rabbit or deer, or beef "borrowed" from the Old Man or from somebody else, but no matter—we were brothers, *compadres* of the wild—and Tom and I would grab a plate and eat with a knife and fork if they had them, or with our fingers if they did not.

All the Indians had remarkably good teeth. I think the reason was because they ate nothing but natural food. Acorn mush, corn, wild roots, herbs, and game were their staples. They never brushed their teeth but sometimes cleaned them by rubbing them with charcoal daubed on the ends of their fingers.

After dark there'd be a fire in the center of the hut and the smoke got out where it could while we talked and told stories.

When time to sleep came I lay down on the floor with, as the Old Man said derisively on hearing of it, "the rest of the Indians," and rolled myself in my blanket, while Tom was out tom-catting with the unmarried girls and widows.

Tom was something of a celebrity to our local Indians—the Viejas, Capitán Grandes, and Lagunas—and had plenty of girl-friends, and men-friends too, wherever he went.

For a few years he and I were inseparable and then as I grew older I developed other interests.

# 4.   Guns and Girls

Billy was my particular pal at this next stage. He'd come out from St. Louis to visit an aunt and uncle who had a homestead on the Mountain, taken to our life, and stayed. Billy was likable and easy in his ways and even the Old Man cottoned to him and let him board and bunk with us and lend a hand as needed.

We used to spend hour after hour in the bunkhouse, when the Old Man wasn't around, lying on our bunks practicing with empty six-shooters, aiming and pulling at a tack on the wall. Our pistols were the long-barreled, single-action, .44s that had to be cocked and pulled for every shot. With practice your thumb and forefinger learned to work automatically on hammer and trigger. As frequently happened, my left hand became better than my right, perhaps because the left knows less than the right to start with and so has less to unlearn when it comes to shooting.

For the fast draw, we used holsters of sole leather split and well oiled. Their smooth surface didn't interfere with your gun's barrel and we cut away a portion in front to permit your thumb to close freely over the hammer. We estimated it took one twenty-fifth of a second for a good man to draw and hit something.

Not that we were gunmen. Or pretended to be. But guns were part of everyday life and it was a good idea to wear one and, for survival's sake, you had better know how to use it.

For practice we used flying quail or jackrabbits. We'd be riding along. A covey of quail would get up. We'd draw and fire at one bird, then another and another. Maybe we shot at five hundred quail before we learned to connect regularly. Jackrabbits were easier. We'd wait till they reached the tops of their bounds and knock their heads off. Similarly with a small block of wood or

[32]

coin tossed in the air, the trick was to wait till it reached the crest of its rise. There if you hit it just right, you could knock it higher and hit it again. And so we shot away thousands of rounds which we loaded at home by the fireplace in the bunkhouse, with our bar of lead, can of black powder, and bullet mold.

Constant practice was the basis for whatever skill we attained. I think the reason comparatively few Indians and Mexicans became good shots was because they didn't have enough ammunition to practice with.

All serious shooting, when things came to that, was aimed shooting. You held your pistol in front of you slightly above the hips where it came to rest naturally after drawing. There was little or no hip shooting and, despite what you see in the movies today, absolutely no fanning of a six-shooter except as a stunt. Most gunfights were personal matters, no law or order involved, and the sheriff seldom bothered to come up the fifty miles from San Diego to investigate. He had plenty to do without riding around the back country looking for work.

More often than not Mexicans were involved in these shooting scrapes. Only twenty-odd years had passed since we'd taken the land on our side of the border, and though relations on the whole were good and people came and went across the line regularly, some of the Mexicans wanted their territory back. A few years earlier they'd invaded our nearby settlement of Campo and tried to take it over, as Pancho Villa tried to take over Columbus, New Mexico, years later, and there'd been a bloody battle. In fact the border was dangerous ground. My father's blood had gone into it. So had the Old Man's. So might mine or Billy's or any of our gang's but we gave little thought to such subjects. We were too busy living.

Five or six of us had gotten together by this time and were looking for ways to make money, as young men will. A Winchester carbine cost us sixteen dollars but an Indian south of the line would give us eight to ten cows for it. Maybe he'd stolen those cows from some Mexican; that was none of our business. On our side, cows were worth twenty dollars a head. All we had to do was start them up one of the rugged canyons like Robber's Roost that ran up into the United States and they drifted along following the grass and water and soon became American cattle.

There was a ten-mile-wide strip on our side of the border where the Mexicans could come and gather their cattle and a similar strip on their side where we could go and gather ours, but nobody knew exactly where the line ran. There were no fences, no markers, no law enforcement to speak of. The *rurales* patroled the Mexican side pretty haphazardly. On our side "General" Cadwallader, reputedly an ex-Union Army officer, had charge of the line riders who were responsible for the border between San Diego and Yuma, a stretch of rugged country an army couldn't have kept watch over successfully. The General and his handful of ex-cowboys didn't try very hard; they preferred poker. So if we were planning to move cattle across, one of us would get into the card game at the hotel in Campo, where the General and his men headquartered, and take care to lose. What if it cost fifty dollars? If fifty head crossed the line during the night we made money.

Sometimes we brought a bunch across legitimately, paid the duty on them and got the papers to prove it. Thereafter those papers could be exhibited as evidence that any cattle in our possession were legally ours.

It was foolishness, of course, but we didn't think of it as law-breaking but as fun.


Girls had come into the picture by this time. For a month or two on Saturday nights Billy and I would steal out the Old Man's team of matched grays while he was asleep and take our sweethearts riding in the surrey—until he came to the barn early one morning after we'd arrived home late and found his horses still sweaty. That put an end to that.

After working all day on Saturday we thought nothing of riding horseback ten or fifteen miles to a dance at Alpine or a party at Will Fairley's up in Pine Valley. Sometimes these get-togethers were simply play-parties with taffy pulls or games like truth and consequences, post office, or spin the bottle. Sometimes they were formal dances with a floormaster in charge. Before you could dance with a girl you didn't know you had to ask the floor-master's permission and be formally introduced to her. As always there were the "nice" girls and the other kind and we quickly learned the difference. Sex was no mystery to any of us growing up on ranches among animals but it was a more serious and on the whole more precious matter than it has become. We valued it because it was not easy to come by and because the risks involved were considerable. I was far from a Romeo in appearance: short, towheaded, bowlegged, but tried to make up in energy what I lacked in beauty and got my share of attention.

Girls, however, compounded our financial problems. When pressed for cash, Billy and I would ride mean horses for neighboring ranchers for five dollars a ride. When sorely pressed we'd take a couple of the Old Man's yearling steers and drive them to the butcher in San Diego. After all, they were my cattle, weren't they? Or would be when I came of age and inherited my share of the ranch. The Old Man didn't see it that way. Just as he didn't see why we needed to take a girl to the bullfights in San Diego and to dinner afterwards at the Horton House. Accordingly he and I began to part company, and Billy and I and our gang turned to other ways of making money.


We'd done pretty well running cattle past Cadwallader at Campo. Now we decided to go into Sonora where the Old Man had been going for years—I'd been down there too—and buy a good-sized herd, pick up strays as we came back toward the line, fatten everything on our side, and maybe make enough money to visit Chicago and New York, get married or do whatever else might seem appropriate.

I left from the ranch alone because I did not want the Old Man to know where I was going. It was September when the weather is good and there have been rains south of the border to start the green grass. I rode a buckskin mare who was tough as leather and gentle as a cat. I'd named her after my best girl, Adele. On more than one occasion she'd lived on cactus when there was nothing better to eat and I'd often carried water to her in the hollow of my hat. The bay packhorse that I took with her liked her and would be found with her when I turned them out. Packed on him were my bedding roll, grub, grain, cooking utensils. In my saddle bags were smoking tobacco, razor, a clean shirt, and in the money belt next to my skin I carried some of the gold that would be needed to buy the cattle. A Fish-brand slicker and blue denim jumper were tied across the back of my saddle, my .44 carbine traveled in its scabbard and my Colt .44 in its holster. My saddle was one of our low-horn, low-cantle models, single-cinch, designed for hot country, where you need a saddle that moves around and doesn't stay fixed and scald your horse's back, as the two-cinched or double-rigged models are apt to do. Its blanket was made of yucca fibre woven by Indian squaws, the yucca being porous as well as absorbent and allowing air to penetrate.

I met Billy down the road. Johnny joined us at Campo. Shorty and Charlie fell in along the line. They'd brought Mexican and Indian kids to act as camp helpers, so we made a party of about a dozen as we went down the Meyer's Grade into the desert. The grade was named for the Old Man because he'd laid it out by sighting over a yucca stalk to make a trail for taking cattle down to the grass of the Colorado overflows. Later the wagon road followed it and later still the highway.

We followed it east toward Yuma, the weather very hot. A few miles before reaching Yuma we swung off to the south and hit the river near the site of the old date ranch where the stumps of giant palms were visible, supposedly left from the time the Apaches had massacred a Spanish settlement there many years before. We swam the river at our usual crossing place and struck off through the sand hills toward the Spanish trail that ran from Yuma to Mexico City, the one used by the conquistadors and padres.

The mouth of the Colorado was, as I suppose it still is, in reality many mouths, and there were sloughs and waterways and islands and thousands of deserted beaver houses. The beaver were trapped out before my time but Kit Carson is reported to have said, when he reached the mouth of the Colorado, that he had never seen so many beaver houses in any one place in all his life. Doubtless Kit skinned a few before he left.

We hit the Spanish trail and headed south. Our destination was a ranch two hundred miles below the border where I'd been with Joe Lopez and the Old Man. The people were friendly and fair in their dealings and would show us a good time. We followed the road along the Gulf for a couple of weeks and then back in the hills, and at a point where the desert and the mountains were merging and you could find palms and pines within a few miles of each other, we came to the hacienda. It was situated in the middle of a green valley watered by *cienagas* or natural seeps and was surrounded by a high wall. From a distance it looked like a fort. An old retainer was standing guard at the gate.

"Good afternoon, old one," I greeted him, "is all well at the hacienda today?"

"Very well, God be thanked!"

"I am the Americano who was here year before last with the stout man with the beard and José Lopez, the great roper, you remember?"

"I remember very well!"

He had touched his forehead at first but now we were talking like friends.

"Is the Señor at home?"

"Alas, he is in the hills but will be back soon."

"And the Señora?"

"In good health, thanks be to God."

"Any of the girls get married?"

"Many would have them—but they are particular, being so beautiful."

"Well said! And the young master?"

"Growing like a weed, with the help of the Saints!"

He stood aside and bowed us through. We entered an enclosure of fifteen acres containing fruit trees, flower and vegetable gardens, huts of mestizo and Indian retainers built against the inside of the wall, corrals and stables at the rear, and in the center the house. It was a low rambling building in the shape of a rectangle, two hundred feet long, by one hundred wide, made of adobe, with a tiled roof and a veranda all around the outside.

The Señora herself came onto the veranda to greet us. She was in early middle age, one of those stately women of graying hair and queenly carriage who distinguished the Spanish-speaking aristocracy wherever you found it. I explained we'd come on business and didn't mean to impose, and she laughingly corrected me and said we had come to spend the night and give them the pleasure of our company. I confessed there was no-

thing we'd rather do. Johnny, Charlie, Shorty and Billy made
their bows, and an Indian girl in sandals and bright calico
brought us a bottle of brandy and tiny glasses on a tray and we
started the process of refreshing ourselves. Pretty soon we heard
a commotion at the back of the house and knew the Señor and his
men were returning from the hills. His boots clumped on the
flagstones of the inner court, a green glimpse of which we had
seen through an archway, and we heard him speaking to his little
son. He spoke the soft musical Castilian with a distinct "th"
sound, quite different from our California corral Spanish with
its "s" or buzz, and then he came out onto the veranda, a squat
figure dressed in white, dusty from all day with his cattle. He had
homely good looks—long nose, long jaw, a light complexion—
and a sense of humor.

"Well this is a treat for my girls," he exclaimed, shaking hands
all around. "I'm the father of three unmarried daughters, you
know, and whenever young fellows come around we get our
hopes up!" Then he clapped me on the back and asked how the
Old Man was. I said the old rascal was too ornery to be anything
but well and told how he and Rancho Santa Margarita, now the
Pendleton Marine Corps base, had imported two carloads of
white-faced cattle from the East, the first to reach our part of the
world; and then he asked me what I'd been up to, and I told how
Billy and I had been spearing stingrays from a skiff in San Diego
Harbor and letting them tow us up and down past North Island
where the naval base is now and where there used to be the
remains of a Spanish whaling station. Then the triangle rang to
warn us it was time to get ready for supper and a *mozo* showed us
to our rooms.

Billy and I bunked in one, Johnny and Charlie and Shorty in
the other. Our beds had interlaced rawhide for springs and
mattresses of cotton ticking stuffed with cornhusks. There was a
piece or two of dark heavy wooden furniture that maybe came
from Spain in a galleon, and Indian rugs and goat and deer skins
on the floor. The service was first-rate. Our *mozo* promptly
brought us water to wash with and took our dirty shirts to be
laundered and returned to us next morning while we changed to
clean ones and headed back toward the veranda.

A long hall ran around the inside of the house and at nearly every corner was a crucifix or figure of the Virgin with candle burning. I remembered there was a priest in residence and chapel somewhere on the premises. Out on the veranda the whole family was waiting: Señor and Señora, Chiquita, Graciosa, and Maria looking mighty sweet—as I had predicted—in evening dress with flounced skirts, tight bodices, and high combs crowning their heads, keen to see the Norte Americanos; and the young padre who wore the gray robe of the early Franciscans or Gray Friars. The boy, Felipe, was having supper elsewhere with his Indian mammies, and our young helpers were out back with the Indian girls and other retainers.

While we bowed and acted gallant, the padre took charge of the conversation. He was the Señor's advisor on temporal matters as well as spiritual ones and knew the price of steers at Chicago and current rates of monetary exchange. He also conducted the hacienda school which was chiefly religious in nature and, for most of his pupils, went little beyond the rudiments of reading and writing. The daughters had been away to school in Mexico City and perhaps Europe and were accomplished young ladies who could sing, embroider, and smile and above all talk and make themselves attractive.

When the triangle rang we went to the small family dining room where candles burned in wrought-iron candlestands as tall as modern floor lamps, and there was a fire in a fireplace and Indian girls standing around waiting to wait on us. We sat at a table of black ebony wood so hard that a burning cigarette wouldn't mar it. The padre said grace, in Latin, then lifted his head, made a joke and the talk became general, while the serving girls brought us huge platters of roast beef, bowls of potatoes, pink beans, corn tortillas, biscuits, butter, red wine in a decanter, cake and pie to top off with.

After supper the ladies adjourned to the parlor while we lingered at the table for brandy and cigars. I knew the ladies were probably having their smokes, too. They did it privately, rarely in front of men or in public. Almost all California-Spanish and Mexican women smoked, as did many pioneer Anglo women in California until different notions of behavior came in, and smoking went out of fashion until the 1920s.

"We're thinking of buying some steers, Don Guillermo," I said finally. "Four-year-olds or threes. Not a great number because we're young fellows down here to make our first stake, but Joe Lopez said you might have a few fours you could sell us, and we would like to do business with you if possible."

"By all means," he replied. "In the morning we'll ride out and take a look, but tonight the ladies are waiting to entertain us."

We went to the parlor and listened while they sang *Cielito Lindo* and *La Golondrina* and played harp and organ, and did pretty well. After things warmed up there was dancing. We whirled them, counted their numerous petticoats, did the schottische and gavotte, got a squeeze of a hand here and there and an implied promise of more intimate favors. About 1:00 A.M. we tried to go to bed and about 2:00 made it all the way, flopped on our rawhide springs, and were asleep before the *mozo* pulled our boots off.

At 7:30 next morning he was back with hot water for shaving, after which we joined the Señor and his two foremen in the dining room for breakfast, no women present, this strictly business, and then we rode into the hills. His cattle were the same Spanish stock as ours and carried a diamond on the right hip. He would, as part of the sale, vent it by duplicating it on the shoulder on the same side, and we would slap our rattlesnake on the other side.

"Would six dollars be satisfactory for these three-year-olds?" I asked. We had hoped for fours, the standard beef of the day. Four-year-olds would bring $20 (gold) in the U.S., but they would cost us more than threes and he had not showed us any.

"These are excellent three-year-olds," he replied, "and I must have seven dollars a head for them."

That was all there was to it. At seven dollars a head (Mexican) we would make a profit of about sixteen dollars (U.S.) on each animal.

Next day when his men had gathered the cattle at a point near our road home and vented his brand, and we'd applied ours, we paid him in gold and he made out a bill of sale. Then having bade fond farewells to the femininity at the hacienda, we hit the homeward trail with around 200 head of three-year-old steers. It wasn't a fortune but would make a nice stake and it might grow larger if we could pick up strays en route to the line.

Shorty and Johnny took the points of the herd, Charlie and Billy were the swing riders. I followed at the rear shoving the drags along assisted by our Mexican and Indian youngsters and the pack string.

With help from the Don and his men we moved them along pretty lively for the first day until we got them out of country they knew and they quieted down, and then we grazed them forward slowly on a wide front, keeping to the foothills where there was grass. "You'll have something to write home about now," I told Billy. He'd gotten a kick out of the hacienda visit and here was an honest-to-god cattle drive. There was a girl back East he was writing to but she didn't interfere much with those nearer. Like all of us he wore a gun though he'd never had to use it seriously except in his imagination. Sometimes we'd talk of Wyatt Earp, Bat Masterson, John Wesley Hardin and other famous gunfighters of the period and speculate on what they were really like and what they would do in various situations. And when far enough away from the herd so a shot wouldn't spook them, we'd bang away at a rabbit or rattlesnake.

In this fashion we spent nearly a month, avoiding settlements, and covered most of the distance to the line without any trouble when we came one evening within sight of a barrio that looked inviting. After the herd quieted we drew straws to see who would visit the twinkling lights and who stay behind. We should have known better. But we were starved for some human companionship beside each other.

The *tienda* was like a hundred others below the border. At the left was a bar, at the right card tables. Straight ahead was an adobe archway leading into another room and in there were the girls and the dancing. After a drink or two I wandered over to the monte table and, after watching the deal, sat in. It was Mexican monte played with a forty-card Spanish deck. I wasn't having much luck, didn't expect to. I noticed Shorty had established himself at the bar and Charlie and Billy had gone to the inner room and were dancing with the señoritas. There wasn't the slightest indication of trouble. When the music stopped the girls came to the bar with their fellows and stood with them while they drank. Billy and Charlie came and went with a couple of cute tricks. Everything was harmonious and I was watching the cards, when all of a sudden everything was wrong. You sense it more than you think about it. There is an instantaneous change in the pitch of the sound, in the atmosphere.

I turned my head in time to see the fellow draw his gun and empty it into Billy's stomach. Billy sagged forward to the floor by the bar with the life shot out of him and the girl who'd been standing with him jumped away and started sireaming. I saw the fellow who had shot him working the trigger with an expression of hatred on his face. I jumped up and started across the floor. Our yell was up and I could see that Shorty and Charlie were tangling with a bunch at the bar and that the fellow who had killed Billy was now shooting at me. I was wearing a gun but didn't think to use it. I wanted to get hold of him. I wanted to feel him between my two hands. Something hit me low in the right leg and I went down. I didn't feel any pain, just the surprise of being down among the chair and table legs. I kept crawling forward among them and I guess he was overshooting because the last thing I saw before somebody shot the lights out was his surprised look—that he hadn't stopped me, that I was still coming.

Then I had him between my two hands. He hadn't given Billy a chance. Something like that went through my mind. You go crazy when you are like that. When I got through with him he lay still.

Things had quieted by then and I heard Charlie's voice in a corner of the room say, "Fred, you all right?" I said I didn't know. Shorty struck a match and we saw what I guessed we would see: Billy wasn't with us any more. The fellow had simply shot the middle out of him.

They asked me if I thought I could walk and I said I thought I could. Carrying Billy and helping me, they stepped gingerly out of doors. Not a sound. Not a light. Moving fast we put Billy's body across Shorty's horse and they helped me onto mine. On the way back to camp I nearly fainted but decided I'd better not. We'd passed near a garrison town a day or two before, and the thought of a Mexican jail was worse than the pain in my leg.

The boys were already rounding up the cattle—daylight coming—but Shorty insisted on doctoring me before we went any farther. My leg was so sore and swollen and my boot so full of blood he couldn't pull it off so he cut it off, and we found the bullet had gone clean through the upper part of my calf. The hole was still oozing a little. He poked Indian salve into it on the end of a stick. I howled. Then we mounted and hurried for home, taking Billy with us. We didn't want to bury him on foreign soil.

Late next afternoon when we reached one of the mouths of the Colorado and felt sure we were on American territory, we buried Billy.

Johnny and Charlie dug the grave. Shorty and I gathered sticks for the cross. When all was ready we stood around in a circle, as they do now in storybooks, our heads bare, while Shorty recited the Lord's Prayer. I think he got most of it in though there were parts I didn't quite recognize.

Then he talked a little about what a good pal Billy had been, how he'd always done his share, how we'd all liked him, what a shame it was he'd had to stop so early and not go on. We buried him complete: pistol, clothes, and all. Piled rocks on top. Left him there on the bank of the river. Swam our steers over. Took them up into the hills and made our profit as planned. But we didn't go to Chicago for a gala on the proceeds.

You die a little with each of your friends.

My uncle and guardian, Dr. F. D. C. Meyer, sometimes called "the millionaire cattle baron of Descanso," was an imposing figure afoot or on horseback.

Indian Mary was our housekeeper and my "mammy." (*Irving Lee Palmer*)

San Diego wasn't suffering from overdevelopment when I first saw it. In the background, beyond Point Loma, is the Pacific. Billy and I used to spear stingrays in the harbor in the foreground. (*Historical Collection, Title Insurance and Trust Co., San Diego, California*)

At permanent camps, Siberian Eskimos lived in skin-covered igloos like this one. Eskimos on both sides of the Bering Strait built snow-block igloos for shelter when on the trail in winter. (*Photography Collection, Suzzallo Library, University of Washington*)

# II

# GOLD ON THE YUKON:

## 1894 - 1907

# 5.  The Far North

When my leg healed I got a job as field man with the Mexico, International, Pacific, and Gulf of California Steamship Company which operated two coastal trading and passenger vessels, the "Carlos Pacheco" and "Manuel Dublán," from San Diego along the coast of Baja and into the Gulf of California. The company also operated and speculated in mines, ranches, and nearly everything else south of the border. It was useful experience. It took my mind off recent events and enlarged what till then had been a rudimentary knowledge of mining, shipping, and commerce and business generally.

Returning to San Diego I fell in love, love of the marrying kind. She was a local girl I'd known for years but suddenly saw with new eyes. A prospect opened more golden than any I'd yet envisioned. In it Adele and I occupied that imaginary hacienda I'd dreamed of, surrounded by our adoring children. But when she told me we could always be friends I knew the truth. It fanned my natural desire to roam. There was nothing to keep me. The Old Man was getting crankier, sinking deeper into spiritualism and old age. The economic depression of the nineties was hitting him hard and he regarded me as a scalawag and wouldn't hear of me having my father's share of the ranch "at this time." I didn't want it at any time because it meant living with him and I didn't want to do that. So I looked for greener pastures. The one I chose was more white than green.

Charlie Tufts and I reached Dyea, Alaska, at the head of that glacial inlet known as the Lynn Canal in February 1894. Dyea, port of entry to the Yukon region, consisted of a trading post operated by Captain John J. Healy, a warehouse, a handful of Indian cabins, and that was about all. The Gold Rush was still years away. Gold had been discovered, yes, but in limited quantities. Cassiar had been struck and the boys had come down the Hootalinqua working the bars. And in '86 Skiff Mitchell had wintered at the mouth of Stewart River, instead of coming out to Juneau as usual, and Johnny Miller had taken a few thousand out of Miller Creek. But it was nothing sensational and made little stir in the outside world.

They told us at Dyea we would need about a ton of grub and gear for our journey into the interior. We bought it—flour, bacon, tea, sugar, rolled oats, dried fruit, axes, saws, picks, shovels—and two sleds made of hardwood in Juneau—and sledded our stuff by hand and backbone up to the Sheep Camp, the headquarters of wild sheep hunters, at the foot of Chilkoot Pass; and there in the lee of the Sawtooth, everything frozen white, not another living soul in sight, we broke it up into small lots and backpacked it to the top of the pass. Then we packed the sleds up, crosswise on our backs, along with our war bags and camp kit.

The Chilkoot goes over the divide into the headwaters of the Yukon. From the top it's an easy downhill slide. You take 500 pounds on a sled, put yourself in harness, grab the gee pole and away you go. The trail was broken after a fashion, which was a good thing because neither of us had much experience in snow. We were desert rats. But here the idea was the same—catch as catch can, make do, learn quick.

We slid and rolled, overturning at least half a dozen times, reloading, laughing and whooping till we came to the shore of Lake Lindeman, first of the series of lakes that form the Yukon headwaters. We continued to Lake Bennett and around on the ice into its west arm where the best camp sites were and the best timber. There we pitched our camp and prepared to saw lumber for the boat that would carry us down the river after the spring thaw.

To make our saw pit we selected four spruce trees growing in a square about fifteen apart, cut them off eight feet above the ground, and tied their tops together with cross-logs to make a frame. Up onto this frame we skidded our saw log, peeled it, marked it off—with the help of charcoal and fish line—into one-inch boards thirty feet long. Then we went to work, little realizing what lay ahead.

Whipsawing broke up more partnerships than anything else in the Far North, I am prepared to state, women included. It was sheer misery. Charlie climbed on top of our saw frame. I stood below. Between us lay the heart of our problem, our eight-foot saw. Its teeth were set only one way. You couldn't saw two ways with it. Charlie pulled up. I pulled down. Charlie lost his balance. I got sawdust in my eyes. After an hour we were ready to kill each other but gradually our profane efforts turned trees into boards.

When not whipsawing we trapped or hunted, going up onto the Sawtooth north toward Mt. St. Elias and I got a Dall sheep and on our way back Charlie killed a woodland caribou. The woodland variety remain in one locality and don't migrate like barrenland caribou. We trapped a few beaver and then the days got warmer, avalanches began rattling off the slopes and the bear emerged from hibernation.

The first thing the bear do when they emerge is look for peavine. They want to rid themselves of the wad of dry grass that's been clogging their systems throughout the winter. That wad is the cap or seal overlying the last food eaten in the fall, the one that nourishes them during their long sleep. By spring it's served its purpose and must be got rid of. Hence the search for peavine, a natural laxative, which grows on the bars of creeks.

We spotted our first grizzly on a bar about 200 yards upstream. I slipped around through the timber on the opposite bank until I could get a clear view of him. Then I looked back at Charlie who was sneaking up the creek toward him and raised my hand in the agreed-on signal so that we could fire together.

I thought we had. I knew the bear was hit and was coming straight for me. I didn't know that eight times out of ten a bear runs straight for the sound of a gun. I kept pumping lead into him. He kept coming. Where was Charlie? He wasn't firing a shot. The bear had nearly reached the bank at my feet when he keeled over. Then I saw Charlie coming slowly up the creek. "What happened to you?" I yelled. "Why, he had to climb a bank to get to you!" he snapped back. "He had a downhill run at me!" He was enormous and harder to kill than anything I'd met so far. My .40-65 slugs had penetrated downward through his back, hitting kidneys, lungs, heart and finally stopped him. We cut steaks from his loins and kept his foreclaws as souvenirs. They were nearly six inches long.

While waiting for the ice to break up, we'd finished our boat. She was a double-ender (pointed at either end), thirty feet long, five in the beam, long and narrow so as to offer least resistance when poling upstream. We had difficulty caulking her. We'd brought oakum but forgot the pitch. So we dug spruce gum out of live trees, melted it over a fire, poured it into her seams, ran a red-hot pick point over it to drive it into the oakum, and it worked.

When the ice broke we launched and loaded her until she had only a five-inch freeboard. For a sail, we rigged a bed tarpaulin at her forward thwart, which gave her a nice lateen rig, and away we went down the lake, chasing the ice, avalanches crackling and roaring off the slopes around us, snowflowers in bloom. It was that first wonderful moment of a northern spring, and in the water below us we could see fish waiting in schools to ascend the streams—grayling, skinfish, trout, each in its respective group; and the mosquitoes had come out from behind the bark of the trees where they'd spent the winter and were walking around on the snow. Some of them were as big as spiders—literally as long as a joint of your little finger—but were numbed by their winter sleep and didn't bother us much.

We sailed from lake to lake until we came to The Canyon where the water raced between rock walls forty feet high. It went so fast it humped in the middle. They had warned us at Dyea to stay on that hump and we did, thanks to the help of our spruce-limb steering oar. Those who didn't usually drowned. Next came The Rapids where the trick was to swing out far enough so that the current carried you clear of the rocks, and we managed that too.

At the junction of the Hootalinqua—the Hootalinqua (or Teslin) and the Lewes formed the Yukon proper—we saw huge blocks of ice as large as houses tossed high and dry on the bank by the breakup of a few weeks before. On still days you could hear the noise of that breakup for forty miles and its force was of course incalculable.

Above the mouth of Five-Finger Rapids where the steamers came up later by means of winches and cables, we lashed a log at each side of our boat to prevent her capsizing and sailed safely down to Sixtymile, where we stopped at the trading post and sawmill run by Joe Ladue, a French-Canadian pioneer, who told us of placer gold in pay quantities on the creeks out of Fortymile further downstream. So we floated on, stopping at an Indian village at the mouth of Klondike Creek, then called Deer Creek. George Carmack, the squaw man who later made the strike that started the Gold Rush, was living there with his Indian woman in one of the village cabins. He gave us some fresh salmon he'd just caught.

On reaching Fortymile, a major tributary coming in from the west side of the Yukon, we poled around into the stream's mouth to get clear of the drift logs floating down the river, tied to some willows that overhung the bank, and went to pay our respects to Jack McQuesten at the trading post. The settlement at Fortymile consisted of Bishop Bompas' Church of England Church, McQuesten's store, Billy McPhee's Saloon, plus a few other saloons and a dozen or two miners' cabins, all log buildings. The fact that they were in Canada, not the United States, made little difference, such distinctions as national boundaries being reserved for later eras.

McQuesten, a big, hearty, generous fellow, often referred to now as "the father of Alaska," made us feel at home right away. He'd come to the region in the seventies and knew it as well as anyone. He gave us a key to a cabin where we could store our things and told us how to reach the diggings at the head of Fortymile.

Taking our boat and a light outfit, Charlie and I poled up Fortymile to Chicken Creek and there made camp and looked the country over. We staked claims on Chicken and Jack Wade Creek, put down a few holes, twelve to sixteen feet to bedrock, but there was no rich pay on either creek. Our holes started out four feet wide by six feet long and ended up as big as a room. To dig them we thawed the frozen ground by means of a daily fire (cutting and hauling the wood), hoisting the gravel out with a bucket at the end of a rope and homemade windlass, then washing it in our sluiceboxes.

We had a good summer, however; plenty to eat; made friends, built a cabin on Chicken Creek, got our wings built for a fish trap, so that when the freeze started and the fish turned around and headed down for deeper water we could catch them, gathered up a few dogs as we went along. We didn't know much about dogs, so got skinned at every turn until we learned.

As the days grew shorter, Charlie grew homesick. I didn't blame him. He had a wife and children back home. I was free. Before the snow flew he left. I stayed.

One evening when I went to the creek for water, I saw crystals of ice floating down with the current and knew I was a sourdough. I'd seen the ice break up and form again in a single season.

We—Frank Manley, Riley Dingman, and I—wintered in the cabin Charlie and I had built and, speaking of sourdough, we kept a box of it hanging from a rafter at the back of the stove where it stayed warm. Our recipe for it was a standard one. We took dried potatoes, boiled them, saved the water, put it in our sourdough box which was watertight, added some flour, then a quarter-handful of sugar and some corn meal, then a yeast cake as starter. When the mixture began to bubble, we added rice or oats—or flour if we wanted bread. Then we removed about a quarter of the dough and put it in a mixing pan, added more flour and pounded and worked it and let it rise.

When it had risen, we kneaded in all the flour it would accept and let it rise again. After the second rising it was ready to put in the stove. And when we had eaten bread like that we didn't need to eat again for a while.

Our first winter was a starvation one nevertheless. The steamer "Arctic," coming up-river with supplies, was wrecked on a reef below Fortymile, and we went down to her with sleds. Jack McQuesten rationed out the grub. Instead of 300 pounds of flour we got 100. Instead of 200 pounds of sugar, fifty. Instead of five twenty-five pound boxes of dried apricots, peaches, and prunes we got one. Thus the normal daily requirement of three pounds of dried stuff per man per day was drastically curtailed, and as consequence some people developed scurvy. Those who stayed in town and didn't get outdoors and exercise much were hardest hit. One fellow turned black from the waist down. But those of us who stayed in the hills and got plenty of exercise and plenty of fresh meat (caribou, moose, ptarmigan, rabbit) remained healthy.

We worked, too. The gravel piles beside our sluiceboxes grew steadily larger. In the spring we'd wash them out, pay our bills, and maybe have a little left over.

Before the spring thaw came, Frank Manley and I went up the Yukon to Sixtymile and east from there to unexplored country in the Rockies at the head of Stewart River. We found some good rock and Frank went back to it years later and opened a silver mine. Though we carried only three days' grub, we managed comfortably for thirty, living almost entirely on moose, caribou, or sheep. But coming back the thaw caught us in the marshy lowlands of the Stewart and we had to abandon our sled, pack everything on the dogs, and scramble, half-starved, across the niggerheads (clumps of swamp grass) till we reached the Yukon. There was no way to cross to Sixtymile Island where a settlement was located so we built a raft, cut limbs for poles and poled like hell, hoping the current would carry us against the island instead of past it. We barely made it, caught an overhanging limb, boosted the dogs up and then ourselves—and found we'd been reported dead. Knowing we'd started out with only three days' grub, the Mounties stationed at Sixtymile had looked for us, not found us, reported us missing. Somehow the word reached San Diego. For years afterwards I met people in various parts of the world who thought I'd died of starvation in the Yukon.

The Old Man got the report and promptly accepted it. If I wasn't dead, I ought to have been, was apparently his reasoning. But I was writing Bess Pennoyer whose father was foreman for the Old Man and Bess would show him my letters. "Nope," he'd snort, according to Bess, even though he knew my handwriting, "that's an imposter! The boy's dead! Mounties say he is! Mounties can't be wrong! Anybody can imitate handwriting!" He was afraid of losing his property.

Back on Chicken Creek Frank and I washed our gravel and paid McQuesten what we owed him, heard of the strike at Circle 200 miles down the Yukon and went down there.

Circle City was situated inside U.S. territory where the river emerged into broad marshy flats. It'd been established the year before as a trading center and point of departure for the gold-

bearing creeks fifty miles to the southwest. The original strike on
Mastodon Creek had been made by Jack Gregor. Discovery claim
was staked by Gregor, Clum, and Cornelli and produced a fortune. Then Pitka and Walaska struck Pitka Bar on Birch Creek
and took out enough dust to start the stampede which we were
part of. Eagle, Harrison, Independence, Mammoth, Deadwood,
Frying Pan, and Greenhorn Creeks were all staked and within a
short time Circle became the metropolis of the Yukon and
claimed the title of "the largest log-cabin city in the world." Supposedly it lay inside the Arctic Circle but was actually ninety miles
outside.

Although the best ground had been taken, I got Fourteen
Above (the fourteenth claim above Discovery) on Mastodon
Creek and two or three other claims. None of them proved
valuable. You could own dozens of claims in a strike area and
never make a nickel. My Mastodon claim epitomized this. Its pay
dirt was covered by solid ice. Years later the syndicates came with
steam drills and took good money out of it but for the time being
I was stumped, so leaving Frank and Riley to work their claims, I
decided to explore the country. Who knew what lay beyond the
next ridge?

Hearing from friendly Porcupine Indians who'd come
down to Circle to trade that there was a valley to the east where
there was a live mastodon, I went back with them over the divide
toward the Mackenzie. They traveled with ten-foot-long tobog-
gans made of birch wood two feet wide, bottoms scraped and
greased with fat to let them slide easily over the snow. Eight or
ten dogs on individual lines fanned out ahead, and behind ran a
squaw at the end of a rope to steer the toboggan or act as brake.
The women wore their usual short traveling skirts of red or blue
cloth, mukluks (sealskin boots), and blankets, no hats, because it
wasn't very cold yet, their hair in long braids and their babies
tucked inside blankets on their backs. The men dressed in skin
trousers and parkee as I did.

I drove a team of seven dogs led by a smart old bitch, hitched
tandem, Yukon style (Eskimos used paired style), to a long and
narrow eleven-foot basket sled with handlebars. It carried my
light tent, a small wood stove with bake-oven that fitted inside its
chimney, an axe, my rifle, a rabbit blanket (the warmest lightest

fur in the Arctic), a sack of flour containing a wad of sourdough, some salt, tea, and dried salmon for the dogs. There would be caribou in the hills and fish in the streams and I had beads and trinkets for trading.

I didn't really believe the story of a live mastodon but it was as good a reason as any for taking a trip. And actually we were digging up fossilized mastodon and mammoth bones on the creeks every day, mixed with gold-bearing gravel, so why not a live mastodon in an unexplored valley where there was gold-bearing gravel? Stranger things were happening.

At night my Indians "Siwashed it" by fires in the lee of canvas lean-tos. A single piece of canvas, pitched at an angle against the wind, reflects the heat back onto you and keeps you warm. Later in the winter they would construct dome-shaped homes, tepees, if you will, of caribou skin stretched over willow frames. But long before we'd seen anything resembling a mastodon or a secret valley, they dropped away to their respective stamping grounds and I continued alone.

Thirty miles from the sea I met my first Eskimos. They were camped beside a stream about to head homeward after their autumn hunt, their sleds loaded with caribou and sheep meat. They were friendly. I traded trinkets for some of their meat, but they weren't ready to travel yet so I went on to the coast and found a deserted village of drift logs and sod huts.

Between me and the pack ice, close offshore, lay a strip of water, the Northwest Passage, still untraversed in its entirety by human beings. The discovery of the Pole also lay in the distant future.

As I went eastward along the coast the going became rougher. Soon I was chopping a trail through salt ice with my axe, the dogs following of their own accord. You develop a relationship with your dogs under such circumstances which is both sentimental and practical, a combination that may result in the best values. Some of my dogs were malamutes, some huskies. Some had a good deal of wolf in them. Later, when breeding dogs to wolves, I learned that pups with as much as fifty percent wolf blood would make good sled dogs but given more wolf than that they wouldn't pull the hat off your head.

Later still, during the rush, some of our best dogs came from

Siberia, but as yet we had none of them.

After a few more days I met a band of Eskimos busy cutting up the carcass of a blue whale they'd killed from open boats in a method their ancestors were using long before our first whaling ships put out from Nantucket. I traded for some seals they'd just killed and for some white fox skins and saw my first ivory-and-driftwood sleds, the finest, lightest things of their kind in the North. They had runners of walrus ivory morticed so smoothly together that you could hardly see the joints. Unlike wood or metal runners, ivory runners never stick no matter how salty the ice.

The remainder of the trip was uneventful until I came to Herschel Island where about a dozen U.S. whaling ships, sail and steam, were trapped by the ice. They were in no serious danger of being crushed because they were in the lee of the island which protected them against the main pack. Though short of grub, supplies were reaching them from the Hudson's Bay Company posts along the Mackenzie and from local Eskimos. I boarded several and talked with their crews. Whalers had been coming into the Arctic Ocean for five or six years, I learned, and wintering in the lee of the island, trading with the Eskimos, employing them as meat hunters, romancing their women, and traveling up and down the coast and inland. Some of the boys had recently grown restless, jumped ship, and headed for the legendary riches of the Yukon. I could have told them not to.

I continued to the Mackenzie, talked to the traders there, found what I'd expected: the fur trade was tightly controlled, there was no room for an independent, and if there was gold in the country nobody was saying where. The only mineral I'd seen was some coal as I came along the coast. It was time to go home. Retracing my steps I reached Circle on the last day of 1895, having covered around 1800 miles. I hadn't made any money but had enjoyed myself thoroughly.

Squaw pickets stopped me as I approached Circle, reminding me that the last day of the year was Squaw Day—Women's Rights Day—throughout the Far North. For twenty-four hours a turnabout occurred. Men abdicated. Women took over. They had the absolute right to exact a contribution from every man they met—a can of tomatoes, a bag of prunes, a kiss, an ounce of dust. They would come right into your cabin and roll you out of your bunk if necessary. If you tried to dodge them, they'd chase you through the snow, tackle you, then toss you in a moosehide blanket to teach you better manners. The blanket was like the modern trampoline. Oldtimers like Jack McQuesten could fly as high as a second-story window and always come down feet first.

I paid them off with the last of my trinkets and went on toward Jim Chronister's Saloon to get the news and tell the boys what I'd seen during my travels, hoping Gus Leiendecker would have cooked one of the feasts with which he nourished the hungry. The annual Christmas-New Year's celebration was in full swing (though liquor was banned from the district, it was openly sold and prodigiously consumed) and Jim's saloon was full to overflowing with nearly every species of human including Bill Ewing, our first Negro in the North.

Bill, a strongly built man of middle height, came from Tacoma, Washington, and had worked for the fire department there. He was a hard worker, always mining when I knew him, always with a white man as a partner, one of them being Dick Rice later a partner of mine. He and Dick worked a lay (lease) on Discovery at Hog 'em Creek out of Circle. Later, at Fairbanks, Bill had a piece of ground out from the Indian village at the mouth of the slough where he struck good pay. We called him "Nigger Bill" not as a term of opprobrium but to distinguish him from another Bill Ewing who was white, and he came and went as he pleased and was treated the same as anyone else.

Now and in the days following I experienced fully the grass-roots democracy of the North. If you were a man you were treated as one until you proved yourself otherwise. At a miners' meeting at Chronister's Saloon, the question arose as to how old a man should be before he could legally hold ground, and it was unanimously decided that if he was old enough to be in the North, he was old enough to hold ground there. The question also arose as to how much ground a man could own. By law, claims were limited to 1320 feet in length along the gold-bearing streams. This could be decreased but not increased. By miners' meeting we decreased it to 500 feet but allowed an additional 500 to the discoverer, so that he might have a total of 1,000 feet.

Infractions of law were infrequent and were dealt with summarily. When a man was found guilty of stealing food from another man's cache, we put him in a canoe with a sack of flour and told him to float downstream and not come back. On another occasion Chronister shot and killed a man who'd threatened him with a gun. He was tried by miners' meeting and found not guilty. On still another occasion a young Indian girl complained about a young white miner who'd gotten her in a family way. It was unanimously decided he should marry her, then and there, and the union was solemnized with the help of a sled-dog preacher.

Many miners were legally married by the traveling priests and ministers of the Yukon, such as Father Judge and Bishop Bompas, and many more were as good as married to the Indian women they lived with.

There were almost no white women in the Yukon at this time. Wives and daughters of steamboat captains or traders sometimes traveled on the river but few if any became permanent residents ashore. Consequently when we heard that our first "girls" were due to arrive, excitement reached fever pitch. Oscar Ashby and Billy Leake, our local impresarios, recruited them in San Francisco and Seattle and brought them in over Chilkoot and down the river on scows. They were so-called "variety girls"—entertainers with a variety of skills. Some, like Grace and Myrtle Drummond, whom I was to have as friends for the rest of their lives, were tap dancers and contortionists. Some were ventriloquists. Some like Annie Merle were singers. Annie's sweet voice was perhaps the first white female's ever to warble its notes in our Arctic wasteland.

I was in Al Morenci's Saloon the day they arrived. Circle rushed as one man to the waterfront. Several of the girls received offers of marriage before they stepped out of their boats. We escorted them in a body to Ashby and Leake's unfinished two-story theater building which had rooms upstairs. While the girls changed out of their trail clothes, the building was finished forthwith and before the sun set a memorable party began which lasted all that night and into the following day—a sailor from one of the Herschel Island whaling vessels being among those furnishing us continuous music from fiddle, mouth harp, and accordion.

By November 1896, we had such an up-and-coming community that we decided to hold our own Presidential Election. By law none of us could vote—Alaska being only a district, not even a territory—but that made no difference. Our candidates were the national ones: William McKinley who favored the gold standard and William Jennings Bryan who advocated free coinage of silver. Republican Headquarters were at Jack McQuesten's Alaska Commercial Company Store, Democratic Headquarters at J. J. Healy's North American Trading and Transportation Company. The polling place was Morenci's Saloon. Your vote was challenged automatically and in response you were expected to buy drinks for the house. When all votes were counted McKinley and gold received 202, Bryan and silver 101, and those 303 votes represented virtually every white man in the Yukon and probably included Bill Ewing and an Indian or two.

That night there was a celebration and torchlight parade. Casey Moran led it on a mule. The girls had made him an Uncle Sam suit out of some red-and-white bunting. Casey looked like a million and so did the mule, the only mule in the Arctic Circle. The torchlight procession followed them, in through the wide doors of the saloons, into Ashby and Leake's theater, and there everybody except the mule had to get up on the stage and do something, sing a song, dance a jig, say a prayer, anything. There was Montana Pete, miner and gambler, in blue woolen shirt and Prince Albert coat. He made us cry with laughter as he recited *The Boy Stood on the Burning Deck.*

By now, however, we were beginning to hear of a rich strike up at Deer Creek, or Klondike as it later was called. Jack Carr, our mail carrier, who had the longest mail route in the world in all probability—Dyea over Chilkoot and down the river to St. Michael on Bering Sea—a round trip of about 5,000 miles—all done on foot with dogs and sled—brought us the first word. Jack said they were getting twenty-dollar pans on Deer Creek. Next reports put the pans at fifty dollars. Then a hundred. Then five hundred. When Jack McQuesten received confirmation from his agent at Fortymile that there really *had* been a rich strike,

Frank Manley and I decided to go up over the ice and see for ourselves.

We found a tent-and-log city springing up at the mouth of Deer Creek across from the Indian village where Charlie Tufts and I had stopped and talked to George Carmack on the way in in '94. George had figured prominently in what had happened.

# 6. Strike at Seventymile

Dawson (as it became known) was struck the seventeenth day of August 1896 by George Carmack and two Indians, one of them Skookum Jim his brother-in-law. They'd traveled from their village at the mouth of Deer or "Klondike" Creek over the hill, to what we later called Hunker Creek, in response to friendly word from Bob Henderson, Al Dalton, and others, who were getting sixteen-dollar pans there, to come and stake. On their way back they stopped at Rabbit Creek, later called Bonanza—and for good reason—to make tea. Skookum Jim went down to the creek with the teapot. As he stooped to fill the pot at a spot where a reef happened to cross the creek and bedrock was exposed, he saw a nugget shining in the water. He called George. When George saw the nugget he went and got the frying pan, burnt it out clean, came back and scraped the contents of a rock crevice, just above water line, into the pan. When he washed it he had two or three ounces of gold. He kept on washing and got two or three more ounces.

George, who'd never had much luck, became excited. He staked, and Jim staked, and the other Indian, Tagish Charlie, staked, and then without a word to Henderson and the boys working just over the hill who'd tipped them off in the first place, the three of them hiked for home. There George got into a canoe with Skookum Jim and floated down to Fortymile to record their claims with the gold commissioner. And there at Willy McPhee's saloon George exhibited his dust on the bar and announced: "The drinks are on me fellows! I'm rich!" George died broke as so many did.

Frank and I staked a residential lot at the foot of the hill near the big spring where the Catholic Hospital would be built later and looked around for ground. It was going fast but we bought Discovery on Gold Bottom and a bench (hillside) claim where Gold Bottom and Hunker came together, Whiskey Hill on the left, Temperance on the right, as close as whiskey and temperance ever got, as the boys liked to say.

We eventually took around a hundred and thirty thousand from our creek claim but failed to hit the really big pay. The stream slid over smooth rock, and the gold had collected either above or below. Our bench claim produced well for a while, a number of its pans going to ten and fifteen dollars. But its face grew too steep and we had to tunnel and that got us into more work and expense than was profitable.

Dick Lowe's fraction was another matter. It was located where Eldorado and Skookum Gulch flowed into Bonanza. Dick got it while he was asleep. He was with the government survey party that came up the creek surveying the claims. After lunch, he lay down for a nap under a spruce tree. When he woke the others had gone on, so Dick decided to stake a fraction, or small slice of apparently low-value ground that they and he had happened onto and which could not lawfully be included in the claim of an earlier staker.

It became perhaps the richest ground in the world. I've walked the length of it—eighty-seven feet—on sluiceboxes covered solidly with gold. Dick took out a couple of million and his deepest pay was only about thirteen feet.

Frank and I kept busy—staking, trading, or working claims. We didn't walk, we ran. Everybody was on the go. The atmosphere was charged with excitement. You'd see a man trot into town, do his business, trot back to his claim. Sometimes we didn't take our boots off for a week, going on stampedes as strikes were made on the various tributaries of the Klondike and fresh discoveries were reported from up and down the Yukon.

After one stretch without sleep I was in our cabin taking a snooze on my bed of spruce bows when Frank came in, fresh from downtown, and announced, "There's been a strike at Seventymile!"

I tried to express interest. "Big one?"

"They say she is. Some of the boys just came up-river with the word."

"We always knew Seventymile had color in her."

"Ground that's been worked has often panned out later. Some people have already left."

What Frank was meaning without saying was that it was my turn to go on this stampede if either of us went. He'd just returned from our claim on Dominion Creek. Frank had been a peace officer in west Texas before coming north and he had an even-handed sense of justice that carried weight. He and I were "one-sack" partners—that is, we shared the same sack of dust, each dipping in as needed and settling up when he felt ready—and I wanted to keep it that way.

"All right," I said, "I'll catch a little sleep and leave early in the morning."

We kept a dog team in a corral beside the cabin but by the time I waked I'd decided to make the trip without dogs or sled. Anywhere within reason, say 100 to 150 miles, a man can beat dogs. Dogs have to be fed and rested every fifty or sixty miles. A man doesn't. Or if he does he can do it more quickly than dogs. I knew that the snowtrail down the ice of the Yukon would be in excellent condition. My moccasins would hardly get damp. I knew that my cross-country pace was six and a half to seven miles an hour on a good trail, because I'd checked it several times between Dawson and Dominion, fifty miles over two ranges, in seven and a half hours. On the comparatively level downstream-going of the Yukon it might be faster. And I knew that though I was nearing my thirties, after four years of the northern grind I was in good shape and would give boys or dogs a run for their money.

It was still dark when I started for the river. I was wearing moosehide moccasins, tanned, smoked and soft as chamois. There was a layer of dry grass for insulation between them and my three pairs of wool socks. I wore red flannel underwear, gray wool shirt, blue denim Levi overalls, parkee of white drill that came down to my knees, Yukon cap of beaver fur with earflaps, and gauntlet mittens of moosehide, white wool-finger gloves inside them. My snow glasses, of the kind the Eskimos have been using for ages, were two pieces of wood about the size of a small matchbox with a slit big enough to insert a quarter in. For protection against sunburn I'd reached into the stove before I left the cabin and smeared my cheeks and lips with charcoal. I carried a small backpack of possibly fifteen pounds consisting of two extra pairs of moccasins, three extra pairs of socks, matches, tea, tobacco and a small ax.

It was a warm March morning, not more than fifteen below. Sounds and odors of breakfasts and departures were in the air. I called to a few neighbors and went on down to the river bank, and as I moved out onto the ice I could look back and see the smoke drifting straight up from the cabins of Dawson into the windless early dawn and hear the sledrunners popping. There was a fine canopy of stars. Behind the town rose Moosehide Mountain. Upstream beyond the mouth of Klondike Creek were the lights of Lousetown, the Indian village—its new name speaking for the degradation it had undergone.

Directly in front of me was the island where Hoochinoo Albert ran his hooch mill, and beyond, sheer bluffs rose dark against the sky.

The surface of the river was roughened by ice jams left from the fall before—huge blocks of ice, big as boulders, loomed up here and there. The snowtrail, pounded hard by hundreds of sleds and thousands of feet throughout the winter, picked its way where best it could, generally close to the bank on one side or the other.

There were a number of people moving out onto the ice with me. I could see dark shapes, some solitary as I was, some with one-dog bobber sleds, some with large ten-foot basket sleds—all with the same objective, the strike at Seventymile.

I hit an easy pace and warmed up slowly. When you are going to travel all day, perhaps for several days, there is no use to start fast. I stretched my legs and rambled five or six miles, then slowed to a walk and raised my earflaps. I'd found my pace—had my "shakedown cruise" as they say of ships—and was ready to go.

I'd already passed a few slow-movers like Dolf Leggett who played tortoise to the hares of many stampedes, yet left the country better fixed financially than most of us. He was driving a regulation Yukon sled with gee pole instead of handlebars.

"I'd hate to have you building the fire for me if I was freezing to death," I kidded him as I went by.

"Better save your breath, wise guy. Mother Woods is ahead."

Luckily it wasn't Fay Dalzean or Judge Coke Hill or Scotty Allan. Those fellows could really cover ground. Mother Woods, however, was our leading feminine stampeder. Many a night in a bunk cabin on the trail, its floor covered with sleeping men, I've seen her come in, kick a place for herself among the bodies, lie down, wrap up in her lynx robe and sleep tight till morning. She'd come to the North to seek her fortune as many women did. She had a daughter at finishing school in the States and that daughter gave rise to a famous story by deciding to pay Mother a visit. Mother was running a roadhouse not far from Nome at the time. When she heard her daughter was coming she called the boys together. "Look here, you dirty so-and-so's, my daughter's coming to visit me and she's a lady, see? I don't want anything but gentlemen on the premises while she's here. You bums understand that?" The bums understood. The bar was closed, the card games shut down. During Mother Woods' daughter's stay, butter would scarcely have melted in the mouths of some of the roughest men in the Arctic—they were so well behaved.

"How long's she gonna be here?" one of them finally asked with a sigh.

"Not any longer'n I can help it!" Mother snapped.

Mother and I were on the best of terms friendly enemies can be—I having just got the better of her in a dog trade—and now I saw her ahead of me, driven by Big Jack, her driver and close friend.

"Hi, Wolf!" Jack greeted me as I drew alongside, using the nickname I'd acquired through breeding dogs to wolves.

I winked at him. Mother was sitting on the sled wrapped in her lynx robes, a good-looking woman, nothing of the dance-hall floozie about her.

"Good morning, Mother! Those dogs I sold you pulling you pretty lively?"

Her face got white with anger under its coating of rice powder. Profanity was one of her strong points. When she'd finished exercising her vocabulary on me, she concluded, "You cheated me in that dog trade!"

"Why, how do you mean?" I asked innocently.

"Those dogs you sold me were no damn good!"

"You didn't say you wanted good dogs. If you'd said you wanted good dogs, I'd have sold you good dogs. You thought you were fooling me by getting three-hundred dollar dogs for hundred-dollar ones!"

The air turned blue.

"See you at Seventymile!" I called back over my shoulder.

I was feeling good. The sun had come up at a low angle far to the south. Pretty soon I was passing the site of old Fort Reliance, once the Hudson's Bay Company's headquarters in the Northwest, now just a grassy clearing covered by snow. Then a pair of young wolves came down and crossed the trail oblivious of me. It was almost spring and they were pairing off. A little later I saw a caribou who had wintered all season on the banks of the Yukon. He was watching me from among the frozen trees. Not far beyond him a smoke rose from a cabin chimney. That was what I was hoping to see. I was hungry. It was mid-morning and I had been going since before daylight.

Inside the cabin I found half a dozen fellows sitting around, some the owners of dogs resting outside, the others woodchoppers who occupied the cabin and spent the winter chopping wood for the steamers to use next summer, and cording it up like breastworks along the bank. I first knew Tex Rickard, later the famous Madison Square Garden fight promoter, at such a woodchoppers' cabin. Tex was selling wood to the steamers at eight dollars a cord.

"Hi, boys," I said. "What are you doing here when gold's cropping out of the ground on Seventymile?"

They were skeptical. "Those fellows claim a three-grain pan. I don't believe it. I've worked that creek, once in '89, once in '94. There's no pay in her."

They gave me some of their Siwash tea that was on the stove and some pink beans that had been cooked till your breath peeled the skin from them—the perfect test—and then frozen instantly by the natural quick-freeze of the Yukon. Add a little bacon grease and heat and you have beans to eat in ten minutes.

Nourished, I moved on. The day was a perfect corker, not too hot, not too cold. The snow underfoot was perfect. I didn't even stop to change socks or moccasins. I rambled on at six to seven miles an hour feeling I could run the entire 2,000 miles of the Yukon clear to the ocean.

Toward the middle of the day I was passing Fortymile, fifty-two miles from Dawson.

Fortymile, one of the oldest camps in the Yukon, was deserted. Her fine "punkinseed gold"—shaped identically like a pumpkin seed—could not compete with the more plentiful supplies of Dawson, though it assayed the highest in the region at twenty dollars an ounce. You could make a grubstake at Fortymile but that was about all. In later years the syndicates with their dredgers took more from her worked-out diggings than we ever took by hand.

In the open rapids below Fortymile steam was rising and mallard ducks were floating. The sight of those ducks in that open water in wintertime was a strange one. They didn't startle when I ran by and I wondered if many ahead of me had passed them, or if I was nearing the head of the pack. I'd passed quite a few already. Those fellows with the dogs at the woodchoppers' camp had left Dawson the night before. Others had stopped to feed their dogs the half-pound of salmon. Others had hit a slower pace than I. But I guessed there was one ahead and guessed who he might be.

Bill Hunter was a crackerjack stampeder. He stood better than six-feet-two, tall for those days, and had a stride to match. He'd established a reputation for himself a year or two earlier by Siwashing it—that is, traveling with not much more than a rabbit blanket and an ax—from Juneau to Circle City, 900 miles, alone.

As I went down into the Narrows toward Eagle and the American boundary I was looking for Bill. I knew he'd been in Dawson and doubted he'd miss a chance to stampede. Now the hills were closing in and it was beginning to get dark. I didn't know the time I was making but had a feeling it was good. I was going to run on to Seventymile if it took all night. I knew I'd recognize her mouth. She's a wide-wash creek and her bars would be shining in the starlight. John the Bear Hunter, a veteran squaw man, and two or three other fellows had cabins at the mouth of Seventymile and I planned to stop there and recoup and borrow snowshoes for the trip up-country into the creek, where the going would be mostly on unbroken trail through heavy snow.

I passed the American line where there was no marker but the deserted camp of Ogilvie and the surveyors who had run the line along the 141st meridian years before. The river began to widen again. I hadn't passed anybody in quite some time when I saw a figure ahead of me. I knew right away it was Hunter.

Then I saw with a start he was limping. That took away some of my satisfaction. There were, you should understand, no trophies in these runs but satisfaction. Stampedes were not so much races as friendly trials among friends.

"What's the matter?" I called as I drew up.

"I turned my ankle."

That was all there was to it—bad luck. I walked beside Bill for half a mile. He'd left Dawson about the same time I had and been a little ahead of me all the way.

"You should have clear sailing from here on," he said. "Since most of the Fortymile boys were at Dawson when the word came, not many could have got the jump on you."

I ran on into the spectacular Arctic night with its aurora playing like many-colored lights against the blackness of the north. The Yukon is the only place where I've *heard* the northern lights. They make a peculiar whirring sound which is eerie when you're alone. The hours began to flow together now. My feet and legs were working automatically as were my lungs and heart. I'd reached that condition of equilibrium when your body becomes like an efficiently functioning machine. Toward midnight I saw lights in the trees and the welcome wide washes of Seventymile. Even then I didn't feel very tired, just comfortably worked out.

I trotted up through the trees and found John the Bear Hunter's cabin and John himself sitting next the stove drinking hooch with two pals, their whiskey having given out back around Christmas. Hooch, I might explain, was concocted from anything that would ferment. Practically every cabin had a hooch mill at the back of its stove: a mash barrel into which went leftovers such as raisins, potatoes, prunes, dried apples, and a cake of yeast. The warm effervescence of this brew was distilled through a piece of worm-shaped pipe and the clear product was usually enough to stand your hair on end.

"Dawson?" they said. "You're the first we've seen. Thought maybe you guys had struck it so rich you wouldn't stampede any more!"

"How far up the creek is she?" I asked, meaning "Discovery."

"Six or eight miles."

Now John broke in emphatically. He was a Dutchman, a German, that is, who'd worked for the Hudson's Bay Company for thirty years before I knew him. He was one of the dirtiest men I ever knew. His whiskers had originally been black but were now a mottled gray and so dirty and tangled no mowing machine could have gotten through them. They ran right up to his eyes. His hair hung down around his shoulders except where it had got so long it bothered him and he'd chopped some off. He wore a pair of old yellow mackinaw pants he'd worn for years, and over them a pair of Levis patched and full of holes. You could see the yellow mackinaw through the holes.

"Tree grain of gold! Tree grain of bull-con!" he bellowed. "I live on dis creek half my life. If dey get tree grain to de pan, dey brought 'em wid 'em!"

The boys who had struck it were outsiders who'd come in the autumn before and sunk their hole. By the light of John's dip—what is impolitely called a bitch, a dish of bear grease with a bit of twisted moss for wick—I listened, sipping tea, eating beans and moose, while John told how he had been appointed recorder for the creek by the first of us to go up, and how he hoped to record nothing but rich claims for old friends like me who'd been "in" before the crowd arrived. The hooch had a powerful influence on John's English. It soon made him completely incoherent but not till he'd agreed to lend me snowshoes so that I could make the trip up-country next morning. They would be the big Yukon shoes built on willow frames five to six feet long, ten to twelve inches wide, curled at the nose. I fell asleep in one of John's bunks on the slough grass he used as mattress, feeling his lice crawl over me but too tired to care, while he argued with the others whether it was 110 or 120 miles to Dawson. I'd been something like twenty hours on the trail.

In the morning I went up the creek to stake. Seventymile is a fairly steep stream running back into high hills on the west side of the Yukon. Eight miles up, slogging on a half-broken trail, I came to Discovery, a hole twenty feet deep in one of the bars a few feet above present water. A double tent (actually two tents, one inside the other to provide insulation and warmth) was pitched on the bank where three or four fellows were looking at samples of gold in a bottle. It was fine gold, grains the size of a pinhead or less, and looked genuine enough.

As Frank and Riley and I had done during our first winter on Chicken Creek, they'd sunk their hole through frozen ground by means of a daily fire, cutting the wood to make the fire, bending their backs over shovels, and lifting out tons of gravel by means of a homemade windlass.

"I hope the pay streak holds," I said. "Is there room for me?"

"Waltz to it," they said. "This is a free country."

Following the last fellow's tracks, I found his right and left limits and staked my claim, a spruce post "four inches or more in diameter, hewed square and clean," bearing a paper proclaiming that I, Fred Schroder of Dawson, was lawful owner of Two Above Discovery on Seventymile Creek.

So I was located. I went down and recorded my claim with John for two dollars in dust and went home. The strike never amounted to one that you could work profitably by hand. The dredgers came later and took out a fortune. All I got out of it was the exercise and a new nickname, Seventymile.

# 7. Dawson

Until that summer the population of Dawson had consisted mostly of those of us who'd been "in" when the strike was made, a few hundred all together, but after the breakup in May 1897 hundreds more began arrriving. Along the river on Front Street, saloons, stores, dance halls, and restaurants shot up. Joe Ladue had moved his sawmill down from Sixtymile so there was plenty of lumber available. Soon we boasted most of the appurtenances of civilization including an opera house, board sidewalks, and even a volunteer fiire department.

Frank and I bought a scow and hoisted her up on pilings and converted her into a restaurant, the Skookum, which made us a nice income and saved us paying $10,000 for a waterfront lot. Our regular menu consisted of caribou or moose steak, beans and potatoes, bread, tinned butter and coffee for $3.50. Moose nose—cut off at the eyes—a popular delicacy—cost $4.50. Finding we had more meat than we needed we opened a butcher shop where we sold moose at $1.00 a pound, caribou 50¢. We shot most of our game up Stewart River and floated it down in scows. There are four to five hundred pounds of usable meat on a bull moose, and one or two would keep us going for a week or more.

We also operated a string of packhorses. They were mostly poor skates from Canadian ranches brought in from the coast over the White Pass route or along the trail Jack Dalton had opened from Pyramid Harbor. It was less arduous than Chilkoot and had grass much of the way. It hit the river below the bad rapids and from there Jack floated his horses down on scows. We charged twenty-five cents a pound (the equivalent of about two dollars today) for packing supplies to the creeks and fifty cents a pound for bringing gold back—gold being such a concentrated weight and so hard on a horse that we could carry much less of it, seldom more than 100 pounds per animal. Even with a 200-pound load of ordinary freight, though, a horse could earn you fifty dollars or more per day. Rates varied with distances traveled, a standard trip being the fifteen miles up to the Grand Forks junction of Bonanza and Eldorado one day, and back to Dawson the next.

There was little or no grass available so we fed them corn meal and rolled oats from a ten-pound sack. When winter came it was more economical to kill them for dog food than to feed them. Later we tried turning them out during the winter and found they could fend for themselves in the sheltered valleys by pawing their way through the snow to find grass, as the horses of lower Canada and our Great Plains did.

Our horses plus our restaurant made us more money than our claims except when we struck our best pay.

Transportation became increasingly a problem as Dawson's population grew. In addition to horses and dogs—there were thousands of dogs by now—oxen, goats, and even bears were pressed into service. One fellow I knew on Upper Bonanza had a black bear and a black-and-tan shepherd dog with which he made regular sled runs to town. He hitched them in tandem, the dog in front. Once the dog got the bear started all the dog had to do was keep out of the way. And when you met them coming down the trail, believe me, brother, you stepped aside!

Jack McQuesten's Alaska Commercial Company's store served as our first bank. Moosehide bags full of dust worth thousands if not millions were stacked like cordwood against the back wall. Each was labeled with its owner's name. When you wanted some dust, Al Whistle, Jack's clerk, sorted through the pile of bags until he found yours, weighed out what you wanted, and tossed your bag back on the pile.

At first the dust from all the creeks was mingled indiscriminately. Later it was assayed and segregated according to source. Upper Bonanza was worth $18.25 an ounce; Lower Bonanza around $18.00; Eldorado, almost as pale as silver and the best of all, brought $19.00. The regular commercial rate was $17.00 per ounce. In '97 the Canadian Bank of Commerce came in and was going strong by '98, shipping out dust for you, issuing paper money on it, and doing a regular banking business.

By then the population of Dawson and her gold-bearing creeks had reached thirty thousand. Some of the newcomers were celebrities such as Captain Jack Crawford, the famous scout who'd been with Buffalo Bill and fought the Sioux and wore his hair down to his shoulders. Crawford opened a shooting gallery on Front Street where I saw Arizona Charlie Meadows, perhaps the best shot of his time, perform. Charlie could split a bullet on a knife blade at thirty feet or put one down the throat of a bottle and break its bottom without touching its neck.

Frank P. Slavin, the Australian heavyweight whom John L. Sullivan declined to meet, was on hand as was Frank Gotch, world's champion wrestler. For some reason Gotch got the idea he wanted to be a boxer, and he and Slavin met one night in a ring on the stage at the opera house. Slavin toyed with him for a few rounds, tormenting him with punches from every direction until Gotch got mad, ripped off his gloves, picked Slavin up with a crotch hold and threw him into the orchestra pit. The referee, Charlie Gleason, a former middleweight titleholder, declared Slavin winner of the boxing match, Gotch of the wrestling.

Also on hand were men who became notable later but were relatively unknown then, like Jack London. London had a reputation for extreme laziness. He was among those occupying a cabin on the Klondike Flats claim at Ninety-seven Below on Bonanza which I visited on several occasions while packing supplies and gold to and from the creeks. It was dirtier than the hubs of hell and Jack was unable or unwilling to get out of it often enough, or to eat enough fresh meat with plenty of fat in it, to stay healthy. Consequently he developed scurvy and went home.

Joaquin Miller, the California poet, took better care of himself while becoming one of our most disliked citizens. Miller had the unfortunate habit of not going outside trail cabins to relieve himself on cold winter nights but used an inside corner as *pissoir*.

Major Frederick Russell Burnham, a Los Angeles boy who'd distinguished himself in the Matabele Wars in South Africa, appeared among us, as did Joe Boyle, a colorful Irishman, organizer of the Princess Pat Regiment of Klondikers and frontiersmen in World War I and later a close friend of the Queen of Romania.

Wilson Mizner, scion of a prominent San Francisco family, later a New York playwright and Hollywood celebrity, came in over Chilkoot with a dance-hall girl as part of his luggage and became known as the "Yellow Kid"; and Klondike Kate Rockwell, a popular belle, staked a saloon keeper named Alexander Pantages who became a theater magnate.

The Oregon Mare was there, too. She would whinny when she stepped up to the bar to order drinks. Like most of her kind she was generous to a fault. I've seen her spend five or six hundred in one evening buying drinks for the house.

Dawson like Circle was a rough but honest town and there was little or no crime. If you got obstreperous, the Mounties put you to work on the woodpile next their log barracks. They didn't wear guns and neither did we, though most of us had them.

Well, by May 24, 1898 Queen Victoria had reigned longer than any other British monarch and the time had come for her to take her place in Dawson's history, too. Good Queen Vic, as she was commonly referred to, had celebrated her diamond jubilee several years earlier and Kipling had written his poem, *Recessional*, about it. Out here on the farthest fringe of her empire her portrait was constantly in view and patriotism probably keener than on Piccadilly. Her birthday meant as much to the frontier Englishman as July 4 did to the frontier American. The fact that most of us in Dawson weren't Englishmen didn't matter; one excuse for a party was as good as the next.

May 24, 1898 dawned bright and clear. The ice was gone from the river, the snow was off the ground. Flags and bunting were up. The town band, a truly democratic organization, was sounding off. Anyone who could blow, saw, or bang anything resembling a musical instrument could play in it. A rival group of bagpipers squalled up and down Front Street wearing kilts. Then Harry McCullough from Eleven Above on Bonanza, our "mayor," made some appropriate remarks. He announced that Captain Constantine, head of our Mounted Police detachment, was to be chief referee for the day's events and that we had better behave or Constantine would put us to work on his woodpile. "Go to it, boys!" said Harry and the show was on.

Most of the sporting events took place on Front Street. Usually a quagmire, it had received a coating of sawdust for this occasion. First came the lifting of the anvil. The idea was to pick up a 200-pound anvil by the horn with one hand and walk as far as you could with it. Harry Somers of Rampart took top honors, as I recall. He and Captain Al Mayo were probably the strongest men in the North, though I've seen Manuel Gularte, who came to us from the Azores by way of Wyoming, lift 200-pound flour barrels by the chines and stack them three high. Some of the finest physical specimens in the world had been attracted to Dawson. They'd come literally from the earth's four corners. Others had been hardened by years of life in the North. Consequently some of the performances that day were near record level.

The winning toss in the shot put was around forty feet, a distance not much exceeded by the best in the world at that time. Then came the caber tossing, or "throwing the tree trunk," done American style for distance, rather than Scottish style for grace. Three husky miners from Butte, Montana, won the dust.

In the pack race, the contestants ran to the top of Moosehide Mountain carrying a hundred-pound sack of flour on their backs and wearing heavy gum boots to negotiate the swamp behind town. Thirty or forty started. Five or six finished.

The hundred-yard dash was the chief event of the day as it usually is, and rivalry ran high between oldtimers and newcomers. I was among those who felt called upon to defend the honor of the sourdoughs against the cheechakos, fleetness of foot having been one of my strong points since boyhood. Ten yards from the finish the fellow a step ahead of me, a semi-pro from the Olympic Club in San Francisco, stumbled over one of numerous small pieces of wood interspersed among the sawdust of the street, and I won first place, a sack of dust, and my side bets. A good morning's work.

At dark the bonfires were lit and the party really got going. After all, Queen Vic was seventy-nine today and she might not be with us for another year!

With no intentions whatever of seeing the Queen, I headed for London that summer with samples of dust and claim certificates to sell wildcat gold shares. Frank and Riley and I had combined our less promising holdings with those of several friends and were hoping to cash in on the boom market in Klondike claims. Gold fever—Klondike fever—was sweeping the world. Dick Rice would go with me as far as Seattle. We carried our samples in moosehide bags, each weighing around twenty-five pounds and each containing five to six thousand dollars worth of nuggets or dust. Joining forces with Fred Burnham and George Burke who were also heading for London with samples for the South Africa Company, we went by steamer up the Yukon, portaged around the rapids, took the lake sternwheeler that now carried us in style to the head of Bennett. Things had changed drastically since Charlie Tufts and I had come in four years before. At Bennett we hired Indians to pack our gold over Chilkoot Pass. We chose Chilkoot rather than the easier White Pass route to Skagway because of Soapy Smith and his gang who controlled Skagway and waylaid incoming miners.

Reaching Dyea without trouble, we chartered a tug to take us across the inlet to the Skagway docks where the "City of Seattle" was lying. Boarding her from the seaward side to stay out of Soapy's way, we learned that he'd been shot and killed the night before by a man named Reid, and his reign of lawlessness, the first of its kind in the North, was ended.

On reaching London I submitted our samples to two brokerage houses that specialized in mining claims and they eventually marketed nearly a quarter million for us in wildcat shares. I found the names of our creeks almost as well known in London as in Dawson. Thanks to the courtesy of friends, I stayed at the Thatched House Club near the Marble Arch, a rendezvous for sportsmen, adventurers, and military men. The club had once been a pub and its large main lounge had a fireplace at either end that could accommodate a six-foot log. Trophy heads looked down from the walls and there was a rather sacrosanct atmosphere of imperial power. There I made the acquaintance of R. K. Douglas, of Wilson & Company, and of representatives of other trading firms with whom I did business later in China, and there one afternoon I encountered His Royal Highness, the Prince of Wales, a patron of Arctic exploration among other things, and a member in good standing of the Arctic Brotherhood. As a fellow member (though my formal membership came later as perhaps his did) I had the right to keep my hat on in his presence but since I wasn't wearing one the issue never came up. He wasn't much taller than I, five seven and three quarters, but much heavier. We shook hands; he asked a few questions. I said things were booming on Bonanza and Eldorado. He impressed me with his knowledge of Dawson and surrounding territory. That was about it.

On another occasion I met Fred Selous, one of the leading white hunters of the day, prototype for Alan Quartermain in Rider Haggard's popular novel by that name. Among other things, Selous told me he'd known native African hunters who could smell a white man at half a mile when the wind was right. I later found much the same to be true of Manchurian hunters. They could smell a white man at about the same distance they could smell a bear.

I visited the London Fur Market, then as later the center of the trade, and the British Museum of Natural History where I saw my first Siberian, or Manchurian, tiger. He was mounted alongside one of his Bengal cousins but there the similarity stopped. Though marked the same, the Siberian was more than half again as large. His enormous bulk and bow legs would stay in my mind until I saw them in the flesh years later.

I spent nearly two months in England, traveled through Wales and considered crossing the Channel and visiting Hanover (the Old Man always spoke of us as Hanoverians, never as Germans) but headed for home instead. On arrival in New York I found a wire from Frank Manley, sojourning at Hot Springs, Arkansas, with a new wife, saying Riley Dingman had died of a fever in Dawson and there was no one to look after our interests.

Hurrying to Seattle, I teamed up with Al Dalton and Dick Lowe of The Fraction. At Skagway we got dogs and sleds and joined Jack Carr who was going in with the mail. In addition to the mail, Jack as usual carried a few supplies for sale. Included was a five-gallon keg of whiskey.

Al and I broke trail because we were light. Next came Dick. Then Jack. We hurried, hoping to reach Dawson in time for the St. Patrick's Day celebration, always a big event.

Around seven o'clock on the evening of March 17 we were still several miles from town when we saw a lantern bobbing toward us along the right-hand limit. We were on the left, picking our way down the snowtrail through rough ice. A voice hailed us and pretty soon here came little Jimmy Carey, one of Dawson's leading saloon keepers, with a half-dozen dogs and an empty sled.

"Where's Jack Carr?" he demanded. He'd heard Jack was coming.

"Back yonder!"

"He got any whiskey?"

"A little."

When Jack caught up, Jimmy went to his sled and without a word picked up the five-gallon keg. "How much will it cost me?"

"A hundred dollars a gallon!"

Jimmy didn't bat an eye. "Sold! Come on, the party's already begun!"

Our dogs weren't as fresh as his so he was well ahead of us when we reached town but we saw him silhouetted against the lights as he topped the forty-foot bank. When we arrived he was running down the middle of the street, holding the keg of whiskey high above his head with both hands, yelling at the top of his lungs: "Come on, you sons-of-bitches, I've got whiskey! Real whiskey!" Dawson hadn't had much but hooch to drink since Christmas.

The saloons and dance halls shelled out. Everybody who could squeeze into Jimmy's place did so, while one of his bartenders inserted a spigot in the keg and Jimmy himself climbed on top of the bar. "Keep your dust, fellows!" he announced, as pokes were tossed at his feet. "This one's on Mother Carey's boys and the Seventeenth Day of Ireland!"

Everyone got a free drink if it was only a sip. Jimmy watched to see that nobody double-shot the turn.

The Klondike Strike was a realization of a dream which has led men westward after wealth and happiness since human history began. It was a realization, too, of my boyhood dreams of wealth and fellowship. Somewhere toward the sunset, the legends say, lies the promised land. Here we were, plain ordinary people who had made our way to prosperity and comradeship. It was a kind of paradise—rough but real.

# 8. Nome

Early in 1900 word reached us that Nome had been struck. George Friend, Dave Englund, Charlie Mulcahy and I took sleds and went down the Yukon, across Kaltag Portage, and up over the ice of Bering Sea to Nome. There at the mouth of Anvil Creek we found a tent-and-board city springing up on frozen ground along a beach.

The big pay was at the water's edge. Some of the beach claims were only sixteen feet square and yielded a thousand dollars or more per foot, or $256,000 from a piece of ground no larger than your living room floor if pay were uniform throughout. The work was all done with wooden rockers which sifted out the flour gold.

George and I bought a residential lot near the Alaska Commercial Company's Store, put a tent on it, began to look the country over. There was no good ground available so George began hitting the faro bank and I headed north toward Port Clarence on Bering Strait to the strike reported in the Kougarok district but found nothing suitable for handwork. I bumped into Three-Fingered Jack McKay whom I'd known at Dawson and who was living in a tent on the beach with his wife, where he had one of the biggest polar bear skins I'd ever seen, and at Mary's Igloo I saw several dozen Eskimos dead of the Spanish flu, and by midsummer was back at Nome to find a madhouse atmosphere.

Twenty thousand people were in the process of landing on the beach at Nome. Included was a substantial criminal element. At Dawson there'd been the tough overland trip to weed out the riffraff, but here anybody who could scrape up the price of a steamer ticket could come. Before the troops were called from

[81]

St. Michael to preserve order, I went over to Council, fifty miles east, and staked. I bought Discovery and One Above on a creek close to town, met Charles D. Lane, head of the fabulously rich Wild Goose Mining Company, the man who later led the successful fight against the claim-jumpers and corrupt politicians at Nome. And then a group of us bought Three and Four on Crooked Creek, a gamble, right on a rock slide. Complicating matters, there was not even timber enough to make sluiceboxes, let alone what would be needed for a mining operation.

The demand for lumber and other supplies was so acute and the possibilities for trading so promising, that I came outside on the last boat in the fall of 1900, got with Captain Charlie Samuelson whom I'd known at Circle and who knew sailing ships, and in the Estuary at Oakland found what I was looking for.

She was a little two-masted schooner of eighty tons register called the "Ralph J. Long." She drew three and a half feet of water on a flat bottom, which made her ideal for coastal trading, and had a fifteen-foot centerboard which could be lowered so that a storm would not upset her. I gave three thousand for her in the name of the Crooked Creek Mining Company and we pulled her out of the water and scraped her, found her sound as a nut though her rope rigging and canvas needed replacing. Then we took her across the bay to San Francisco and into the creek near the Third and Townsend Street depot of the Southern Pacific. There we began loading her with the kinds of merchandise and supplies that would be needed in the North: gum boots, shovels, raincoats, slabs of bacon, sacks of flour, sugar and beans, canned stuff, hammers, nails, saws, and so forth. Finally we put a deck load of lumber on her. She must have been carrying nearer 100 tons than 80 when we sailed.

For crew I'd signed a boy who claimed he could cook, two Scandinavian deckhands, and Captain Graeder, a little fighting cock of a fellow who'd been an instructor in a nautical school in San Francisco, lost a couple of bouts to John Barleycorn, and needed a change of scene.

One afternoon in mid-April 1901 we untied the bow, the "Ralph J. Long" swung around with the tide, her jibs caught the wind, up went a piece of foresail, then a piece of mainsail, and soon we were passing Alcatraz Island which had a prison on it even then. After a rough crossing of the "potato patch," the bar outside Golden Gate, we headed her up the northwest coast. She took the swells like a gull and would log 200 miles on a good day. But Alaska lies 2,000 miles west of San Francisco. Opposite Oregon we headed her out to sea and didn't make land again until we reached Unimak Pass in the Aleutians three weeks later.

There at Dutch Harbor, the entrance to Bering Sea, eighteen or twenty steamers were waiting for the ice to go out. The cutter "Bear" was chasing the ice for them, hunting for leads, trying to get them through.

While waiting we fished for tom cod and salted away several boxes for use at the Crooked Creek mine. Then we followed in the wake of the steamers and reached Chinik at Golovin Bay on June 23, three months out of San Francisco.

At Chinik we unloaded part of our cargo and the tom cod to go by sternwheeler and poling boat up the Niukluk River to the mine, and that was how I made the acquaintance of John and Molly Dexter.

John was the trader at Chinik, Molly his Eskimo wife. Her people, the Niukluks, occupied cabins surrounding John's post and John was unofficial leader of the tribe into which he had married.

John was a conscientious man. He didn't sell the Eskimos whiskey, at least not too much of it, didn't cheat them out of their furs and ivory, at least not very much, and in general treated them as if they were members of his family which they were. He was crippled and walked with a cane. His game leg and how he acquired it and Molly's role in the matter, were the substance of a story often told by northern campfires.

Several years before I knew them, John was coming home with dogs and sled across the ice of Norton Sound from a visit to St. Michael when a storm caught him and the ice started breaking up under his feet. Molly and her people knew he was out there riding a floe but nobody dared go to him, the storm was so fierce. Finally Molly announced: "I'm going!" She took an umiak, an open skin boat, and paddled out alone and rescued not only John but his dogs. He was half frozen and limped for the rest of his life but the episode cemented his relationship with

Molly and her people as probably nothing else could have done. I saw that cement tested in an unusual way.

In 1902 in conjunction with our Crooked Creek operation, I was operating a sternwheeler between Chinik and the head of navigation on the Niukluk River, transhipping cargo from steamers and carrying it to the camps. When not busy I'd often spend an evening with John and Molly in their cabin, talking or quietly watching John teach her logarithms by the light of a whale oil dip. John had been a sea captain in his younger days but why he wanted to teach her logarithms I never discovered, unless it was to bring him closer to Molly who was many years his junior.

That fall was a particularly stormy one. The big blows started early. As consequence the herring didn't make their usual run into Golovin Bay, the caribou changed their migration routes, the walrus and white whale stayed far offshore, and the food caches of the Niukluks on the spit of land beside John's post were nearly empty.

As food grew scarcer, an increasing number of the tribe wanted to go to the Mission down the bay, or up the river to the gold camps, for handouts but John counseled patience. He knew the demoralization that would result if they became dependent on the Mission or the camps. Bad weather continued and hunger and unrest grew. The breaking point had been reached one night when I was sitting with John and Molly. We heard the wind beginning to rise around the eaves again. Another storm was coming. John shook his head gloomily. I said something hackneyed about it being an ill wind that blew nobody good. "How can it blow us good?" John asked. I had to shrug.

Next day and most of the following night I was busy transhipping cargo from a steamer to our sternwheeler. The wind kept blowing and the surge kept building up until good-sized combers were rolling into the bay. Riding with them, we took the sternwheeler and its cargo up the bay and up the Niukluk to White Mountain where the poling boats met us.

On our way back, we found the wind blowing harder than ever and the sky turned dark gray. The water covering the mud flats at the bay's head was churned white by big swells. We were following a course marked by fifty-gallon oil drums converted to buoys and I was sitting on a stool in the deckhouse, relaxed and dozing after two nights with little sleep, when my pilot jabbed me in the ribs with his elbow. "Look there!"

At first I thought one of our oil-drum buoys had drifted away from its moorings. Then I realized I was looking at a walrus.

What was a three-thousand pound bull walrus doing up here in the mud flats at the head of the bay? Then I saw another. Then a whole pod. Then another pod. It was unbelievable. By now we were beginning to see whales, too, the white belugas about nine feet long, schools of them, lifting their bottlenosed heads as they poked along the shallow channels. Then it dawned on me what was happening.

The storm was driving game into the bay. The wind was blowing us good. But where were John and his hunters?

As we approached the landing at Chinik I was holding down the whistle cord. The weather had kept people indoors and they hadn't realized what was happening but now they came pouring from their cabins. I saw John hobble out of his, Molly beside him carrying a rifle and a chair for him to sit in.

The water around us was alive with game by this time, walrus, whale, and many kinds of seal, and men were jumping into kayaks and bidarkies, with their rifles, spears and bladder floats, while women, children, and dogs raised a hubub that carried to us above the wind. We made a wide turn toward the landing, waved to John and Molly, yelled at the nearest hunters to throw us lines so we could tow them to the head of the bay where game was floundering in the mud.

On the bluff above us, Molly settled John into his chair and began to shoot at seals in the water below, taking deliberate aim with her .30-30. Around us skin boats were racing in every direction tied to seal or whale. And the wind and huge swells kept bringing more game into the bay until it looked like a crowded corral at roundup time. We chased whale and walrus into the shallow channels of the mud flats, as you herd cattle into chutes, shot them, attached lines and towed them back down the bay, while behind us the kayaks and bidarkies and spears and harpoons weren't idle either.

As we approached the landing, towing our last load of meat

behind us, try-pot fires were lighting up the beach and smoke was beginning to rise from the long-darkened council house. At the water's edge men, women, and children were busy butchering dozens of carcasses and hoisting the meat into the stilt-legged caches, while the dogs fought among the entrails.

Later we joined John, Molly, and the others at the celebration. The council chamber was a big one, roughly 150 feet by 50, made of drift logs which had floated down the Yukon and been distributed by the tides of Bering Sea. Along its walls, on half a dozen stoves, washboilers full of meat were bubbling. We men sat around the ceremonial fire in the center and drank tea and ate bannock cakes prepared and served by the women and girls.

When the keen edge of hunger had been relieved, there was dancing and singing. The younger fellows pounded around in a circle giving off explosive grunts to the accompaniment of beating drums and a monotonous *hee-hee-hee, haw-haw-haw* from the crowd. Now and then one of the dancers would select a woman from among the spectators and dance with her. Sometimes a couple would start dancing at random, apparently unrhythmically, yet taken together it was part of a pattern—part of that larger rhythm of up-beat and down-beat to which we all dance.

Finally John and Molly, their patient counselling justified, stood up and did a little shuffle. Everyone cheered, and a young buck ran out from the crowd and showered them with the feathers of good luck.

With our remaining lumber and supplies, we sailed on now in the "Ralph J. Long" to the boomtown of Teller, north of Nome, port of entry to the Kougarok district, where we disposed of our lumber at $150 per thousand and the balance of our cargo at a comparable good price. All but one of my crew left me at Teller in the belief they'd soon become rich, though I'd warned them that most who went rushing to the strikes at Nome, Dawson, Circle, and elsewhere ended up working for wages until they earned enough money for a ticket home.

A few evenings later Captain Graeder, Otto Rapp, our remaining deckhand, and I were sitting on the deck relaxing. The temperature was well into the 80s and we were smoking our pipes to keep the clouds of mosquitoes away, when the question of what to do next arose.

"How far is it to the Siberian coast?" Graeder inquired.

"About fifty miles." You could see across on a clear day.

"Perhaps we could trade for a few skins?" Otto suggested.

"If the Czar's revenue cutters don't catch you."

"They're few and far between, I hear," Graeder put in. They were.

"We've got the ideal vessel for coastal trade," Graeder continued. "She can slip in and out of shallow water and up streams if need be."

I was more than willing. I'd long wanted a look at Siberia. We caught a wind that night. Aided by the tide that pours down through Bering Strait at the rate of two or three knots an hour, we crossed before morning. On the Russian side tundra reached back toward barren mountains. Low willows grew along the streams. We swung south keeping a mile or so from shore, watching for native villages, intending to avoid Russian ones. With no maps or charts to guide us, we relied on sextant and binnacle and Graeder's know-how.

Thirty or forty miles below East Cape, we came to a village of drift logs and whalebone at the mouth of a good-sized stream. Fish were drying on racks. Lines strung with multiple hooks were stretched across the stream to catch sturgeon. Women and children were out attending the lines or hunting for berries while the men sat by their igloos, their faces turned our way. A schooner usually meant trade. It was late afternoon, good visiting time. Graeder ran us close to the beach and I took the dinghy and went in the rest of the way.

The first man to meet you at an Eskimo village is usually the headman. He is a recognized leader according to custom, rising to his position by being best hunter and wisest councilor. This one was middle-aged, shrewd looking, and smoking a pipe with a tiny brass bowl shaped like a cuspidor such as were common throughout the Far East.

"*Icka-nacka-ticka-cum-tuck-Chinook-wa-wa?*" or "Do you speak Chinook?" I greeted him in Chinook, the international jargon of the North. It was composed of Indian and Eskimo words plus a dash of English and maybe a bit of Russian. Three hundred words of it got you along in any camp in the Arctic.

"*Bos'n man* [American]?" he asked.

I nodded, and though I was interested primarily in his furs, I asked about his fishing. He led me to his drying racks where the catch ranged from 800-pound sturgeon to 12-pound sea trout. Still not wanting to seem eager, I asked about his catch of Japanese crabs. Each winter when those huge spiderlike crabs came into Bering Sea to spawn, the Eskimos fished for them through the ice with scraps of meat on barbless hooks, and each time one of the crabs was caught—and flipped out onto the ice where it froze stiff—the fisherman would toss it a spoonful of water. Why a spoonful of water to a dead crab? To placate the Crab Spirit. Otherwise his crabs might not return to Bering Sea next year and there would be no food for Eskimos. I said I'd heard it had been a bad year for furs, for which I extended my sympathy.

"Our furs were never better," he rejoined. "This is the best year I can remember!"

"Do you have some you might show me?"

"The Russian trader was here and paid me a fine price but I saved some of the best!"

I doubted that the Russian trader had been around so early in the season, but to say so was part of the game.

After a few minutes more of such negotiations he led me to his igloo. His furs were stacked on the sleeping bench that ran around the inside. A driftwood fire burned in the center of the floor. An old woman, his mother or mother-in-law, crouched over it tending a pot. In a few years her usefulness would end and they would send her out into the snow to die. Bags of oil and shreds of meat hung from the ceiling. Dogs and children were underfoot.

"Here are my choice skins," he said, showing me some third-grade stuff with rub spots such as the animals make in the spring when they start to shed and rub against trees or rocks.

I threw them down and, to make my disgust plain, started to walk away. He discovered better skins. Finally we got down to his good ones, taken before the long hair of winter comes but after the underhair has grown long enough to make them good. He had some really choice white fox, ermine, polar bear, mink, wolf, hair seal—no fur seal—mukluk seal, reindeer by the dozen, one black fox worth $500 in London. No sable. The sable, or dark marten, comes out of the timber country farther south. Nor was there any wolverine. The wolverine or carcajou was the one exception to the rule that a fur was worth twice as much in London as in the North. With wolverine, it was the other way around. Because wolverine is the one skin that won't collect frost no matter how cold the weather. It makes ideal lining for the openings of parkee hoods, and for that purpose I've paid a squaw as much as ten dollars for a strip of it two inches wide by eighteen inches long.

"These aren't bad," I conceded. "We might come back with trade goods for yourselves and your women. Are there other igloos with skins such as these?"

He showed me. Then we put across to Nome for a cargo of trade goods.

Nome was in chaotic state. Claim jumping, robbery, murder were rife, as were prostitution, drunkenness, and dope. Prominent citizens included Wyatt Earp. Far from maintaining law and order as he was supposed to have done at Tombstone, Earp kept to himself and operated a saloon in partnership with a fellow named Jack Hoxsie. In contrast to later years when the publicists got hold of his story and made him famous, Earp had a small reputation while in Nome. However he was reliably reported to have close connections with the unscrupulous courthouse crowd who, as Rex Beach accurately stated, ran Nome for their own advantage and chiseled and swindled their way to fortunes at the expense of many innocent people. Years later I learned that Earp had operated three gambling halls in, of all places, my own San Diego during the wide-open years there in the late '80s, but had kept very quiet about it.

Tex Rickard, Mother Woods, and many others from Dawson had come to Nome to get in on the show, and Lucky Baldwin from California had opened a sensationally big saloon and dance hall complete with gilt and girls.

If I'd had my doubts about the success of our Siberian trading venture, they were laid to rest when I met young Arthur Eaton. Arthur, short, chunky, not yet old enough to vote and a friend of mine for the next fifty years, had been doing exactly what we proposed to do. In company with an experienced captain named Allen, he'd acquired a little schooner like ours and was trading for furs on the Siberian side. Arthur's personal story gives as clear a picture as any of the kind of people who led the way in those days. Arthur was born in Swansea, Wales. At the age of fourteen he sailed as an apprentice aboard the full-rigged ship "Flintshire" bound around the Horn for San Francisco with a cargo of coal. Aboard were men of many nationalities including two Barbados Negroes and one white American (the renegade son of a minister) and another fourteen-year-old Welsh apprentice named Charlie Smith.

As apprentices in the British Merchant Marine, Arthur and Charlie did not bunk in the fo'castle with the men but on the half-deck next the captain's cabin. Their duties included striking the hours on the ship's bell and measuring her speed by means of a reel and a line cast over the side. They wore blue serge uniforms with brass buttons and small visored caps.

For the first ten days they were deathly sick but by the time the first Falkland Island pigeons perched in the rigging they'd become good sailors. Arthur was still gullible, though, and when the veteran seamen told him "the Falkland Island natives" would soon come aboard from canoes wearing war paint and breechclouts to trade gold for trinkets, he arranged his valuables on deck in anticipation. Of course no such natives existed. He learned to climb the mast and furl the skysail in wind and sleet, the smallest lightest men being sent to the highest, most dangerous heights.

Off the Horn they were dismasted by a violent storm which blew them as far south as Weddell Land. The ship nearly foundered. Rigging jury masts, they proceeded up the Pacific side to the doldrums where they lay becalmed for twenty-one days. The ship stuck as tight as that painted ship upon a painted ocean in Coleridge's poem. The only person allowed "to whistle for the wind" during this period was the Captain walking the deck. For hours his whistling was the only sound that could be heard except for the squeaking of the ropes as the vessel rocked almost imperceptibly from side to side.

At last a breeze sprang up and took them swiftly up the North American coast till they came to a bank of fog and out of that fog came a pilot ship, and they knew they were at the mouth of San Francisco Bay.

They unloaded at the old Howard Docks in Oakland and continued up the east side of the bay to Crockett to take on wheat. The central valleys of California in those days were one of the world's great wheat producing areas. Ships from many nations anchored in the roadstead or moored at the docks. Freight cars were lined up thickly on the shore and bags of wheat were unloaded from them onto the ships. The duties of apprentices like Arthur and Charlie included tallying the bags of wheat from the cars onto their ship. While doing this, the boys saw the chance to run away they had been waiting for. Life on shipboard had been hard, discipline rigorous, the food worse. Aside from soft bread on Sunday and pea soup twice a week they ate mostly hardtack. Every day at noon they lined up with the crew in front of the Captain and drank their lime juice. In the promised land of California things might be better.

At first they weren't, much. Arthur got a job at the Spreckels Sugar Refinery where he worked twelve hours a day, six days a week, for forty-five dollars a month.

Making his way to Seattle, he shipped on the steamer "Portland" bound for Skagway, and, with her, he brought back the first gold brought out of the Yukon—the gold that started the Klondike Rush.

In 1900, Arthur went to Nome for the strike there. Prospecting and working as a longshoreman, living at a cabin out on Belmont Point, he attended school at night in a building where Jimmy Doolittle—the same who would later bomb Tokyo—and other youngsters attended during the day.

While working a claim on Anvil Creek, Arthur got acquainted with a prosperous looking elderly gentleman who owned the adjoining claim. The elderly gentleman turned out to be H.M.H. Bolander, the "snuff king," a major stockholder in the American Tobacco Company. Bolander took a liking to Arthur and backed him to the tune of $65,000 to lead an expedition into the unexplored headwaters of the Kuskokwim region. Arthur's party made the rich strike at Ophir and then, following an Indian trail described to him by venerable Chief Nicolai, he hurried to communicate the news to Bolander in Chicago, covering 350 miles of wild country alone over the mountains to Cook Inlet.

There he was caught by the bore of Turnagain Arm and nearly capsized and drowned but rode the crest of the tide in a dory with dogs and sled, reached Seward and, finally, Seattle with the news of his strike.

Arthur had many other adventures that took him from the Arctic to Patagonia. When I last heard from.him he was facing one more: licking arthritis, doing fifty knee-bends when he felt the stiffness creeping up his spine; or he would rush into his garden, grab a spade and start digging.

Encouraged by Arthur's success on the Siberian coast, Graeder, Rapp and I stocked up on flour, sugar, tea (Nome having no such shortages as Dawson, thanks to its relatively easy accessibility by sea), piece goods, trinkets for the women and ammunition for the men. When we dropped anchor again off our Eskimo village, the trade room in our hold was ready.

Beginning with the headman, they came aboard to barter furs for merchandise. The women picked over the earrings and bracelets while the men examined the ammunition. They were using mostly an old eight-millimeter Russian army rifle of outmoded design and the Alaska Commercial Company stocked the ammunition to fit it. The trade might take anywhere from three hours to three days, the era being long past when you could stand a rusty musket upright and tell a native he could have it if he would pile his skins until they reached its muzzle, such a pile of course representing hundreds if not thousands of dollars.

Cruising on down the coast we reached Indian Point, an open port. Any ship could stop there for water or supplies. It consisted of a handful of igloos and cabins on a bleak spit of land inhabited by Eskimos, Russians, and halfbreeds, and from them we heard of the Siberian tiger, a $500 skin, who followed the reindeer herds to the Arctic Circle, and of the sea otter, perhaps the most fabulous skin of all, whose highly prized pelts had led to Russian exploration and settlement of the Bering Sea area, much as beaver furs led to the similar exploration and settlement of our American Northwest.

The Russians of the early 1800s had followed the otter across Bering Sea to the Aleutian Islands, pressed Aleut Indians into service, continued after the otter as far south as San Francisco Bay and even to the islands off the Southern California coast, slaughtering them by the hundreds of thousands. I'd heard how our Yankee forefathers got into the act. Ships rounding the Horn picked up otter skins in California for sale in Canton where the mandarins used them to trim their robes of state. One shipload is supposed to have sold in China for a profit of $300,000 on an investment of $50,000. Otter skins made many a New England fortune. Dandies in New York and London caught the fad. Otter facings to their coat collars and cuffs cost around three thousand dollars—quite a sum for Thomas Jefferson's day.

We left Indian Point to find otter if any could be found. We didn't expect a fortune. One or two good skins would pay us for our trouble. We would cross Bering Sea to the Aleutians where the very last of them existed, wild, wary and all but extinct.

Standing out from the Point with a good wind, we passed our first Russian cutter. She looked like an ocean-going tug, deck overall, blue-and-white ensign of the Czar's navy at her stern, guns fore and aft. We had nothing to account to her for, so passed her and went down to the Pribilofs, where our own cutters were standing guard over the fur-seal herds, and on to Dutch Harbor. There we tied up at the dock of the Alaska Commercial Company and went up the street to the trading post to dispose of our skins.

The town was so chuck-a-block with cheechakos, dance hall girls, get-rich-quick boys, that we could hardly squeeze through. The strike at Cook Inlet across the sound was going full blast and, in addition, every vessel en route to the North, or returning, usually stopped at Dutch. At last we spread our skins on the counter at the rear of the two-story log trading post. I wished there'd been time to hang them in the sun and let the wind blow through them but gave them each a shake and hoped for the best. Then the buying began.

White fox was par-value at one dollar. Polar bear brought ten dollars a foot or a hundred for the average skin. Ermine was cheap, about a dollar or a dollar-ten. As a matter of fact summer or brown ermine had a top price of only twenty-five cents. Sometimes the buyer and I got into a wrangle over whether a skin should go into the number-one or number-two pile. Or I might try to repair a rub spot with a little "lip-stick" and he might catch me. But mostly it went all right. We saved two black fox skins for consignment to the London market. Then we asked about sea otter.

"The Aleuts bring one in now and then. There's no organized hunting. There aren't enough of them left."

We said we'd try our luck anyway but needed some experienced native hunters to help us. He told us where to go. We removed the bulkheads to make more room below decks, cruised down among the islands to the Indian villages, parleyed with the headmen and agreed to pay a dollar a day plus a percentage of the kill. As a result, sixteen Aleut hunters came aboard. They looked more like Eskimos than Indians—short, dark-skinned, jolly fellows wearing hip-length rain jackets made of seal bladders, denim overalls, and wool trousers beneath. They brought all necessary gear including kayaks and bidarkies, rifles which they carried in waterproof seal gut or bladder cases, and throwing spears. Then we cruised westward among the islands.

For two weeks we saw nothing but fog and rain. Then one morning as we poked our nose out between two headlands into Bering Sea, the Aleut in the crow's nest let out a whoop. I glanced up in time to glimpse a dark object shoot from an offshore rock into the water.

The Aleuts in their kayaks and bidarkies hit water almost as quickly as the otter. Paddles flashing, they fanned out in a wide semicircle to try and surround him and bring him to bay. Two of them rowed me after the others in the dinghy, while Graeder and Otto nursed the schooner along behind. Pretty soon I heard a shot. It wasn't aimed at the otter, I knew, but in the air. It was intended to frighten him the moment he appeared so that he would submerge and be unable to fill his lungs. Repeated often enough, this would leave him exhausted on the surface where I would have a chance at him.

The next shot came from an entirely different direction. During his five-minute dive he'd swum a quarter of a mile. So our game of hide-and-seek continued back and forth across Bering Sea for two hours. Finally I saw that the kayaks had formed a circle about a hundred fifty yards in diameter. The Aleuts were holding their rifles muzzle up ready to fire. Their shots had been coming with increasing frequency which meant he was tiring and surfacing more often.

As my boys rowed me into the circle of kayaks, I was standing in the bow with my .40-65 lever-action Winchester ready. When he surfaced my job would be to shoot him through the head and kill him instantly while there was still air in his lungs. Otherwise he would sink and be lost. In a rocking dinghy on a choppy sea it wouldn't be an easy shot. The Aleuts were looking my way. It was the test of my medicine.

When he surfaced about forty yards off, his head didn't look much bigger than a drowned rat's, but in between two pitchings of the dinghy I caught it in my sights and squeezed the trigger. A general shout went up and we all pulled toward him as fast as we could. But it was a clean kill. He didn't sink.

When we'd hauled him aboard I saw he was about the size of a good-sized dog, his face whiskery like an Airedale's, his tail haired, feet webbed. His fur was a gorgeous dark brown. Smooth as silk. An inch and a half long. The most valuable fur in the world, in all probability. As good in summer as in winter. And when I breathed on it it lay down evenly in all directions. He was an old male, scarred from many a fight, a second-grade skin that would bring us no more than $600 at Dutch Harbor.

We skinned him, fleshed him, fitted him to a drying board, skin-side in, hair-side out, till he was snug as a glove on your hand, then dried him in the sun and hung him in the hold to keep.

Our hopes ran high. A dozen skins like that would make us a nice stake.

To mock our hopes, the first big storm of the season hit and we ran for shelter behind the nearest land and dropped the hook. Hardly had she blown herself out when another hit, and another, and then the fog wrapped us up. For days we lay to, the Aleuts passing the time telling stories or singing in a kind of humming gargle or throwing their spears at objects in the water. They were astonishingly accurate and could hit a piece of wood or a seal nearly every time at thirty yards. Sometimes I shot seals for them with my Parker 12-gauge, nine buckshot to the cartridge, swabbing the barrel clean afterward with sea water and it never pitted.

When the fog lifted we hunted. Once, creeping along the shore of a cove at sunset, I spotted an old male otter before he saw me. He was busy feeding. After making a dive he would float on his back clasping a rock against his chest with one paw, while with the other he cracked shellfish open by pounding them against it. After eating their meat he nonchalantly flipped the empty shells away over his shoulder.

On another occasion I watched a mother otter bedding down for the night with her baby in twenty feet of water. She took a strand of seaweed and, with movements as deft as a shop girl's tying up a package, wrapped it several times around her lower body. Thus securely anchored, she turned on her back and cuddled her baby beside her with one paw. Rocked in the cradle of the deep they fell asleep. I didn't wake them.

One day we noticed the sea ice beginning to form in crystal patches. It was time to go home. At Dutch Harbor we sold our second-grade skins at prices ranging from three to six hundred dollars. The best went on consignment to the London Fur Auction where they brought a top price of twelve hundred. Despite commissions and other expenses we were money ahead. But the work had been long, hard, and tedious and we'd had enough. After we'd sold the schooner, Graeder and Otto headed south and I got back to Golovin before the ice formed solid.

Our contribution toward the extinction of the sea otter was fortunately not fatal. After 1910 they were fully protected by international agreement and are now plentiful again in the Aleutians and also off the California coast where the Russians and the Aleuts once hunted them. It's strange to think of the Russian counterpart of the "Ralph J. Long" following Aleut kayaks around San Francisco Bay and along the Santa Barbara Channel but it happened. When I drive the winding Big Sur Highway and see one of those bobbing heads far below me in the water, I think of all it represents.

During the winter of 1902-'03 word reached Crooked Creek that Fairbanks was struck and I went over there and staked, got a number of pieces of ground on Cleary and Pedro Creeks and met old friends including Bill Ewing and Frank Manley. The pay was good at first and the ground wasn't deep. The camp, centered around Captain Barnette's trading post on the bank of the Chena River or slough, one of the tributaries of the Tanana, a major branch of the Yukon, had more than its share of card sharps, whores, and bunco artists, it being easily accessible from Nome, Council, and elsewhere. In fact it had nearly everything but food. Fairbanks might literally have starved to death that first winter except for the moose who had "yarded up" by the hundreds in the Tanana bottoms. To winter they'd, as usual, chosen an area with ample willows and similar browse. It soon became honeycombed with their trails. As the snow grew deeper, so did the trails, until their "yards" were virtually traps from which they couldn't escape, especially when a freeze hardened the surface.

Within a radius of a few miles from where Fairbanks stands now we killed at least 300 moose, and they made the difference between a hungry camp and a happy one.

As at Dawson, I made more money from meat than gold. And I had fun, too. Exploring new country high at the head of Big Delta, I shot a blue or glacier bear, nearly as big as a grizzly but narrow rather than wide, and then I crossed the divide into Copper River Valley and saw what looked like a green meadow several thousand feet above me on the face of Kennecott Glacier. In reality it was the fabulous Kennecott copper deposit, six thousand feet up on the face of twelve-thousand-foot Kennecott Peak, its greenness caused by its verdigris leaching out onto the surrounding ice and snow.

The Big Bonanza, as we called her, had been staked three years earlier by a group of prospectors who'd sold it to Stephen Birch, a New York engineer, nephew of Mrs. Havemayer, the "Sugar Queen." It was seventy-two percent glance ore, nearly pure copper, one of nature's more generous accidents.

With Johnny Barrett, who later developed the town of McCarthy in the valley below, I bought an interest in some of the Bonanza extensions and Johnny and I built a claim on the "v" of rock where the glacier splits, packed a stove up to it, did some hunting, and later we helped George Baldwin, Kennecott's first superintendent, install the first machinery and carrying cables needed to extract ore. By now Birch and Mrs. Havemayer had sold out to the Guggenheims who were building the Copper and Northwestern Railroad up the 200 miles from Cordova on the coast, a remarkable engineering feat for its time—tunneling and pylon-hopping up the Copper River gorge—to carry the ore to tidewater from where ships could take it to the Tacoma smelter. The Guggenheims mined tens of millions of dollars' worth of virtually pure copper from the Big Bonanza which helped finance development of their lower-grade but more extensive Chuquicamata deposits in Chile.

But by 1907 the excitement and adventure was over. The country was settling up and once again I was looking for new frontiers. I'd spent twelve busy years in the North, attended every major strike, built more than three-dozen claim cabins, made a little money, had a lot of fun, but now the fun and money were coming to an end. I decided to "go on west" and try my luck in the Far East.

Membership in the Arctic Brotherhood included the right to keep your hat on in a king's presence.

Black miners like Bill Ewing were rare but not unique. Here Dick Smally and George Williams are shown mining not far from our claim on Dominion Creek. (*University of Alaska Archives*)

This was Dawson's main street, Moosehide Hill in the background. (*University of Washington Library*)

The settlement at Fortymile looked like this during my first winter in the Yukon. At the time of the spring break-up, the flood water sometimes came right into town, as shown here.

Though not present for this picture, I was among the early members of the Yukon Order of Pioneers (see Appendix I). Leroy Napoleon ("Jack") McQuesten, the pioneer prospector and merchant who founded the order and did so much to develop the Yukon region, is the major figure in the front row, center. His name was regularly mispronounced and misspelled "McQuestion."

Street scene, Pao-ting-fu.

I talk with the Queen of the Beggars, my ally during the troubles at Pao-ting-fu.

A flatcar like this one with a mounted machine gun and a detachment of soldiers preceded our train during the trip from Peking to Pao-ting-fu.

Some Mongols from the western provinces were nearly nine feet tall. The man on the left is average size. This giant was sent by the Emperor of Mongolia as a present to the Czar of Russia.

This was the bungalow in our compound at Kalgan on the Mongolian border.

# III

# CARAVANS
# IN CHINA AND MONGOLIA:
# 1907 - 1919

# 9.  China

The China I was stepping into was still Ancient Cathay, the Imperial Cathay my colleague there, William Ashley Anderson, later described as "an empire of walled cities, and mandarins of the seven orders, the Manchus of the Nine Banners, of huge palanquins carried on the shoulders of massed porters, of gold-encrusted and embroidered dragon robes, of men with shaven heads and long queues and women on pinched lily-feet." It was also the China of half-naked toiling coolies hitched like work-horses to carts piled high with freight or merchandise, while others balancing long poles on their shoulders were nearly hidden by loads suspended at either end, and still others pulled rickshaws carrying people or their belongings. It was also the China of the twentieth century.

The docks along the Shanghai Bund were lined with ships of many nations. Across a broad avenue bordering the waterfront rose a wall of modern-style commercial buildings, clubs, and hotels, and I could see trolley cars, bicycles, men wearing business suits and women in smart dresses who might have stepped off the streets of London or San Francisco.

This was also the China of the dominant foreigner. The Bund and everything I was looking at were in Shanghai's Foreign Quarter, where there were signs in the parks prohibiting dogs or Chinese.

The British-American Tobacco Company's headquarters, a four-story brick building, faced the waterfront avenue. A stream of men wearing long blue gowns, their hair in queues down their backs, flowed in and out of it, mingling with those in modern business suits I'd noticed earlier. An Otis elevator made in the U.S.A. lifted me to the top floor.

[105]

As I walked along a corridor toward the office of James A. Thomas, British-American Tobacco's Far Eastern manager, I glanced through an open doorway and was astonished to see, sitting at an executive's desk giving dictation to a pretty Chinese secretary, a friend of mine from Nome days, Tom Cobbs. "Why Cra—!" I broke out, almost using the nickname "Craphouse" by which we'd known Tom at Nome. Tom was a big, boisterous, irrepressible Virginian who'd been among the 20,000 gold-seekers landing on the Nome beach during that memorable summer of 1900. Too late to find a claim, Tom who was nothing if not enterprising, got a bright idea when he ran foul of the camp law requiring a man to walk a couple of hundred yards beyond the fringes of settlement before relieving himself. He built a rickety pier into Bering Sea, erected privies on it, sold tickets at twenty-five cents each. By the summer's end he was making a small fortune and Tom Cobbs and his tickets were the standing joke of Nome.

He'd recognized me the same instant I'd recognized him. I saw him flush with embarrassment as he heard his nickname half out of my mouth. When his secretary turned to see who'd interrupted them, he raised a finger to his lips and tipped me the wink. I smiled and walked on, feeling myself already at home.

I found J. A. Thomas an impressive, soft-spoken North Carolinian, with the natural directness and good manners some topnotch people have. As a younger man he'd revolutionized the tobacco business in the Orient by asking himself a simple question: How many cigarettes per package would yield a reasonable profit and still sell for a coin worth about two U.S. cents? After extensive calculations he came up with the answer, five. He took his idea to James B. Duke, his boss in the American Tobacco Company. Amalgamating with British Imperial Tobacco, they built a trading empire in the Far East second only to Standard Oil's; and the Chinese, pipe smokers for hundreds of years, became cigarette smokers.

Though he received a salary of sixty thousand a year from B.A.T., an enormous sum for those days, and had immense power, Thomas was no ruthless exploiter. The Chinese had been growing tobacco for centuries but it was heavy pipe tobacco, not the aromatic variety used in cigarettes. He brought in experts from North Carolina who taught native farmers how to cultivate fine-quality cigarette tobacco. Seed and fertilizer were also imported from the States, and Shantung Province, the center of the new tobacco culture, became one of the most prosperous in China where before it had been one of the most depressed. Fine tobacco was also grown in Manchuria and many other parts of the country. As the demand increased, Thomas built cigarette factories in China and more jobs and more prosperity were created.

When we'd talked a while and he'd read my letters of introduction, he offered me the job I wanted. As an independent operator, I would receive a small salary from the company but could engage in any business not directly competitive with B.A.T.'s. It sounded good. I wanted freedom to act on my own and see the country and I liked Thomas and the far-flung nature of his operations, which were bound to take me to the frontiers and outdoor life I was used to; and with Cobbs at hand I would be starting among friends. But first I wanted to acquaint myself with the language and customs of China. I told this to Thomas. I said I wanted to immerse myself completely in native surroundings without any foreign influence. I argued that I would be of more use to him and to myself in the long run if I could do this now. On the map on the wall he showed me where the railroad ended far up in Anhwei. I asked leave to go there and steep myself in Chinese life. He agreed, and I went back down the hall to settle accounts with Cobbs.

At the Long Bar at the Shanghai Club, said to be the longest in the world, we reached an agreement over gin-tails. I would say nothing about Tom's pierhead privy at Nome. But every time I was in Shanghai he would have to buy the drinks. He'd taken his stake made at Nome, invested it in British-American Tobacco, and was now general manager of the company's Shanghai office.

He thought my idea of going into the hinterland a crazy one but helped me find the indispensable first ingredient, a good personal boy. Having a good Chinese servant was like having a benevolent genius looking after your needs. With Lu to guide me I boarded the train for Nanking. He carried a basket of food and personal belongings in his lap. As we sat opposite each other, he would hold up an object, say its name, and I would repeat after him. By the time we reached Nanking I'd learned how to say "What is that?" From there on, things got easier.

At railhead on the unfinished line running northward toward Tientsin, we got off. I put my finger on the map a substantial distance into the interior and said we would go there. He shrugged. "All right. We go there." I made him understand we would need a cart for our luggage and horses for ourselves. He disappeared but soon returned with some sample carts and their owners. I selected a high-wheeled, cloth-hooded model and left arrangements to him. Next I tried to explain that we would need riding horses. He brought me cart horses and draft horses. Finally I got my saddle out of my dunnage. It was a lightweight California model made to order by the Visalia Stock Saddle Company of San Francisco, California's premier saddlemakers for many years. I held it up and indicated I wanted something to go under it. Lu got the idea but suggested we postpone our purchases. "Horses no good here! Up-country better!"

Up-country we went and in the recesses of Anhwei we stayed five months while I did little but observe, listen, get acquainted with the people and their customs. The language presented no difficulty. I'd been exposed to so many that Chinese was simply one more. I found the people admirable in many ways: intelligent, industrious, and for the most part friendly, though now and then I heard the shrill derisive shout of *yang kwei-tse* (foreign devil) as I passed. They were very tidy in their habits. Shops, houses, and courtyards were swept clean. As summer came on, dust was laid by sprinkling. Every bit of waste was used. Instead of being dumped into rivers or lakes, human excrement was collected and placed on the fields to fertilize crops. Clothes were washed at every pool and stream, the dirt beaten out (as the Indian women of California had beaten it out) because there was no soap. The Chinese had no knowledge of modern hygiene yet blew their noses on bits of paper which they discarded, a hygienic measure we didn't practice till years later. Even the smallest towns had public hot baths, and the most numerous among a myriad of commercial peddlers and travelers were the barbers who shaved heads and cheeks, trimmed queues or filled them out with pieces of string, cleaned your eyes, ears, and nostrils—using the same cotton swab for all customers!

Opium pills were a standard remedy for most ailments. You could buy a handful from any apothecary. For the more discerning there were the traditional herbs, potions, and acupuncture treatment which, with the antibodies developed in the national bloodstream over the centuries, combined to keep the people surprisingly healthy. There were sufferers from disease, smallpox, leprosy, typhus, yes, but there were few weaklings or mental misfits. Attrition, the inexorable demands of survival, weeded out the unfit.

Both men and women wore long loose jackets of blue cotton or blue or purple silk, fitting closely at the neck, with wide sleeves, and wide short trousers. Hats were of close-fitting silk or wide-brimmed straw. Shoes were commonly of cotton or silk with thick felt soles. Both men and women carried fans, sometimes sticking them at the backs of their necks, as I later learned to do with Mongolian and Tibetan prayer wheels when shooting game for my caravan crews. Both sexes smoked pipes or cigarettes. Both were abstemious in their habits and as a rule modest and decorous in their behavior, though they privately looked down on all foreigners including me.

Every household I visited had a wall niche or shrine where a tablet displayed the family genealogy. Candles burned in front of it, keeping alight symbolically the family's eternal flame of life. Offerings were set out on special occasions. This was the traditional ancestor worship associated with Confucianism but there was little other evidence of religious practice except at funerals and weddings, or in the form of pilgrimage to sacred places. At deeper level, though, there was a primitive superstitious reverence for the forces of nature. *Feng-shui*, this reverence was called, or literally "respect for wind and water"—wind representing the breath of life, water the force that both nurtures and destroys. *Feng-shui* expressed the precariousness by which we all exist in the face of the forces of destruction and creation, which also move within ourselves.

For entertainment I joined the crowd around the storyteller under the sacred tree or at the village streetcorner, listening to his tales of ancient princes and princesses, dragons and demons. From time to time he accented dramatic moments in his recitation with a sharp *ping* of his tuning fork as Homer did by plucking the strings of his lyre ages earlier. And there were the games: mahjong, go, fan-tan, or the poker which I taught my Chinese friends. They were inveterate gamblers, more so than any people I had encountered.

Food was plentiful and good. There were thick tasty soups made of birds' nests, ducks' tongues, or chickens' brains, served with toasted unleavened bread. There were game birds such as pheasant and duck, fish dipped in batter and fried whole, morsels of pork simmered in hot fat until deliciously crisp, plus rice and vegetables of many kinds. Eggs were often preserved in a solution of salt, lime, or wood ash and served fresh after months or years of storage. And there was *samshu,* rice wine, served hot in small bowls. Dinners were apt to be incredible events lasting most of the night and including twenty-four, thirty-six, or as many as seventy-two courses (always a multiple of four) depending on the expansiveness of the occasion.

And yet the good nature of the people could be misleading. Underneath lurked a latent violence, ready to break out on provocation. The bloody events of the Boxer Rebellion, the popular uprising against foreigners, were only a few short years away. China had paid dearly for that bitter experience in the form of cash indemnities and economic or territorial concessions to foreign interests. But I remembered Thomas' warning: "Always move boldly. Always exercise authority." Several B.A.T. men had been killed by Chinese mobs which turned suddenly ugly.

Both Thomas and Cobbs were surprised by my familiarity with Chinese life when I returned to Shanghai.

My first assignment took me to Chinkiang, a major port, strategically located for trading purposes at the junction of the historic Grand Canal with the Yangtze River. My partner there was J. W. G. Brodie, a husky, jut-jawed Englishman fresh from Oxford, whose family owned a substantial quantity of B.A.T. stock and who later became one of the leading businessmen of Wellington, New Zealand. Brodie and I lived in style in a bungalow formerly occupied by an official of the Matson Line. It was situated on the crest of a hill overlooking city and river, surrounded by extensive grounds, stables and outbuildings. We had a total of twenty-seven servants to wait on us, and learning to play my role among them as gentleman-master took some study. After years of helping myself, I had to learn how to stand aside and *be* helped.

If I found a bone one of our hunting dogs had left on the lawn, I couldn't pick it up without seriously jeopardizing the order of things. I must call our number-one house boy who in turn called our number-two house boy who in turn called our dog coolie, whose responsibility it was to pick up the bone. Such were the ways of my new world.

If Brodie and I went down the hill into the city, we each had four chair-coolies to carry us. Yet this division of labor was welcomed. It had existed for centuries. In an overpopulated country it provided a maximum of jobs, no matter how meagerly paid, plus a chance for kumshaw, food, housing, status.

At the foot of our hill was a park and tennis club where we occasionally had tea with the gentry from the consulates and their wives and daughters. On more enjoyable occasions we played baseball or cricket with the crews of the gunboats "Helena" and "Duck," or went hunting in the New Forest three miles away where there were deer and leopard; or we prowled the old trenches, not far beyond, dating to the days of the Taiping Rebellion and the British General, "Chinese" Gordon, who'd commanded Chinese Imperial troops there aided by an American general named Ward. Together they had put down that earlier uprising against foreigners and Manchu rule.

To entertain us at home we had our hunting dogs, riding horses and a tame cheetah we used for hunting, and from time to time we gave wild parties, when sing-song girls with their fantastically painted and powdered faces sat on our respective knees and sang to us in their high-pitched off-key voices to the accompaniment of their *hu-hus.*

On a hill nearby lived a missionary family who disapproved of our carryings on. Years later when I read her autobiography I learned that it was the family of Pearl Buck.

From Chinkiang, Brodie and I covered a wide trade territory. Traveling in a forty-foot houseboat towed by a motor boat (the houseboat having plenty of room for servants, merchandise, and our native sales crew), we traversed the historic Grand Canal and its tributaries southward toward Suchow and Hanchow or north through the rich coastal lowlands toward Peking. Parts of the canal had been built as early as 400 B.C., and it had once been the chief artery linking north and south China, while also providing a means for the traditional rice tribute to reach Peking without the hazards of a sea voyage. In some places it was a hundred feet wide, its sides faced impressively with stone. In others it was merely a tortuous muddy channel winding monotonously through level country.

At strategic settlements where roads and feeder canals led into the interior we stopped and called on leading local merchants to persuade them to become our dealers. Or if we already had a dealer in the community, we helped organize his sales forces and went with him to visit stores where our products could be sold. Sometimes, surrounded by the street crowd which always formed when foreign devils were present, we lit sample cigarettes and after taking a few puffs ourselves, handed them to bystanders or thrust them into the toothless mouths of grinning old men who in eighty years had never puffed anything but pipes. All of this was accompanied by much good-humored banter and by-play, occasionally by resentful catcalls reminding us that we were interlopers. Meanwhile our trained crews would be roaming the streets, plastering the walls with advertising posters, distributing additional samples, and generally drumming up trade. It was all part of the white man's potent big medicine that was changing the face of Asia and the world supposedly for the better.

One night when we were moored to a levee whose top had loomed four feet above the deck when we went to bed, I felt a gentle lifting sensation while sleeping. Next morning we found ourselves nearly level with the levee's top and with the roofs of houses beyond. Soon the water was spilling over the levee, inundating miles of fertile land. It was the terrible Yangtze flood of 1910.

Cruising across country at housetop level we rescued as many survivors as we could carry, taking them to the nearest high ground, depositing them, going back for more. Sometimes we had to push dead bodies away with boathooks, sometimes resist the clutching hands of the living in order to save ourselves and our passengers from being swamped. Hundreds of thousands lost their lives. Millions were left homeless and starving. But in the long, often grim story of China it was merely an episode, one of time's little gestures.

Soon afterward I became the B.A.T. representative at Shih-kia-chwang, a strategic railroad and trading junction a hundred miles or so south of Peking. I traded on my own there, too, and also at Pao-ting-fu nearby, and then was posted to my final and favorite billet at Kalgan, on the Mongolian border, where the Great Wall dipped and rose across barren mountains, and the wild country beyond stretched unbroken for thousands of miles, across Mongolia into Siberia and Turkestan, or to Sinkiang and Tibet. I'd come to the jumping-off-place for the Far West of Asia, Asia having its Wild West then just as we in North America did, and its West being by that time remoter and wilder than ours.

At Kalgan the 150 miles of railroad from Peking ended in a dry watercourse. The town with its shops, stalls, earth-walled dwellings and compounds, sprawled along this watercourse for several miles. Its unpaved main street, which was also the caravan trail that led up through the huge gate in the Wall into Mongolia and all the hinterland, swarmed with strings of camels, ox carts, flocks of sheep, mule trains, horses, dogs, and people of many kinds. There were fierce-looking slant-eyed Outer Mongols dressed in their native sheepskins, somewhat smaller but equally slant-eyed Manchurians, turbanned Mohammedans from the Far West, the ever-present ever-industrious Chinese, Siberian Russians with fur caps, and we English, American, German, and Scandinavian traders.

B.A.T. headquarters was situated in a compound built by Chinese railway engineers a short distance from the railroad station. Within its walls were godowns (warehouses), servants' quarters, stables, and our central bungalow with bedrooms, dining room, tackroom, storeroom, and offices, surrounded by a wide verandah—and by enough space to assemble and load a camel caravan.

These were the last great years of the caravan trade, of methods and routes almost unchanged since the days of Marco Polo. Thousands upon thousands of camels departed and arrived in Kalgan annually. They carried tea, cigarettes, tobacco, candles, silks, cottons, and all the varied merchandise of the coastal lowlands to be exchanged for the wool, hides, and furs of the interior.

In and around our compound were men cut in a mold to do this work: the Norwegians Oscar Mamen and T. A. Rustad, embodying a Viking tradition turned landward rather than seaward from their Scandinavian homeland; W. B. Haughwout, a veteran American trader-adventurer; Frans August Larson, the Swedish missionary, trader, explorer, often called the Prester John of the twentieth century, and in fact an honorary Duke of Mongolia and one of the most effective yet modest persons I ever met. Larson later assembled the camels and guided Roy Chapman Andrews on the American Museum of Natural History's expedition into the Gobi that discovered the fossilized remains of dinosaurs and brought them back to New York. Without Larson's influence with the Mongol authorities at Urga, Andrews could not have accomplished what he did.

I was soon conducting camel caravans along the border and into the interior, meeting native leaders, dealing for livestock and merchandise, feeling in many respects as though I'd come full circle and was back to the life I'd known on the ranch. Even the countryside reminded me of Southern California with its vast deserts, barren mountains, and fertile grassland.

But now the violent forces I'd sensed underlying Chinese life broke out. The Chinese Revolution of 1911 had two basic purposes. One was to overthrow the tottering and corrupt rule of the Manchu Dynasty in Peking, the other to free China from foreign domination. Overriding both and often obscuring them was the terrible need of most Chinese simply to survive. Even in the best of times about ten percent of the population, pressed by hunger, was ready to rise, loot, rape, and murder at the least provocation. Millions more lived near the verge of starvation. Other millions had recently been rendered homeless and hungry by the floods.

Nevertheless it was, of all incongruous things, the proposed construction of a railroad in, of all unlikely places, the remote "tea province" of Szechwan that actually triggered the revolution. Szechwan lay isolated behind mountain ranges in the remote southwest corner of China bordering India, Burma, and

Tibet. A controversial railroad was proposed there that would cut through the mountains and link Szechwan with the rest of the country. But the railroad would disrupt an age-old economy of carriers and carters and all their associated interests. Resistance to construction of the railroad became resistance to the Imperial Government in Peking—which had proposed it and proposed financing it by foreign loans. Imperialists and foreigners would be building the hated railroad.

This sparked riots in Szechwan in the spring of 1911. The spark spread to students, young soldiers, and other reformers led primarily by Sun Yat-sen. Even in faraway Kalgan we heard rumblings of this. Our local commander declared himself irrevocably loyal to the Imperial Regime.

Fighting broke out at Wuchang on the Yangtze early in October 1911. It spread quickly to Hankow and Nanking. Both sides fought with extreme bravery. A number of foreigners participated in the field and behind the scenes. Most of them including Thomas and other British-American Tobacco leaders strongly supported Sun Yat-sen and the Republican cause. They believed that a republican government led by Sun, who'd been educated in the U.S., would be best for China and the Chinese and for foreign interests. Most of us in the field agreed.

My involvement came through a telegram from Thomas telling of trouble at Pao-ting-fu, the provincial capital ninety miles south of Peking where I'd done considerable trading, and asking if I could go at once to Peking for further information. Peking was said to be in turmoil. But I took the next train, got through without difficulty (learning later that they had recently removed piles of severed heads left in the streets after the fighting), and went directly to the B.A.T. office which was located on a side street just off the Chienmen or main thoroughfare.

There Jimmy Hutchison, our Peking manager, explained the situation at Pao-ting-fu.

Regional military leaders were seizing power as the central government at Peking weakened. Two warlord armies were jockeying for control of Pao-ting-fu. Fighting and pillaging were rampant. Our native dealer was holding a substantial quantity of silver which needed transportation to Peking. Numerous sub-dealers in outlying districts were in a similar predicament. Transporting the money under armed guard as was usually done was out of the question. Armed guards would be almost certain to attract the unfavorable attention of riotous mobs, bandits, or marauding soldiery. What was needed, according to Hutchison, was a small-scale, fast-moving operation which would collect the silver unobtrusively and bring it quietly to Peking. I had no illusions that the job would be an easy one but it could yield me a substantial bonus, enhance my standing with Thomas and B.A.T., and result in useful contacts I might exploit later.

I stayed overnight at Peking (our headquarters there included a dormitory and piano bar as well as offices and godowns), talked further with Hutchison and with Charlie Coltman, Standard Oil's district manager. Standard employed many of the same native agents in the Pao-ting-fu area as B.A.T., its chief stock-in-trade there as elsewhere being paraffin candles and coal oil. Standard had developed an inexpensive oil lamp, the *Mei-foo,* which provided light in millions of Chinese households and burned millions of gallons of U.S. kerosene. Like the rest of the Far East, China was becoming an important market for our mass-production and mass-marketing techniques.

Hutchison and Coltman furnished me lists of their agents in the Pao-ting-fu area plus letters of authorization and next morning I was on my way south by train accompanied by Lu, who by this time was a second-hand edition of myself in appearance. He wore my old clottes. They saved him money and made him fashionable since many Chinese were adopting western dress. Under his coat he carried a .38 Smith & Wesson in a shoulder holster, as I did. In addition I carried a .303 British Winchester in hand.

Our train was preceded by a pilot locomotive pushing a flatcar manned by a squad of Imperial soldiers wearing caps and dark blue uniforms, commanded by a little Frenchman who symbolized the many foreigners who served the Peking government one way or another. Besides rifle and pistol his men were armed with a tripod-mounted, water-cooled machine gun. Peking was anxious to maintain control of the railroad, its only line running south to Hankow and the Yangtze region.

For reasons real or imaginary, our little Frenchman stopped his pilot locomotive frequently. Consequently we stopped too, never knowing quite what to expect. There were only a few passengers and most of them got off at wayside stations. As we poked along, I had time to survey the countryside which was flat as a pan and dry as dust, now in late autumn, with its stubble of wheat and barley and dry stalks of *kolyiang*—the tall millet—and to think about what to do when I reached my destination. Acquaintances there from earlier days might still be active and I thought of one in particular who might be able to help me—if she had escaped jail or beheading.

As we neared Pao-ting-fu, signs of trouble increased. Refugees jammed the roads. Some led loaded mules. Some pushed large wheelbarrows which had a wooden deck all around a central wheel, the deck stacked high with possessions. Others lined both sides of the tracks hoping for a ride anywhere out of the district.

By the time we reached the station at the outskirts of the city, the crowd had become enormous. I made my way through it to the depot building and sent a wire to Peking saying I'd arrived and the lines were still open. Then I told the first beggar I met to fetch me the Queen of the Beggars. Given such a crowd, I guessed she'd be nearby. Sure enough, in a few minutes here she came. She wore her usual ragged padded trousers and jacket. Her face was wrinkled as a sunburned mummy's. A few gray hairs were drawn to a bun at the back of her head and when she smiled I could hardly see a tooth. For a woman worth in all probability a good many thousands of dollars, she was well calculated to fool a man.

"Illustrious Master is welcome!" she began in her usual vein, twinkling and bowing like a sing-song girl.

"I thought I'd find you and your rascals somewhere in a crowd like this!" I rejoined.

When we'd exchanged pleasantries, I asked her if she would guard my silver there on the station platform while I collected it from outlying districts. I knew it would be as safe in the custody of the beggars and thieves, their accomplices, as in a bank.

Thieves and beggars were an integral part of Chinese life and absolutely dependable if you knew how to deal with them. At

Kalgan, for instance, when we wanted a night watchman we sent for the head of the thieves' guild. "I have just the man for you!" he replied, when we told him our needs. The man he sent us was too old and decrepit to scale walls or break into freight cars and would have been a burden for the union to support unless they found him an easy job such as nightwatchman. We paid him twenty dollars a month, as much as we paid our cook, and he would amble around the yard, rattling his wooden rattle box until ten o'clock to show he was on duty, and then lie down on the verandah outside the front door and sleep sound till morning. Not a thief ever entered our compound. If we'd hired an honest man to guard us, we'd have been stolen blind.

The Queen looked a little incredulous when she heard my proposal. "You'd trust me?"

"Why not?"

I could see she was deeply flattered. She bowed low. "Your silver will be safe! My people will be your people!"

I was counting on help from her people. They might turn up anywhere: professional blind men and women, some with eye-sockets like hideously gaping wounds; hunchbacks; skin-disease sufferers; pickpockets; young girls who hired babies by the day to beg with; ragged young toughs handy with knives; all with plenty of savvy. Harrassment was their usual tactic. If you didn't pay up, they'd dog your footsteps and abuse you at the tops of their lungs, embarrassing you publicly until you did. Merchants and other businessmen paid them off regularly or found a yelling rabble at the front door discouraging customers. At the end of the day, they handed their receipts over to the Queen and she kept her share and the guild's and returned them a percentage. And they had better not cheat. Guild discipline was absolute. Unswerving honesty and obedience were its primary rules. Infraction usually meant death.

With the beggars and thieves on my side I felt I'd made a good beginning. Next I needed transportation into the old walled city which lay two miles away. Pao-ting-fu was the capital of Chihli, a rich fertile province resembling portions of our American Middle West. Produce from the interior reached it by canal boat and caravan trail and was transhipped northward by rail to Peking or Tientsin. The city was notorious because the Boxer

Rebellion had started there with the beheading of American missionaries and had spread over China, involving not only foreigners but their Chinese associates, such as my Lu, and especially Chinese Christians who were murdered by the hundred. We finally found a carter willing to sell us his services though he protested loudly that only persons of great courage such as himself were willing to reenter the threatened city.

Inside the walls there was an atmosphere like that of a quiet autumn day before a winter storm. As the Queen had explained to me, this was due to the fact that in typical Chinese style neither of the opposing warlord armies wanted to risk a battle by advancing into a city which they both coveted. While their commanders negotiated, troops looted the surrounding countryside. Hence the crowds of refugees.

A number of people had elected to remain in Pao-ting-fu, nevertheless. You have to frighten a Chinese badly to make him leave the place his family has occupied for centuries, and though some shops were closed and their shutters down or their boards up, others were open and there was a considerable amount of activity.

At the B.A.T. office, our representative, an unusually apprehensive type, was expecting me. His silver dollars were wrapped in paper in rolls of twenty and packaged in amounts of one thousand with burlap and rope. His bulk silver was in the form of shoes, literally little ingots of silver four to five inches long, cast, so tradition said, in the shape of some long-dead empress' slippered foot. I don't know how far back in time the shoes dated—probably not as far as the bronze knife money I found in one of the buried cities of Mongolia—but far enough. They ranged in value from five taels (about $5.50 Chinese or roughly $2.75 U.S.) to 100 taels, depending on the amount of silver each contained, a tael (approximately 1⅓ ounces) being worth a little less than 60 U.S. cents. There was no gold, China being a silver-standard country, and we didn't bother with paper bills, or cash or other copper coins.

"The soldiers may enter the city at any moment," he warned me. "You must hurry if you are to return to Peking safely."

"I must visit your outlying dealers first," I reminded him, "and collect their money. Have you notified them?"

He assured me he had.

"I'll need transportation. I understand carts are impossible to procure. Are there mules?"

He looked as if I'd asked for flying carpets.

"There is no livestock left in the area. Marauding soldiers have seen to that!"

"Nevertheless I must have mules or horses and carts."

Seeing he couldn't get rid of me or his money until he had solved my problem, he remembered there might be mules at a village nearby.

Lu found us two rickshaws and we went to the village in record time. There I persuaded the owner of the mules that since his precious animals would likely be confiscated by the soldiers anyway, he might as well rent them to me at a spanking good price and get what he could out of them while he still owned them.

They were good mules. Each could carry 300 pounds. With him and two muleteers to help us, we headed for the remotest village on my list. Scraps of red cloth tied to our mules' manes proclaimed us to be under the protection of the beggars and thieves. Sometimes a gang of ragamuffins escorted us armed with knives and even a few guns. More often a solitary figure emerging from a crowd of refugees, and disappearing back into it, informed us which way was safe and which not.

Reaching the most distant village we proceeded along a deserted street until we came to a sign announcing in Chinese characters and English letters that this was the agency for the British-American Tobacco Company or *"Ying-Mei yen-ch'ao kung-ssu"* and also Standard Oil, *"Kong-lee hung-lung."*

Inside a walled compound were huts for coolies and servants, stables, warehouses, the merchant's house, and his office—a small room where the old fellow was sitting behind a counter in a comfortable chair, his sons and grandsons hovering nearby in case he needed anything, while in the background clerks at tables pored over ledgers as if nothing unusual were happening anywhere in the world.

To exhibit anxiety in time of crisis was out of the question here where they were most exposed. He led me through the little gate in his counter and invited me to sit down.

Tea was served. I asked after the health of his family, he asked about me and my affairs. Then I showed him my letters of authority and we got down to business. His accounts were in order, his money ready on the floor of the office packed in burlap. While his boys and Lu marked and numbered the bundles with lampblack, he showed me—never hurrying—through his warehouses. They were well stocked with our cigarettes— Honest Weight in zinc-lined wooden cases of 50,000 capacity that cost $68 each; Peacocks costing $225; Pirate, $190; and the fancy Three Castle brand in round tins of fifty which officials and the military smoked.

When all was ready I signed a receipt for a certain number of silver dollars and shoes belonging to B.A.T. or Standard Oil, as the case might be. Had there been time to count the money I wouldn't have bothered to. The honesty of such veteran merchants was beyond question. Early in its operations, B.A.T. set up a contingency fund for losses, but over the years it grew so large from being unused that they invested it in something else. Bowing, hands hidden in the loose openings of opposite sleeves, the old man wished us on our way.

After several such stops, our mules were loaded and we hurried back to Pao-ting-fu where the Beggar Queen was waiting at the depot. With help from her people, we unloaded our cargo onto the platform while the crowd watched hungrily. It must have guessed what our packages contained. But the Queen's reputation was fearsome. At the first sign of trouble a war whoop would go up from members of her gang scattered through the crowd and out would come their knives, and no one knew but what the stranger next him was a beggar or thief with a long knife. My presence and my Winchester were an additional restraint. Probably weighing more heavily in our favor was the ingrained Chinese respect for authority, plus the dominant role of the foreigner in national affairs.

When we'd unloaded, I handed the old girl a carton of cigarettes. We left her seated on our bundles of silver, puffing away contentedly.

On our third swing through the countryside we encountered the Chinese Jews. The first was a tall straight-backed fellow who approached me while we were loading silver in an agent's compound. He was dressed native fashion with a pigtail hanging nearly to his heels but had unmistakably Jewish features. He stated politely that he came from a nearby village where they'd heard we were transporting money to Peking. Could we be so generous as to transport some for them at proper fee?

I asked why he thought his silver would be safe in my hands. He said his people recalled me from the days when I had traded in their area for B.A.T., based on my headquarters at Shih-kia-chwang. I remembered his village. It was exceptionally prosperous and well kept, had a mixed population, Jews and Chinese, and all the Jews wore Chinese dress. They had their synagogue and the Chinese authorities permitted them freedom of worship. Most of the men were peddlers working the countryside with backpacks or ran shops in town, but some were farmers and tilled good crops. Legend had it that these so-called native Jews were descended from one of the lost tribes of Israel. They were taller by several inches than any Jews I'd seen before and were quite distinct from the commercial Jewish colonies of Shanghai and Tientsin which were of comparatively recent origin.

I said I might handle his money if there wasn't too much of it and that it might end up in the Hong Kong-Shanghai Bank in Peking if we had luck, but I could make no promises and he would have to bring it to me quickly. I showed him how we were packaging it and he sent a runner back. In little more than an hour, his first wheelbarrow arrived, its deck piled high with bundles of silver, one man pulling, another pushing. We took a good many thousand from that Jewish community, mostly in silver shoes.

When we'd collected all the silver from the outlying districts and finally from our Pao-ting-fu dealer, there were many hundredweight of it on the station platform. It would customarily have been transported to Peking by railway passenger car but I had no such car. Also I had more silver than customary. Time was another urgent factor. The military stalemate was breaking up, the Queen informed me. The Army of the West, pushing across from Hsin-chow, was whipping the Army of the South, driving up from the Yangtze, and Pao-ting-fu was due for the kind of rape only half-starved Chinese troops can give a city. "Master has but a few hours to complete his work!" she warned.

There seemed only one solution. I commandeered a freight that was headed south toward Hankow, told the engineer to cut his locomotive loose and back it into the "Y" in the yard with one empty boxcar, and then pull up to our platform. When he hesitated I showed him and the train officials my papers and my rifle. Standard and B.A.T. could, and did, settle later with the government transportation authorities. It was my job to get the silver to Peking.

The Queen's boys and girls helped load it aboard our car, leaving space in the middle for Lu and me to move from door to door. I saw that Lu had performed one of his minor miracles. From somewhere he'd acquired a battered straw armchair. There it stood, between the piles of silver, for Master to sit in.

Before departing I gave the Queen a package containing five hundred silver dollars. Something like moisture appeared in her dry old eyes. She bowed low. "This is too much honor for one so unworthy!"

She'd been sitting on many times that amount and could have sold me out at any moment but like an honest thief had kept her word. The last I saw of her she was bowing and smiling, her gang clustering eagerly around her, the crowd staring in wonder and envy.

Pao-ting-fu was sacked and burned a few days later but I felt sure she had survived, being, in her very Chinese way, an expert in the art.

During the early stages of our train ride to Peking, we kept a sharp lookout, Lu at one door, I at the other. But when all went well mile after mile I sat down in that inviting armchair. Lulled by the motion of the train, I soon dozed off. I was awakened by an unpleasant sensation. We were slowing down. I heard a sharp cry of alarm from Lu. Grabbing my rifle, I jumped to the open door.

Standing waist-deep in a field of dry *kolyiang* stalks a few yards away, ten or fifteen soldiers were deployed as if to waylay us. The engine had separated itself from our car and was pulling off up the line while we coasted to a standstill. I slapped my rifle to my shoulder and put a couple of quick rounds into the cab. They must have ricocheted around in there in convincing fashion because the engineer slowed to a stop. I motioned to him to back up. He obeyed with such enthusiasm that the recoupling nearly knocked us off our feet, while the men in the field watched as if transfixed. I hoped they'd stay that way. To make sure, I was playing my rifle muzzle over them and acting like I knew exactly what I was doing. "Always act with authority," as Thomas had said. I yelled and motioned at the engineer to get going toward Peking. The soldiers continued to watch while we pulled away. I decided they were a foraging party expecting to find something to loot in our boxcar, but I didn't stop to ask.

When we were a mile or two safely up the line, I told Lu: "Don't ever get me another straw armchair! And now throw this one out of here as far as you can!" He did.

We reached the main Peking station outside the Chienmen Gate about four in the afternoon. I'd wired ahead. Carts, armed guards, and B.A.T. people met us and escorted us and our money straight to the Hong Kong-Shanghai Bank, then as later China's most prominent. We arrived after closing time but the crew was still on duty and as soon as the necessary receipts were signed, the clerks began counting our money. With deft movements of thumb and forefinger so quick your eye could hardly follow, they flipped the dollars into their proper bins: Suchow dollars here, Hong Kong dollars there. Almost every province had its dollar, each a little different in value. The national standard was the Mexican dollar worth forty-eight U.S. cents but some were worth only forty-four, some forty-six and so on. It looked like a mess but the clerks got it sorted out and I saw that Standard Oil and B.A.T. funds and those from the Jewish community were kept separate, and then I went off to report to Hutchison at B.A.T. headquarters, enjoy a warm reception at our piano bar, and sleep around the clock.

So ended my first free-lance job for Thomas and the Company. It established me willy-nilly as successful troubleshooter. Thereafter I was apt to get a telegram from time to time offering me similar opportunities.

In the sixteen-mile pass that lay between Kalgan, China, and the crest of the Mongolian Plateau, one of our caravans stops to rest. There were more than 500 camels in this caravan but only about a hundred are showing. I am on the white horse at the far right.

With two of my camel boys. Note the traditional snuff box hanging from the neck of the one at my left.

William Ashley Anderson, later a well known author, was my understudy in Mongolia.

Wong was my number-one camel boy.

Mu-Yan, my Mongolian camel girl, was no beauty but she could sling a pack with the best men of my caravan crew. She was an excellent shot with a rifle and performed well under fire during bandit attacks.

With some of my friends in our Kalgan compound.

Frans August Larson, honorary Duke of Mongolia, sits a female riding camel resembling my Ursha-Sahn. Larson, sometimes called the Prester John of the twentieth century, was a Swedish missionary, trader, and explorer who knew Mongolia and adjacent regions of China and Tibet better than anyone else. To ride camels like this in cross-country races over distances of thirty or forty miles, we wrapped ourselves from head to foot in bandage cloth, in the manner of Mongol dispatch riders, to protect our bodies against jarring and muscular strain. (*F.A. Larson*)

We flew the British flag from the first and last camels of our caravans. Rope slings held our bulk cigarette cases in place.

This large flat-topped pyramid is located near Sian in western China. It may be a royal tomb. (*Acme*)

# 10.  Journey to Kumbum

Back at Kalgan in the lee of the Great Wall, I resumed the life of caravanner and trader and was soon conducting caravans to Urga, 900 miles northwest across the grassy Mongolian Plateau and Gobi Desert, or along the border northward to Manchuria or southwesterly into west China and northern Tibet.

Hampering our movements was the fighting between Mongols and Chinese which had broken out along the border. Taking advantage of the turmoil caused by the Chinese Revolution, the Mongols had declared their independence after several hundred years of subjugation to China. They wisely avoided direct confrontation with an enemy who greatly outnumbered them. Operating in small units they struck at the flanks and rear of the Chinese, annihilating isolated detachments, disrupting supply trains, withdrawing swiftly into the recesses of their plains and mountains after each attack.

The Mongol fighting men were all horsemen, all mounted on the tough ponies whose forebears had carried Jenghis Khan and his forces triumphantly across Asia and much of Europe, earning their masters the name of Tartars, or literally "horsemen from hell." Some Mongols still carried the curved swords of that earlier era in addition to rifle and pistol.

The Chinese were at a disadvantage as they inched forward into Mongolia from bases such as Kalgan, trying to mount a conventional military campaign against an adversary they seldom saw. As consequence, hostilities sputtered along, neither side bleeding much, while marauding deserters, bandits, and freebooters helped make the border unsafe for caravans like ours.

Complicating things further, we were dealing with both

[129]

sides. Our caravans originating in China often reached destinations in Mongolia. Some of them carried contraband of war, as did one in particular which I took to Urga in the spring of 1913.

It was a comparatively small caravan of 200 camels. Each carried 500 pounds of cargo if a female, 550 if a male. Their loads, slung in rope slings, included bales of silk and cotton cloth, candles, tea, whiskey, gin, tobacco and cigarettes, and interspersed among some of the four-foot-long eighteen-inch-deep bulk-cigarette cases—such as those I described in the warehouse near Pao-ting-fu—were special cases containing cigarettes with steel barrels and wooden butts. Others contained ammunition. These special packages of "smokes" reached us through a British trading firm in Tientsin. The rifles were distinguished by the "Peacock" label. Ammunition traveled under the "Three Castles" brand.

Running such cargo through Chinese military lines was risky but profits were high. For protection we relied heavily on the British flag, which was respected and feared the world over. We always flew it from a staff stuck in the pack of the first and last animals in our trains. For further deterrent, there was our own firepower. But if stopped and searched we stood a good chance of losing not only our cargo but our heads.

We left Kalgan on May 1 at 6:30 A.M. and wound up the pass toward the Mongolian Plateau. I remember the exact date and time of our departure because for one of the few occasions in my life I was keeping a diary. And the reason for keeping the diary was because my life insurance was only collectible if I demised in the line of duty (and not in some frivolous escapade), and if I didn't come back from this trip perhaps my diary would and I wanted a certain person in San Francisco to be better off because of me. I'd met her during my last fling there. She was petite, fiery, indomitable, red-haired, and to me very beautiful if no longer young.

Wong, my number one camel puller, a husky young giant, led the way as usual. Behind him, attached nose to tail by a light tough cord or "string," followed ten heavily laden pack camels. Then came Ho-bar with his ten camels. And so on, until we looked like a long dark snake crawling up the rocky pass between the barren mountains. I roved here and there on Jenghis, my gray Mongol pony, to see that all went well. Other outriders, similarly mounted, served as scouts and security guards.

After reaching the plateau, we took the East Road toward Manchuria hoping to skirt the edge of the fighting and reach Urga, the Mongol capital, by a circuitous route. We covered seventy *li* (a *li* is the equivalent of one third of a mile) that first day without trouble and after twelve hours arrived at Da-hung-yo, a border point.

On May 2 we again traveled by day for greater safety. Usually we traveled at night because camels will not graze after dark and consequently must be pastured during daylight hours. We covered the ninety *li* between Da-hung-yo and Hi-swee-ker without serious incident, stopping for lunch at 2:30 with Dalomma, a Mongol duke and military leader who was effectively harrassing, or so he claimed, some 10,000 Chinese with his 600 horsemen. The main body of Chinese troops was several miles farther into Mongolia, so incoming stragglers told us.

We departed Hi-swee-ker at 5:00 P.M. in order to by-pass Chinese posts after dark if possible. When traveling by night we adopted a close-order formation for better protection. All strings drew up abreast forming a phalanx, a few yards between each string, outriders in close, no talking, no smoking. It is astonishing how quietly such an ungainly looking animal as a camel can move. With its bell clappers muffled (as customary after dark when on the trail in hostile territory) a caravan can pass within a few feet of you and you wouldn't know it unless you heard the squeaking of the pack ropes.

On May 3 we reached Hao-to-ho without difficulty, meeting only small detachments of Chinese. They said they were ordered to guard the road against surprise attack by Mongols. At Hao-to-ho we rested a day as customary during early stages of a trip. It gave us a chance to tighten the ropes with which our packs were slung and tied. They were made of new Chinese hemp which always "gave" a little during the first days.

To unload his camels, a boy made his entire string kneel. Then he removed the wooden pin that held the slings together across the tops of the packsaddles and the loads slid gently onto the ground at either side. Leaving the saddles on, he undid the strings that tied his camels one to another, and turned them out to graze, guarded by dogs and mounted men.

Chained to the last camel of each string and always turned loose to guard them when they grazed was a large fierce Mongolian camel dog. Camel dogs were born, raised, and spent their entire lives with camels. They were the fiercest dogs I ever encountered, fiercer than the most ferocious Alaskan dogs. I've known Mongol camel dogs to kill a wolf, something few Alaska-Yukon dogs could do. I've also known them to kill some of the human marauders who invariably attempted to steal our camels or to peel off and steal their valuable hair. Watch as we might, these thieves were so clever that they slipped past dogs and watchmen and stripped hair off some of our camels even by daylight.

At Koku-tu-su on May 5 I shot our first antelope for camp meat. He was one of the large Roman-nosed variety, weighing probably 400 pounds. As customary I shot him while a Mongolian-Tibetan prayer wheel was stuck down the back of my shirt collar. The prayer wheel was made of wood and looked like a child's rattle. It consisted of a hollow top which revolved on the end of a handle. Inside the top were scraps of paper on which prayers were inscribed in Tibetan. In theory the top was supposed to be turning as the result of the motion of your hand or the wind, and the prayers thus activated at the moment of killing an animal whose flesh was to be eaten. This supposedly prevented evil spirits from entering the meat. For morale purpose I was obliged to carry a prayer wheel when killing game for camp use or my boys—and Mu-Yan—wouldn't eat it. There was usually enough breeze blowing to make the top revolve and if there wasn't, no matter, ritual had been observed.

I should say a word further about Mu-Yan. She was a typical camel girl, or woman to be exact. Her husband had been killed in a fight, her children were staying with her parents, and she was out making her living as a number of Mongol women did—caravanning. Generally speaking, Mongol women enjoyed great personal freedom. In domestic affairs they had equal rights with men. Divorce was simply a matter of mutual agreement. Property was divided proportionately to its ownership at the time of marriage. Before or after marriage, a woman was expected to take as many lovers as she wanted. In fact it was common courtesy for a husband to offer you his wife if you stopped at his tent for the night. Or she might offer herself to you. Either way the next move was yours, and the only acceptable excuse was to plead disease. Mongol women conducted themselves as your equals. They rode horses and camels, acted as herders— cowgirls—and conducted business transactions. Some even became lamas and performed religious rites. Our supposedly advanced western nations offered nothing like it. Thus Mu-Yan could sling a pack with the best of my boys and when we were attacked by bandits she would "dzuk" her string of camels down and take shelter behind her own mount and bang away at the enemy over his back with her old Russian army rifle.

At Koku-tu-su a gale was blowing. We were getting out toward the northern Gobi. One flying cobblestone broke a lens in my glasses. I wore motorcyclist's goggles to protect my face during these windstorms. Sometimes they lasted three or four days and blew so hard we had to lie prone under our tarpaulins, because no tent would stand up in them. Our camels lay down too and gradually became covered by sand and pebbles until they were almost invisible, while the shaggy-haired ponies turned their rumps to the wind and bowed their heads stoically.

These enforced layovers, as well as many nights around trail campfires, gave me a chance to talk intimately with my Mongols about many subjects. A favorite one was the big meteor which had passed over Mongolia a few years before and crashed into the Siberian forest to the north, leaving devastation for many miles. Every Mongol was convinced it had passed directly over his yurta, lighting up the countryside as bright as midday. By nature, the Mongols were as simple, generous, cheerful, and brave a people as I ever knew.

I learned of their mystical faith in the God of Earth which they worshipped every midsummer from the top of the nearest hill. They prostrated themselves on the ground and called upon the god to listen to their prayers for relief from drouth, pestilence, all manner of ills. On these occasions, a variety of selected young animals—a calf, a kid, a lamb or foal—were dedicated to the god, tagged with special bits of colored cloth, turned back into their herds to be spoken of for the rest of their lives as the God of Earth's animals and never killed, sold, or used in any way until the god called them to him in death.

Beyond Koko-tu-su Chinese soldiers were blocking the East Road so we moved out across country. From Mongol riders we learned that scouting parties of Chinese cavalry were in the hills ahead. Reportedly they were seizing all caravans claiming "contraband of war." But we managed to avoid them.

On May 7 we covered only fifty *li*, first dodging Chinese troops and then stopped by rain. Rain can be disastrous to a camel train. Loaded camels can't keep their footing on moist ground. They slip and fall and frequently injure themselves seriously. We had to stop and stack goods and spread tarpaulins.

On May 8 we rested all day. I gave the crew a treat by buying a fat-tailed sheep from a nearby camp. Sheep was considered a great delicacy, particularly the fat tail. Sometimes the tails grew so large and heavy they dragged on the ground and became infected, so the Mongols built little wooden carts or "trailers" which could be attached as supports and kept them from dragging. We ate the greasy boiled meat with our fingers or mixed it with millet in our eating bowls—I foregoing my sahib-style tin plate with knife and fork for this occasion.

Five thousand Chinese soldiers were reported forty *li* to the east and four thousand to the west. Twenty-five hundred Mongols were said to be one to two days ahead. Sorting the truth out of such rumors and then choosing the best way to proceed kept us busy.

By now we were zigzagging to avoid trouble, sometimes traveling 100 *li* a day in order to advance sixty. I could not help but side with the Mongols in their efforts to gain freedom from Chinese rule. Since my crew were Mongols, it increased this sympathetic feeling and gave us good standing with the native population as we progressed deeper into Mongolia. From the air we would have looked like a naval convoy on a sea of grass: our heavily loaded camels the cargo ships, our outriders the surrounding cruisers and destroyers.

After thirty-nine days, we reached Urga and disposed of our cargo at a good profit.

I had hoped for a period of rest and relaxation after what had been a more strenuous trip than usual, but such was not to be.

* * *

Urga, capital and holy city of the Mongols, lay in a broad bare valley in the lee of a steep, almost treeless mountain range, where the Mongolian grasslands ended and the Siberian forests began. Like a frontier American town, its streets were unpaved. Some of its buildings and compounds were made of unpeeled logs, some of milled lumber, some of brick and stone. Roundabout it not Indians but nomad Mongols pitched their circular felt tents or yurtas and pastured their herds of horses, sheep, and camels. The twentieth century had hardly touched Urga. Electricity, plumbing, telephones were unknown.

The town was divided into Chinese, Mongol, and Lama districts, the Chinese being the merchants and traders as usual, and the Lama district being the center for a population of many thousands of red-robed priests who lived in its huge lamasery, officiated in its temples, or served in the official residence or palace of the Living God, their Grand Lama and Emperor. In addition there was a scattering of white foreigners, especially Russians, most of them traders like ourselves.

A few mornings after my arrival, Oscar Mamen, our Urga representative, and I were asleep in the house adjoining our compound when a young lama from the Imperial Palace walked into our bedroom shortly after daybreak and invited us to come to a conference. The impromptu nature of the invitation and the earliness of the hour were both in accordance with native custom, and we assumed the conference had something to do with our trading operations, the border war, or both.

As we approached the palace compound, the watchmen swung the heavy wooden gates in its high yellow wall. We rode our ponies into an earthen courtyard, tied them to posts near the main entrance, left our riding whips at the right-hand side of the door as custom dictated, and entered a long low antechamber floored with tile and lit by large candles. One of the lay brothers who officiated there (lamaseries usually had lay brothers and sometimes lay sisters—women beyond childbearing age—who with junior lamas performed menial tasks) received us and led us through corridors dim with age, smelling of dust, incense, and unwashed bodies, until we came to the room occupied by the Living God-Emperor and his advisors.

They were sitting crosslegged on the red-tiled floor on prayer rugs arranged in a semicircle. Overhead was a beamed ceiling, red lacquer between the beams, and here and there around the room low tables of Chinese blackwood and two or three braziers containing live coals to provide heat or to warm tea. "Sain-bai-na! (God be with you!)" they greeted us cordially, bowing over clasped hands. We returned the greeting, assuring them that we came in peace, and then sat down on rugs like theirs, crossing our legs in the standard manner.

Since we supplied them with many necessities of life besides munitions, we were on good terms with them. They operated an enormous business enterprise in connection with their lamasery, owning thousands of sheep, cattle, and horses, selling large quantities of hides and wool, much like the mission fathers of early California days. We bought their raw material and sold them tea, cloth, candles, cigarettes, and whiskey. Personally they were an extraordinary combination of sagacity and naiveté. They were like red-robed Rip Van Winkles waking up into a modern world after centuries of sleep.

Their bare heads were shaved or closely cropped. The God's robe was a richer red, his sash a cleaner yellow than the others, and for this particular council of state—which seemed to be what it was—he had put on his ceremonial headdress, a crown perhaps twenty inches high, inlaid with gold, silver, and precious stones. Though he was the third greatest personage in the Lamaist world, ranking immediately behind the Dalai Lama of Lhasa and the Tashi Lama of Tashilhunpo, the Hutukhtu of Urga was largely the tool of his advisors, the hierarchy of senior lamas who actually exercised power. They indulged his childlike fancies, kept him pleasantly befuddled with liquor and women, and had organized the revolution against China using him as a figurehead. Though only in middle age, he was going blind from syphillis, syphillis being a national scourge because of the Mongols' extreme promiscuity and because so many lamas exercised their privileged status by taking any woman they fancied. The simple-minded Hutukhtu loved practical jokes and all kinds of mechanical gadgetry. When the Model "T" Ford sedan he had ordered as a curiosity reached Urga after being driven overland from Kalgan by a friend of ours Ethan Le Munyon, who traded for the China-American Company out of Tientsin, curious Mongols, who had never seen an automobile before, nearly pawed the car to death before it ever reached the palace. To keep their hands off it Le Munyon wired its magneto to its body so that anyone touching it got a mild shock. This amused the God greatly. He invited a group of councillors of state to inspect his new toy, encouraged them to touch it, and was delighted when they snatched their hands away in consternation at the car's sting.

The God was a bit nutty about clocks of every description. He had a room full of them ranging in size from alarm clocks to grandfather clocks, all keeping time but no particular time, so that the din of their chiming, alarming, and coocooing at odd intervals was truly remarkable. Many of them had been given him as diplomatic presents, and Mamen and I had brought him several including a cuckoo clock purchased in Tientsin. He would stand in front of it till the bird popped out and then clap his hands in delight.

Despite his childishness, he was a good man at heart and sincerely devoted to the cause of Mongolian independence.

He began by apologizing for disturbing our slumbers but explained that there was important business at hand that needed our sagacious attention. In addressing us he used our native names, "Horse Gate," (a literal translation of "Mamen" into Mongolian) and "Sh-lo-ta" which was as close as Mongols or Chinese ever came to pronouncing "Schroder."

The Minister of War, a senior lama who often pedaled over to our compound on his Russian bicycle, continued the conversation. "Unless the military situation along the border improves, our revolution may fail. This would not help your trading enterprises."

We agreed that it would not, and he continued: "So far the princes (the semi-independent nomad rulers whose word was virtually law in their districts) have not rallied wholeheartedly to the support of the revolution. We have about 20,000 irregulars facing nearly 200,000 Chinese. We cannot hold our own indefinitely against such odds. There is one word, however, which will unite all Mongolia and send it against China like the blow of a single sword."

"And what is that word?"

"The word of his Most Sacred Holiness, the Tashi Lama."

The Mongols were devout adherents of the Lamaism which stemmed from Tibet and particularly from its two great lamas, of which the Dalai was the more powerful politically but the Tashi (or Panchen) more powerful spiritually, especially in Mongolia. Later we learned that they had already secured the support of the Dalai Lama and in addition wanted the backing of the more popular Tashi, or "Red God."

"And how will the word of the Red God help?"

"It will legitimize the revolution. When the highest god speaks, even a prince will listen. It will protect your trading privileges, Sh-lo-ta and Horse Gate. It will unite our people. United we cannot fail to defeat the Chinese though they be numberless as the blades of grass!"

"How does one secure the word of the Tashi Lama?"

"By going to Kumbum and requesting it, with your help."

We were taken aback to say the least. Kumbum Lamasery was about a thousand miles away and neither of us had been there or had any previous contact with the Tashi Lama.

We said we felt honored to be considered worthy of their confidence. "Who would accompany us to Kumbum?"

"Our colleague, your friend, the Hutukhtu of Lama Miao."

It was a good choice. The Hutukhtu or High Lama of Lama Miao, was the administrative head of Lamaism in Mongolia. He lived at a comparatively small but important monastery on the border not far from Kalgan and was thus a southern or Inner Mongol, whereas the clique in Urga were northern or Outer Mongols. His support might give unity to an appeal to the Red God. But why they chose to involve us in the matter we were not quite sure. Partly it must have been because we did so much business with them, partly because they knew we were risking a good deal—a good deal more than our Russian counterparts who supplied them quite easily from nearby Siberia—by running guns through the Chinese lines and had thus demonstrated our loyalty; and partly it was because of our connection with the foreign power structure in China and the Far East, which they supposed to be much greater than it actually was. In any event, foreign advisors were in fashion. Larson, our fellow trader, would soon be serving both them and the Chinese government in that capacity.

After thinking it over we decided to do it. In addition to strengthening our relationships in Urga, it would take us into new territory and give us a chance to make contacts we might exploit later.

According to their plan we were to go to Lama Miao, join our friend the Hutukhtu there, proceed with him and his retinue to Kumbum in the high country of northern Tibet.

We decided Mamen had better stay in Urga to look after our affairs while I, who was well acquainted with the border region and with the Bogdo of Lama Miao, made the trip.

I left before noon that day with a half dozen of our best Mongol horsemen.

We traveled at the traditional cross-country pace: lope five or six miles, slow to a jog or walk, then lope again. The distances you could cover in a day's riding in such manner over the rolling Mongolian grassland exceeded anything I had experienced, but even they were exceeded by the professional dispatch riders, forerunners of our pony express, who were still crisscrossing the country on regular routes as in the time of the great khans. Often the dispatch riders wrapped themselves in cotton bandage cloth to support their limbs and reduce jarring and muscular strain. The cloth was applied over the clothing of the entire body, leaving only face and hands bare. We had no such wrapping and, in addition to weapons, carried dried meat and millet in our sausage-shaped canvas riding bags slung across the fronts of our saddles, but we changed horses often at herds that we passed and covered the 850 miles to Lama Miao in ten to twelve days.

Lama Miao, reputedly the site of Kublai Khan's hunting lodge, stands at the edge of the Mongolian Plateau, where it breaks sharply away to the lowlands and the Imperial Forest that lie toward Peking. Wild apricots and rhubarb grow there in profusion. The town was a major trade center where, as at Kalgan, the Mongols exchanged their sheep, horses, camels, hides, and wool for tea, tobacco, cotton, and silk of the Chinese. At the outskirts of the Chinese settlement was the Mongolian community with its temples and a lamasery of some 2,000 persons.

The Bogdo or Holy One—old, shrewd, wise, and one of the best informed and most articulate lamas I ever knew—greeted me warmly. He seemed aware what was up. When I told him the purpose of my visit and he had read the instructions sent him from Urga, he clapped his hands to command attention and began giving orders to his subordinates.

Next day we were riding westward toward Kumbum, following the border road, Bogdo on a beautiful white pacing stallion and his attendant junior lamas mounted on geldings like the rest of us. Bogdo wore a Mongol hat of sheepskin partially peaked, with earflaps; his robe was reddish. A dirt colored sash whose fringe showed that it had once been yellow surrounded his waist. A tobacco pouch made of skin hung from his sash; also his chopsticks-and-knife sheath. Inside the front fold of his robe he carried his silver eating bowl. Once that bowl had been wooden. Now that he was a head lama it was of silver. But he would still wipe it out with his finger after eating and lick the finger.

We numbered fifteen or twenty all together. Such parties were not uncommon in a land where everyone traveled horseback and my presence need arouse no suspicion since my trading operations along the border and business dealings with the lamas were well known. Nevertheless we avoided Chinese soldiers wherever possible.

We went at a brisk pace, the weather beautiful, the larks singing. They rose in circles, singing as they went, until lost from sight, when only their song came falling back to us like a melody out of the sky. Vast herds of antelope and gazelle scampered off to either side as we rode along. To occupy the time I engaged the Bogdo in one of our favorite topics of conversation: antiquities. Antiquities had interested me since boyhood days among the Spanish adobes and missions and my interest had been whetted by the many relics and ruins visible in China and Mongolia. Bogdo was well informed on those of the border region.

"This trip may take us near the pyramids of Shensi," he told me, the actual term he used being something like "man-made mountains."

"You mean burial mounds?" Burial mounds were common

throughout China, many of them eight or ten feet high.

"These may be burial mounds but they are much larger than any you're familiar with. I have not seen them but they are said to be truly mountain-sized ."

"Who built them?"

"No one knows. Our oldest books describe them as old many centuries ago."

"If they are so old and well known, why haven't I heard about them?"

"You foreigners make me laugh," he scoffed. "Because you haven't heard of something, you think it doesn't exist."

I made him promise to show me the pyramids if the opportunity presented itself when we reached Shensi province, and we continued westward along the border, by-passing Kalgan and following the high grassland toward Kuei-hua-cheng, another border town, where there was also a B.A.T. compound. As we approached it we passed near the missionary settlement of the Belgian Catholic Fathers, a kind of natural wonder in itself, which I described to the Bogdo.

Following the Boxer Rebellion, the Belgian Fathers had taken their indemnity—offered by the Chinese Government for losses suffered—in the form of this fertile border land. "Father Rubbens' Valley" it was called after the founder of the extraordinary community there. It was a cross between a communal utopia and a poor farm. Needy Chinese families flocked to it from many parts of the country. Each family was given an allotment of land—ten *mou* or fifteen *mou* (a *mou* is one third of an acre)—depending on its need. The community helped them build their houses and loaned them seed, a pair of oxen, a plow, and food to sustain them until their first crop was harvested. They retained half that harvest. The other half went to the communal granary. Of that half, one half was sold to help pay expenses of the settlement, for such things as roads, mills, water wells, a hospital, police. The other half stayed in the granary as insurance against time of need.

Within three or four years the new arrivals were usually thriving. The Belgian Fathers thus won wide respect. Unlike other missionary groups they were entirely self-sustaining. They had their own flour mills, blacksmith shops, vineyards (the vines grown from cuttings supposedly taken from the Pope's own vineyards near Rome), and tobacco fields. They made their own clothes and even meerschaum pipes, one of which I smoked in addition to my Pierson. To protect their health they followed a regular program. Every afternoon about two o'clock they went to their houses, stripped down to their underwear, drank three eight-ounce cups of mulled red wine mixed with hot tea. After the first cup they were bathed in sweat. These regular sweats seemed to protect them from disease, especially the dreaded, louse-borne typhus which was very prevalent.

I enjoyed many a good sweat treatment with the fathers, stopping by when on trips and leaving them English and American newspapers and magazines, sometimes coursing wolves with them after the pair of greyhounds which I gave them. They were not Belgian only, but French, Irish, and other nationalities as well. They were hardy fellows, brooking no nonsense. When attacked by bandits they soundly defeated their attackers, the whole community rallying behind them using knives, pitchforks and old gas-pipe muskets. Tucking up their robes like battling bishops of medieval times, they and their "troops," led by the redoubtable Father Rubbens, pursued the fleeing attackers so fiercely that a number of the bandits ran right out of their shoes, which the thrifty priests collected and distributed to their needy people.

Perhaps the most interesting feature of their settlement was its girls' school. In most Chinese families a girl child was simply another mouth to feed. Baby girls were often strangled at birth, abandoned on rubbish heaps, or sold into slavery as household servants, concubines, or sing-song girls. Not so in Rubbens' Valley. They went to a school run by nuns and were taught to cook, sew, and keep house so that they might find good husbands. They were not allowed to marry until the age of sixteen. Then they were permitted the almost-unheard-of privilege of meeting and even refusing the offers of their suitors. If approved, a suitor was allowed to "buy" his girl by presenting her with a dowry which consisted of 150 tael, or about $105 in U.S. money. Of the 150 tael, ten went to her in cash, the balance taking the form of household utensils, clothing, and personal belongings. It was a considerable endowment. But there was more. At any time during the first year of marriage she had the right, clearly stated in her marriage contract, to complain to Father Rubbens in the event of mistreatment. There were few such complaints, however, and the demand for "Rubbens girls" as wives continued keen.

There was little evidence of organized religion in the settlement. Freedom of worship was the rule. Services were held but there was no compulsion to attend. Such freedom of choice was a further reason for the success of the colony, which was probably the most successful missionary enterprise anywhere in China or Mongolia.

Bogdo was impressed by my account. He said that such Christianity resembled Lamaism in that it mingled priests and people at workaday level sharing all aspects of life. Many lamas, it was true, lived away from the protection of lamaseries and were members of nomadic camps, or even lived alone, maintaining their own tents, flocks, and herds and, in the role of businessman, doctor, or priest, shared and made substantial contributions to the popular welfare.

At Kuei-hua-cheng we rested our animals, Bogdo and his lamas staying at the local temple while my boys and I went to the B.A.T. compound. The compound was a huge one, large enough to play polo in, and there was always plenty of livestock available, Kuei-hua-cheng being one of the main centers of the border and trans-Mongolian caravan trade. Finding all white men absent, I made arrangements with our Chinese manager, Lu, for a mule train to accompany us into the wild country ahead where we would carry our own food and water. Had there been a white man present it would have made no difference; I would have dealt with Lu who handled all such arrangements.

With a dozen big ungelded mules, probably tougher than any that ever came out of Missouri, packing 350 pounds apiece, and with an old gray bell mare to lead them, we went on west toward the Yellow River. The chief reason for the toughness of the domestic animals of Mongolia and the border region was the fact that they were never sheltered, shod, or fed. They fended for themselves, winter or summer, learned to survive wolves, blizzards, Gobi sandstorms, long cross-country trips that would leave an ordinary horse or mule a wreck. They were like the animals (and the men) of our early West and that was one reason for my affinity for them. Another reason was the gear they wore. Our mules, for instance, wore packsaddles almost identical with the *aparejos* I'd used on the ranch: leather pads stuffed with grass and stiffened with willow twigs, common in Mexico, too, and throughout the Southwest, dating back through the conquistadors to the Old World and time immemorial.

The river at Pao-ling Miao was lower than I'd ever seen it. It appeared impossible to cross with animals because of quicksand, so we turned south and followed the bank thirty or forty miles until we came to a ferry where there was a spectacularly large water wheel, at least fifty feet high by twenty wide, lifting water to irrigate nearby fields, the water being caught and hoisted in five-gallon Standard Oil tins instead of the traditional wood buckets.

We were now entering Shensi, a province largely unknown to the outside world.

My friends R. S. Clark and A. de C. Sowerby had explored parts of it four years before. Clark, a wealthy New Yorker, attached to our legation at Peking as intelligence officer, and Sowerby, the son of missionaries and field collector for the British and Smithsonian Museums, had penetrated Shensi down-river from the spot where we were entering, then turned south through Yenan-fu, a city which gained notoriety during the Second World War as headquarters of Mao-tse Tung and the Chinese Communists, and proceeded to Sian-fu and westward along the old Imperial Highway to Lanchow. Their purpose was to map unexplored territory and collect plant and animal specimens. We would take much the same route.

Crossing the river, we entered the Ordos Desert, a wasteland of shifting sands whose dunes may be the highest in the world. I know they are much higher than those of the Gobi to the north. Some rise fifty or sixty feet. They are the residue of winds that have blown across the Mongolian Plateau for ages, depositing sand and dust always more and more to the southwest. The heavier sand settles out first. The dust or loess carries farther and finally lies to a depth of two hundred feet or more.

There is no possibility of riding against the Ordos dunes.

You must travel with them as with a wind at sea, veering slightly this way or that if you wish, but never breasting them directly. Even when there is no wind their sand is constantly moving and gives off a continuous hissing sound. This is caused by the dunes breaking at their crests as high waves break and crumble. It goes on day and night much as the sea continues to move even in calm weather. Travelers, especially lone ones, are said to have been driven mad by it. It was eerie.

Our water skins, dried meat, and millet sustained us now as we made several dry camps and saw no game.

Continuing southwesterly we came to the Great Wall, completely covered by sand in some sections, only its watchtowers showing; and then we emerged into the region of the loess. Plateaus of pure dust, several hundred feet thick, were cut by sudden watercourses as sheer as crevasses in ice, and you had to be careful not to ride into them by accident.

Here I shot the giant bustard that has three toes and flies with the wild geese flocks. His flesh is as delicious as a turkey's, all dark except along the breast bone where it is white.

We began to see settlements again, some of them wholly or partially in ruins, grim evidence of the Mohammedan Rebellion of several decades earlier, the terrible civil and religious war which devastated western China and cost millions of lives, though the outside world heard little about it because the region was so remote.

From time to time I reminded Bogdo of his promise to show me the wonderful man-made mountains he had mentioned. He made inquiries at the monasteries where we sometimes stopped but no one seemed to have heard of them.

When there was no lamasery or inn available he could be quite arrogant about accommodations, sometimes ejecting families from their huts or tents so that his holiness could be housed. Generally he behaved himself well and collected information or propagandized for the Mongol revolutionary cause as we traveled, often engaging in long conferences with his red-robed brethren at our wayside stops.

When I asked him how the Red God was likely to receive our request for assistance, he shrugged and answered dryly: "He already knows what we are going to say and what he will reply."

This was in keeping with the widespread belief in the omniscience of the Tashi and Dalai Lamas. I remained skeptical.

Descending onto the plain of the Huei, a tributary of the Yellow River, we began to see many burial mounds. This was a region of very ancient settlement and its burial sites were more numerous and elaborate than any I had observed previously, some rising to twenty or thirty feet. Again we made inquiries about man-made mountains but without success.

Farther along on the fertile plain at Sian-fu, the ancient capital of China, we had better luck. Sian is situated on the Imperial Highway or Old Silk Road, the main overland trade route between China and Europe in ancient times. Its population was around half a million and it was comparable to Peking in the impressiveness of its walls and some of its buildings. In the downtown section, watchtowers arched over the streets. The plazas in front of the *yamens*, or official headquarters, were crowded with buyers and sellers. Merchants advertised their wares by yelling at the tops of their lungs from booths roofed with straw matting or blue cloth. There were oranges and peaches for sale in the stalls; the profusion of fruits in China—pears, plums, apricots, grapes, persimmons—was always impressive to me. I wanted to see the stone tablet which supposedly told of the establishment of Christianity in Sian by missionaries from Palestine around 600 A.D. It had stood on a public street but had been removed to a place of safekeeping and I could not find it.

Inquiring of priests at the Lama Temple (Lamaism was prevalent in western China as in Mongolia) Bogdo learned that our man-made mountains or pyramids might be found a day or two's travel westward.

From Sian, we followed the old caravan road that in Marco Polo's time carried the silks and spices of Cathay to the seaports of the eastern Mediterranean. It was a combination of cart track and nearby caravan trail, the trail—like most caravan routes—pounded hard as concrete by millions of feet over hundreds if not thousands of years, and the cart track deeply cut—sometimes as much as six or eight feet—into the surrounding earth. Where it was paved with stone, wheels had worn ruts so deep that the axles of carts sometimes dragged. Sure enough, two or three days west of Sian we heard that the man-made mountains were said to be a day's travel farther north.

After a night at a village inn we headed northward at sunrise. It was farming country, not particularly isolated, villages here and there.

Toward noon we saw something looming ahead that looked like a small mountain but its top was flat and it had regularly sloping sides. Before long we could distinguish the outlines of a huge pyramid. Then others began to appear. I'd heard of flat-topped pyramids in Mexico and South America and had seen photographs of the pyramids of Egypt, but never anything like this.

As we approached the big one we could see that trees and shrubs grew part way up its sides and that the sides had eroded into gullies and ravines. There were cultivated fields around it and a small village nearby. Stopping at the village we made inquiries. No one could tell us anything about the origins of the pyramids. They had "always been there." They were held in great veneration but no relics were known to have come from them. Yes, perhaps they were tombs, but who could say?

Upon close inspection I estimated the big one to be approximately 600 feet high and 1,500 feet wide at the base. It was truly a colossal structure, breathtaking and awe-inspiring. Its sides had been wholly or partly encased by a layer of rock but much of the rock had fallen or was covered by debris from above. The rock appeared to be cut field stone about three feet square. The core of the pyramid seemed to have been made of the pounded earth still commonly used for construction in China. Alternate layers of lime and clay are mixed and pounded. When the lime permeates the clay and hardens, the result is something like concrete.

Here and there at a distance of about 200 yards, the pyramid was surrounded by a low mound of earth, perhaps the remains of a wall that once enclosed a sacred precinct. But there were no signs of altars and temples or of doors or other openings into the pyramid itself.

Its flat top may have been used for worship. Star worship (focused on the North Star, the fixed point in the heavens, the constellation of the Great Bear, and the cardinal compass points) is said to have been practiced by the early Chinese as by early peoples elsewhere, and I noticed that the pyramid was oriented with the compass points so far as I could tell.

At some early period in the history of China, colors were assigned to the four directions. Black was for the north, blue-green for the east, red for the south, white for the west. In the center was yellow. This may explain why the tops of the Shensi pyramids were flat and not pointed like those in Egypt. The flat tops were perhaps spread with yellow earth.

We rode on for a look at the next pyramid, about three quarters of a mile away. It resembled the first but was only about two thirds as large. Nearby was third one, still smaller and then a gap of several miles and then a southern group of four, all smaller still. All of the pyramids were flat topped, all had apparently been constructed by the same method, all were oriented to the cardinal compass points. Together they formed an irregular pattern with its apex at the big northern one.

When I expressed myself duly impressed by what we had seen, admitting it was as remarkable if not more remarkable than anything I had beheld in the world of foreign devils, Bogdo was gratified. We agreed to ask the Tashi Lama about the pyramids, believing that if anyone knew their origins he would.


Old Bogdo began to weary during the later stages of our trip. At Lanchow-fu, a large commercial city where the Imperial Highway crossed the Yellow River, I secured a traveling chair for him. It was a grand lama's chair, upholstered in royal blue, curtains at the windows. With a mule between the shafts at either end of it, Bogdo ascended into the Tibetan high country in style. Now and then he would poke his head out a window and shout or clap hands for something he needed. Often it was the wine skin which one of his young lamas hastened to bring him.

Tibet was regarded as beginning about fifty miles west of Lanchow and the old maps will show it that way. From there, Chinese authority diminished to near zero when you left the highway—as we did about halfway in the 154-mile stretch between Lanchow and Liangchow-fu—and headed southwestward into the hills.

As we entered Tibet the country became steeper and more

barren but there were fertile valleys with good crops of beans and barley and prosperous villages. The blue-clothed Chinese disappeared and we began to see nomads dressed in sheepskins astride camels or tough shaggy ponies, or sometimes herding or riding yaks. Some of them stuck out their tongues at us in the usual Tibetan fashion as they smiled in greeting.

Mamen and I and Rustad went back into that country with a commercial caravan and sales crews several years later, distributing cigarettes and contacting local merchants at Lanchow and Liangchow-fu along the way. Far to the west on the borders of Sinkiang we found an abundance of wild licorice which proved extremely valuable when the regular supplies from Persia and Turkey were cut off from Europe and the U.S. during World War I. We packed out thousands of tons of it and shipped them to the States. We also collected a number of valuable skins, including those of the white-faced bear and snow leopard. They used female urine to tan skins in that high country as was the practice among the Yukon Indians, female urine of course having a different chemical composition from male. A regular feature of hunters' huts was a small pot of it in one corner.

Kumbum Monastery was situated at the foot and up the sides of a barren mountain. It consisted of a scattered collection of buildings, most of them the one-storied flat roofed, whitewashed dwellings of lamas, here and there larger administrative buildings and impressive temples, some constructed in Tibetan style, some in Chinese. At its outskirts was a village and commercial center with shops and inns catering to the thousands of pilgrims who visited the monastery annually. Kumbum had been founded, I learned later, in the sixteenth century in honor of a reformer named Tsong Khapa who allegedly purified Lamaism of corruption and returned it to honesty. He had been born near the monastery site and the locality had become a famous shrine attracting the faithful from Mongolia, Tibet, China, and even Siberia.

A welcoming party of young lamas (news of our coming had preceded us) met us at the gate and conducted Bogdo and his attendants in one direction, my boys and me in another.

En route to the guesthouse we passed one of the main temples. Pilgrims were prostrating themselves before it. Some were working their way up its steps and inside, a prostration at a time. It was not uncommon for them to travel halfway across Asia, prostrating themselves at every step. Inside, as I also learned later, were numerous images in gilt and bronze. In front of each was a metal basin or dish where you could leave your offerings in the form of food, money, goods, or jewels. In this fashion the lamas helped to maintain themselves but they also worked. Each was largely self-supporting according to his talents. Some were laborers, some household servants, stable boys, policemen, traders, students, teachers, doctors, business managers—all the types needed in a community that numbered five or six thousand. Each owned his own residence or rented a room from some wealthier inmate and so the usual hierarchy of talent and property prevailed.

Our guesthouse was located on level ground near the temples not far from the entrance—rather than on the hillside above where most of the lamas lived. It resembled those we had frequently stayed in during the trip. It contained brick beds, or kangs, with small fireplaces or "stoves" built into them and flues to carry the heat throughout the bed; there were also braziers for cooking and warming tea. Perhaps the place had been cleaned once during the past hundred years. The stains where bedbugs had been mashed against the wall decade after decade gave the interior a speckled effect.

We spread our things on our beds and waited to see what would happen. I wanted very much to clean up. There had been little chance to do so during the trip and though I shaved daily (as usual in summer—in winter we let our beards grow as protection against the cold) by this time I was yearning for a hot bath. But no Tibetan bathes unless caught in the rain. I didn't want to attract attention by asking for a tub, so I heated water on a brazier and settled for a sponge-off.

I'd hardly finished it when an elderly lama appeared, clasped his hands, and after the usual bow and "God-be-with-you!" offered himself as my guide and mentor during my stay at Kumbum. This was a customary procedure at most large or famous lamaseries. He was comparable to the professional guides you find today at the Vatican in Rome or at the Acropolis in Athens. Like them he made his living from the tourist trade.

Not far behind him came a young lama with an invitation to

a meeting with His Holiness, the Tashi Lama. Putting on my hat I followed him to a simple dwelling not far away, not by any means a palace but a kind of private residence, flat-roofed, its walls plastered with a white lime sand, windbells at its eaves. Inside, seated on a low round dais, flanked by my Bogdo and two or three other shaved-headed lamas, was a man in early middle age with a quiet, friendly manner who greeted me cordially.

He wore a reddish purple robe of woven yak's wool embroidered with gold, red Russia leather boots with turned up toes, and the tassels of his yellow sash were decorated with turquoises. His rosary beads—108 of them, one for each book of the Tibetan bible—were also of turquoise. He was about my height and build and of a somewhat swarthy complexion.

As we chatted informally, he expressed curiosity about my clothing. My hat interested him particularly. It was a center-crush Stetson such as the Canadian Mounties wore though its brim had been trimmed from four inches to three before it was sent me from the States. "Don't your ears get cold under a hat like that?" he joked, contrasting it to the usual Tibetan hat with earflaps. I said they would if I didn't change it for a Mongol cap with earflaps when winter came.

Then we got down to business and Bogdo explained the purpose of our mission. His Holiness seemed fully aware of what was going on in Mongolia, nodding several times but saying little. I described the kind of supplies our caravans were providing the Urga government and the military situation along the border. I said I thought an independent Mongolia was likely to receive strong support from such commercial interests as I represented. In the end he gave no indication what he would do but suggested we meet again next day.

Two weeks went by. When not conferring with the God and his advisors I saw the sights of Kumbum with my lama guide. The most famous of these was the Tree of Faces, said to possess magic properties. It grew in an enclosure on the level area near one of the major temples and had broad leaves resembling those of a California maple. By looking long and faithfully at its leaves, you were supposed to be able to see, appearing in them, the faces of relatives you would meet during the comimg year. In a region where family ties and tribal life were of paramount importance, such visions no doubt had great popular appeal, even if self-induced. The tree was surrounded by pilgrims staring reverentially at its leaves. To please my guide, I looked long and hard and said I could see the face of an old uncle of mine who lived far beyond the "big water."

The nearby Temple with the Golden Roof had attracted my attention from the beginning. One day when there were not many people in evidence (though visitors were given wide latitude of behavior I wanted to reduce hazards), I asked my lama to fetch me a ladder, ladders being in good supply, often used by the lamas to go from one flat-roofed level of their buildings to another. With its help I climbed to the roof of the temple ostensibly in awe and wonder but actually to apply a few drops of nitric acid to one of its tiles. Sure enough, the surface bubbled. It was solid gold plate.

There was plenty of gold in Tibet. You could pick it up in watercourses after a rain. But no central source or mother lode was known and we were always looking for it. We were always dreaming of that "Asiatic Klondike," and a vial of nitric acid was a regular part of my equipment when in the field. Once a gold bug, always a gold bug.

I'd been waiting for an opportunity to speak to the God about the pyramids. Choosing a moment at the end of a meeting when we were sipping tea, I did so. Stirring the contents of his silver bowl daintily with his finger, he replied thoughtfully: "What did you think of them?"

"I think they're astonishing. Are they very old?"

"Our oldest books mention them as being old five thousand years ago." But "five thousand years" was a term often used loosely to mean simply "very old."

"Who built them?"

"We don't know. Men of ancient time. That's all we can say."

He asked if I would like to see some of his old books, and I accompanied him to a nearby building which housed the monastery library. Instead of standing upright on their shelves, its books were piled flatly according to size. Seated on the floor at low tables of blackwood were two or three lama librarians or scribes. He informed me they were inscribing the daily events of the monastery into a permanent record. They were writing on pieces of parchment with tapered camel's hair brushes. Now and then they rubbed the brushes on bars of India ink resembling bars of black soap. Other red-robed figures, seated at similar tables, studied books.

The Tashi Lama walked over to one of the shelves and picked up a large volume. It was bound in hide, tied with sinew, and looked very old. Opening it, he turned a few pages, saying they were the kind that recorded the existence of the pyramids and other ancient wonders. He held it out to me and I saw its writing: columnar, dim with age, apparently India ink, apparently an alphabet language resembling Mongolian. "We have even older records," he said, shutting the book and putting it back on its shelf.

Walking to a low table on which stood a large wooden box, he removed the lid and took out a clay disc about the diameter of an old-style phonograph record though somewhat thicker. Writing had been inscribed on it, apparently put there by a sharp instrument when the clay was wet. This writing too was columnar and was a kind of picture writing depicting humans, animals, and other natural objects interspersed with hieroglyphic symbols.

"We don't know exactly how old these are, perhaps ten thousand years," he explained, offering me the disc. Again he was using a figure I discounted, though convinced that the disc was extremely old. I declined to take it in my hands, fearing it might disintegrate.

"What does it say?" I asked.

"It tells of the dealings of our ancestors with a people far older who lived on land beyond the great water."

I hoped he would continue the subject but he didn't and I didn't think it wise to press him. As he replaced the disc, I noticed five or six more, and fragments of others, in the box.

Most lamaseries had libraries but this was the largest I'd seen, perhaps because Kumbum was a center for learning. It had colleges of botany, medicine, music, and many other arts and sciences including, as I discovered later, mysticism and the occult. Most lamaseries also had relic rooms, or museums, which contained a variety of strange objects—old bones, fragments of pottery, sacred relics, coins, paintings, statues. In one of them I saw a long thin-bladed sword resembling a rapier, which might have belonged to some European traveler in Marco Polo's time. There may have been such a museum at Kumbum but I didn't see it.

Despite a fear of giving offense, a blunt question led to my most remarkable experience at Kumbum. The Tashi Lama received information about the war in Mongolia with what seemed unbelievable speed. In the course of our conversations, he would casually mention an event as having occurred a day or two before. Nearly 2,000 miles separated us from the fighting front, and no telephone or telegraph lines connected Kumbum with the outer world. How did he get his information? Finally I asked him.

"Come with me this afternoon," he said, good naturedly as usual, "and I will show you!"

At mid-afternoon his runner escorted me to a building not far from his residence. On the floor seated crosslegged in a semicircle on prayer rugs were a dozen or fifteen lamas apparently asleep. At least they were slumped in the manner they usually adopted when dozing in a sitting position. Three or four junior priests and lay brothers waited watchfully in the background. The Tashi Lama stood with other senior lamas near the entrance door. There was absolute silence and an air of expectancy.

After about ten minutes one of the dozing figures stirred. He stretched, yawned, opened his eyes, blinked and looked around in bewildered fashion as if not sure where he was. A lay brother hurried to him with a bowl of tea. He sipped it eagerly. Making a sign to me, the Tashi Lama walked over to him and I followed.

"Where have you been?" the God inquired gently.

The lama replied slowly as if not yet fully awake: "I've been to Koko-tu-su."

I was astonished to hear him mention a place where I'd been myself a month or two earlier and where fighting might be in progress now.

"What did you see?"

"I saw Chinese infantry advance into the hills. The Mongols were waiting in ambush. Eighteen Chinese were killed or wounded. The Mongols escaped on fast horses."

"What else?"

"The Chinese are dragging cannon onto the plateau above Kalgan."

"How many cannon?"

"I saw four."

"What else?"

"That was all I saw."

"You have done well."

The Tashi Lama turned to me. "Now do you understand?" I shook my head. He chuckled, enjoying my perplexity. "It's very simple. He goes there. He sees. He comes back and tells us!" That was all the explanation he would give.

At the risk of offending, I returned to his intelligence center—or whatever it was called—on two later occasions. Finding myself well received, I took the liberty of examining one of the seated lamas as he was waking from what was probably a hypnotic trance. His forehead was cool, his pulse slow. His entire metabolism seemed depressed as it would be during sleep or hypnosis. When I asked what he had been doing, he shrugged and answered enigmatically: "Oh, I went there! I looked at things!"

A senior lama or the Red God himself was always present to hear these reports.

Did the same observer "visit" the same locality during each "trip"? I could not be sure. Not knowing them, it was difficult to tell them apart, since they all dressed and looked very much alike, but I got the impression they worked in shifts and did not visit regions outside the Red God's spiritual domain, perhaps "went" only to places with which they were in some way familiar. I don't think they "visited" Peking, or New York, or London though they may have had the power to do so.

Did they read minds as well as see objects? There was no evidence that they did. Perhaps they could have.

With a view to later corroboration, I made notes on what I heard reported. After I returned to Mongolia I showed my notes to people in a position to know of the events described in the Kumbum reports. Verification was absolute. In some cases, events were revealed to have occurred which my friends in Mongolia were not aware of.

How did such information reach Kumbum? I cannot say for sure. What I probably witnessed was a performance by a talented group of clairvoyants. They were probably experts in yoga who had mastered the arts of astral projection, whereby the physical body is said to remain fixed while the astral body travels.

Were such experts found in other lamaseries? I never heard of them elsewhere, though they may have existed.

The spiritual atmosphere of Tibet and Mongolia was—and probably still is in some degree—conducive to that sort of thing. In the West we have a handful of recognizedly gifted seers and psychics. In the East, they have hundreds, men who devote their lives to the occult arts and have a centuries-old tradition behind them. We have no such tradition.

Similarly in Russia and other Iron Curtain countries where strong occult traditions exist, investigators are reported hard at work perfecting techniques of extrasensory perception which can be used not only for personality development but for military espionage. We may have to hurry or be left behind with respect to such talents.

Our negotiations at Kumbum came to what seemed a successful conclusion. In a final session, the Tashi Lama suggested that financial support for the Mongol revolt against China might be provided by lamaseries directly in the path of the fighting and thus subject to looting anyway. Coming from a supposedly unworldly spiritual leader, it seemed a remarkably practical suggestion. We parted on the best of terms. I said I would send him a center-crush Stetson and he said he would send me some earmuffs.

When Bogdo and I returned to Mongolia we found a new spirit of unity. I never learned all that went on at diplomatic levels at Urga, Kumbum, or Lhasa. But for a while both Mongolia and Tibet enjoyed a substantial degree of autonomy—until the former was gobbled up by Russia and China and the latter by China alone.

I returned to the high country of west China and northern Tibet on several occasions but only once saw anything resembling what I'd witnessed in the occult center at Kumbum. Our party, which included T. A. Rustad, later Norwegian consul at Nanking, was following the bank of a deep, swift stream looking for a crossing place when we noticed a solitary lama approaching the opposite bank. The sight of a lone figure traveling cross-country in those regions where people usually traveled together and on established roads or trails was remarkable in itself. More remarkable was the way the man was walking. He seemed to glide or float a few inches above the ground.

Moving at a rapid pace, looking neither right nor left, he followed a course that would bring him to the stream some distance behind us, rather than opposite us where we might have had contact with him, which also seemed peculiar. We proceeded, however, glancing his way from time to time, and then without any of us noticing how it happened, he was on our side of the stream, proceeding on his course, looking straight ahead, paying us no attention whatever.

Supernatural? Maybe so. But experience was leading me to believe human beings capable of more things than I had dreamed possible as a younger man. Also I was becoming increasingly convinced that there is another world around us. Though we are able to penetrate this other consciousness only occasionally and sometimes by ways that seem strange, it is nevertheless there.

Not long after returning to Kalgan I received word from California that the Old Man had died, which may have been one reason I didn't see his face in the leaves of the Sacred Tree. Quite seriously, the news severed a final bond with my old life and left me free for my new one. He had left me no legacy but perhaps the best one of all: independence and self-reliance.

# 11.  Siberian Tigers and Other Game

Since Kalgan was the principal gateway from China into Mongolia and the border region and could be reached easily by train from Peking, a number of foreigners came to see its sights. They inspected the huge arched gateway in the Great Wall through which our caravans passed and the much smaller gate adjacent, no larger than a bedroom door, the Gate of Sighs, through which for centuries exiles were banished into the barbarian wilderness.

They mingled with the life of our long colorful main street: its blacksmith shops, wheelrights, leather workers, rope makers, hide and fur dealers, sing-song houses, a bank, ox carts and mule trains, feral dogs, stray pigs, and general tumult including occasionally a band of Mongol horsemen dashing by in picturesque costume. Sometimes these visitors went hunting antelope, gazelle, or wolf on the plains above the town, and they often stayed with us since there was no other accommodation readily available for foreigners except the compounds of two or three trading firms like ours or the homes of a few missionaries.

J. A. Thomas came, always bringing gifts and a quiet sense of his own importance and that of B.A.T. affairs; and there were Singer Sewing Machine and Standard Oil men and members of the British and American diplomatic corps, including the intelligence officer at our American Legation in Peking, R. S. Clark, aforementioned. I became acquainted with Clark and he relied on us for some of his information. There were also soldiers, archaeologists, explorers, missionaries. A few years earlier Herbert Hoover, then a young mining engineer, had come to survey the mineral resources of the Kalgan region and to investigate the possibility of constructing a railroad across Mongolia, a project eventually carried out by Chinese and Russian Communists.

Roy Chapman Andrews visited Kalgan en route to his "explorations" along the border and in Mongolia. Although he was pleasant enough, we always regarded Andrews as something of a Boy Scout who periodically left the comfort and security of the States to visit our frontier and had "adventures" which received a great deal of publicity, while we lived through the same sort of thing—and sometimes a good deal more—nearly every day as a matter of course.

However, such visitors enlivened our bungalow and kept us in touch with the outer world.

Left to ourselves on cold winter nights when the temperature fell to twenty below outside, we played checkers or poker, told stories, recited poems (my rendition of Kipling's *Oonts* or "The Commissariat Camel" becoming quite popular), or engaged in such indoor pastimes as boxing, wrestling, jumping from a standstill over the backs of upright chairs (try it some time), walking on your knees, extinguishing lighted cigarettes on your tongue, or biting pieces out of wine glasses.

Practical jokes were staple entertainment. Once when a newspaper correspondent was visiting us, Brodie invited him into his room on some pretext. While they were there the telegraph key on the table began to click. Brodie answered and took down a message of banditry and bloody murder ostensibly coming from somewhere in the Mongolian wilds. Actually it was coming from the next room where I was operating my key.

Thinking he had a scoop, the correspondent wired the sensational story to his Peking paper. (Peking, Tientsin, Shanghai and Hong Kong all had English-language papers.) Next morning when we told him the truth it was too late to cancel his yarn, which made good reading when it appeared and was no more inaccurate than most others, the level of news reporting in the Far East being quite low.

For outdoor entertainment we rode bucking horses or played polo in our compound. Our balls were willow roots. The Mongols who watched us thought us far too gentle with each other, though as result of one collision Brodie got pitched off on his head and turned black-and-blue down to his neck. The Mongols played their polo with a live sheep for a ball and nothing but mayhem for rules. As many players as wanted to could participate. Their mallets were their hands. They snatched the poor sheep this way and that, forward passed him as you might a football, tore him limb from limb—never mind the squirting blood and guts—and whoever carried what was left of him across the line scored a goal. It was their national sport, perhaps older than the Indian polo we played, and was usually played between rival tribes or camps.

It reminded me in some respects of the rooster races held on the ranch at fiesta times, when the rider who successfully snatched a live rooster out of the ground was immediately surrounded by others who tried to take the bird away from him— the more blood, feathers, and confusion the merrier—while the crowd cheered.

Horse racing was another popular pastime with us, as it had been with me in California. Competing against the Mongols of the plains, we developed some fast horses that won good money on the Peking and Tientsin tracks where all the racehorses were Mongol ponies and the betting identical with our U.S. parimutuel system. Our Thamar, a roan gelding, set a track record at Peking by covering a mile in two minutes flat carrying 160 pounds.

We raced our camels in the wide-open country of the Mongolian Plateau, sometimes over distances of forty and fifty miles, wrapping ourselves beforehand in the bandage cloth previously described. It made you so stiff you had to be helped to your saddle like a medieval knight in armor. But once you were there you were really in place!

All racing camels were virgin females around seven years old. A fast one would outrun a horse after the first ten miles. But her stride measured twenty-one feet forward and nine feet from side to side, and would jar you to death if you weren't wrapped for it. On more than one occasion I ran a sixty-mile race for cash stakes, thirty miles out, thirty miles back.

Such activities, interspersed with periodic sojourns in Tientsin and Peking, added variety to our lives as we mingled with viceroys, living gods, bandits, and beggars, sometimes traveling as far afield as Shanghai and Hong Kong on business or holidays.

\*     \*     \*

At the B.A.T. mess in Tientsin the gang was just sitting down to breakfast, Hunter Mann, later an executive of Reynolds Metals, presiding. We'd been at table a short while when Captain Pat Frissel, officer of the day, entered after depositing his side arms in the foyer, and began describing a riot of the night before which had nearly turned into a general uprising. All foreign troops in the Tientsin area had been alerted. But the Japanese had managed to control the situation without additional help. At this point I caught the eye of young William Ashley Anderson who was sitting opposite me and tipped him the wink.

The afternoon before from the fourth-floor windows of our mess on the Rue de France, Anderson and I had watched refugees streaming into the Foreign Quarter until they were stopped by our troops standing at barbed wire barricades. All north China was in a revolutionary uproar. Yuan Shih-kai, the old war dog and former Imperial Army Commander, was said to be bringing order out of chaos in Peking and to be in line for the presidency of the new Republic if Sun Yat-sen, who'd been named provisional president, resigned it, but we didn't see much order in Tientsin. Street executions were commonplace. Severed heads hung from lamp posts. Rifle fire crackled regularly.

The U.S. Fifteenth Infantry, later Eisenhower's regiment, had arrived from the Philippines to join contingents provided by England, Germany, France, Russia, Italy, and especially Japan. It seemed that indeed another Boxer Rebellion was about to occur and again Tientsin would be a base for foreign military operations.

Fires licked above the city's rooftops in the late afternoon light. Mutinous troops were reported gathering downtown at the *yamen* demanding their pay. The prefect would probably make the usual explanation: though he had no money, he believed the local merchants would be willing to subscribe the necessary funds. That would be the signal. The mob would begin breaking into shops. Law-abiding citizens would close their shutters and take to their prayers.

It seemed too good a show to miss. Several of us including Anderson, C. W. Weeks, and Billy Christian who would join us later at Kalgan, made our way past our military patrols and headed for narrow, winding Old Clothes Street in the heart of downtown Tientsin.

Even under ordinary circumstances Old Clothes Street was like something out of the *Arabian Nights.* Its open-fronted shops displayed the furs of the snow leopard and Tibetan panda, Russian sable and ermine, Siberian tiger, incredibly large bear skins from Siberia and Kamchatka, jade from Tibet and lovely flowering shrubs made of multicolored gems. There were silk shops with distinctively musky smells; apothecary's shops with precious medicinal herbs, ephedrine (*ma-huang*—excellent for asthma and bronchial disorders) and ginseng and aphrodisiacs made of unborn wapiti from Manchuria or rhino's horns from Southeast Asia; multicolored ceramics, delicately painted scrolls, embroidered screens, rare books. Crowds of people went about their business unconcernedly while disorder and violence threatened from some indeterminate source we tried in vain to discover.

As usual there was a bedlam of noises, the people shouting even in ordinary conversations as the Chinese do, parakeets squawking, pigeons cooing, long-eared black pigs running freely here and there, grunting and squealing and, with pariah dogs, acting as scavengers.

After wandering aimlessly and finding nothing very exciting, our party gradually broke up and I headed for a certain sing-song house on a quiet side street.

There, since I was on holiday, it seemed appropriate I be given exclusive use of the premises. Other patrons, notably a pair of Japanese Army officers, refused to see things my way. As consequence I felt compelled to begin ejecting them bodily. This was accompanied by no particular animosity on my part; it just seemed like the thing to do. The girls helped me. They had no love for these Japanese who treated them arrogantly as if they were concubines instead of inmates of a number-one house. Mama, who owned and managed them and the house, had no special love for the Japs either because they didn't pay their bills regularly, preferring to sign chits and forget about payment (though Mama, tottering here and there on her tiny bound feet, took care to stay out of sight during the ruckus I had aroused, so that she might be absolved of all responsibility for it later—she was indeed wise in the ways of this world). Her bound feet, incidentally, were not only status symbols but sex symbols. They were absolutely deformed and not more than four inches long. It was believed that they made a woman highly desirable—even though, as was the case here, she had to be helped or carried by one of her servants in order to walk more than a few steps.

During the heat of the battle I saw several girls using their personal needles. If you've never seen a sing-song girl wield her needle in close combat, you haven't seen all that a woman can do. Hers was not quite as long and rusty and crooked as an old-time sacking needle, nor as long and rusty and crooked as the needles I sometimes used to sew a piece of hide to the foot of a lame camel to serve the animal as a shoe. But it would do. Clenched between first and second fingers, it stuck out of her fist like a hawk's claw.

The Japs who emerged into the street unscathed were lucky. I caught a glimpse of the lowly doorman booting one in the behind as the spirit of fun spread.

Japanese plans for the subjugation of China were well advanced. They treated the Chinese like vassals and were cordially hated in return.

I'd enjoyed the proceedings greatly so far though I guessed what their consequences might be. Each night military contingents from the foreign legations patrolled the city to help the police maintain order and tonight was the Japs' turn. But at the moment Mama was serving me French champagne which sold in Tientsin for eleven dollars a case. Our party was going nicely when it was interrupted by a hubub at the front door. A Japanese patrol was demanding admission.

Two minutes later the girls were helping me out a second-story window onto the roof of the adjoining building. After tender farewells I crept to the edge of the roof overlooking the street. Concealed by darkness, I peered over onto numerous helmets of numerous Japanese soldiers. The sight of those helmets gave me an idea. A twenty-pound roof tile landing on them might make them fit more snugly.

In the confusion no one could tell exactly where the tiles were coming from. A noisy crowd had gathered and the Japs began accusing the Chinese of tile throwing. So I tossed another and another.

By now I could hear soldiers ransacking the house behind

me and knew that Mama's delaying tactics had been exhausted. So I departed across the rooftops tossing a tile now and then to keep things boiling in the street below, and by the time the soldiers emerged onto the roofs after me, I was well into the next block. It was no trick to jump the narrow streets—they were only eight or nine feet wide—and the alleys were narrower.

My pursuers, however, handicapped by their short legs and military equipment, showed little taste for midnight broad-jumping at high level, and those who tried to follow on the ground were blocked by the crowd, while bedlam rose on every side. Pretty soon the Japanese forgot about me and got busy quelling the riot. When it had swept off across the city like a receding thunderstorm, I slipped quietly back over the rooftops to the sing-song house.

This time our party suffered no interruption. When sunrise came I began to think about how to get home. The authorities would be looking for me.

I discussed my problem with Mama. "Why don't you use my rickshaw?" she suggested. "It has curtains. I often travel with them drawn. You will not be stopped. The police know my rickshaw!" she said proudly. No doubt they did. And no doubt she paid them as much annually as any of Tientsin's leading merchants. A few minutes later I was on my way out of her compound in her rickshaw, sitting well back in one corner, curtains drawn, her shawl over my head, two boys pulling me.

At the main intersections native police, reinforced by American and Japanese soldiers, were keeping a sharp lookout. But they weren't looking for me in Mama's rickshaw.

When I reached the Queen's Hotel on Victoria Road, I removed my shawl and got out, paid the boys well, and went into the bar for an eye-opener, and then along to breakfast at our mess in the French Concession, passing the Rue de Chemin de Fer where the Western European and American prostitutes lived in style in their own homes with liveried servants, private carriages, and Paris clothes. I liked my style better.

Such escapades were the spice of our life and an expression of the times. They were also one reason why my account at the Hong Kong-Shanghai Bank in Peking was smaller than it should have been.

\* \* \*

While formal hostilities between Mongols and Chinese along our border subsided, thanks largely to Frans Larson who actively promoted peace in Urga and Peking and brought opposing commanders to a conference in the field, freebooting and banditry continued unabated.

Once Mamen and I rode 200 miles into the Gobi to meet the Suchow caravan and escort it safely across the border.

Another time at Pao-tou-chen near the Yellow River, my men and I became targets of opportunity for several hundred mutinous and trigger-happy Chinese soldiers. Luck got us through safely.

In self-defense, I organized what became known as the Black Horse Troop. It consisted of twenty of our best men—Mongol means "brave man"—all of them mounted on distinctive black ponies, I on a white one. Together we patrolled the border north and south of Kalgan, escorting caravans and keeping order generally.

Sometimes, in these and related activities, I used the Dodge touring car Thomas had bought me, he thinking it would enable me to make better time than with ponies or camels, and maybe make a fast getaway from bandits, but it was usually out of order or out of gas, and when I wrecked it during a wolf hunt I gave it up, preferring ponies and camels anyway.

Wolf hunting was a continuous occupation of the Mongols on the plains in which we joined, wolves being a constant menace to their flocks and herds. They seldom wasted bullets on a wolf, preferring to ride it down and kill it with a blow on the head from a steel stirrup or wooden club. They had more fun that way. Sometimes they "hawked" wolves using black eagles as falcons. The eagles would fly at the heads of the running wolves, bewildering them with flapping wings and striking talons until the riders caught up. The Mongols also hunted antelope (there were no pronghorned antelope in Mongolia, all were single-horned) and gazelle in organized fashion, driving them into nets, and selling them to Chinese merchants. Railroad cars stacked high with their frozen carcasses were a common sight at Kalgan in late fall and winter. Frozen pheasants, too, went by the hundreds of thousands to Peking and other markets.

Some of the game along the border was rare and unique and much sought after by collectors as well as market hunters. Up in Manchuria, for example, were the blackcock, or black grouse, the gorgeous blue-black males weighing up to twelve pounds, the drab gray females six, and neither found anywhere else in the world, so far as I learned, except northern Scotland. Also in Manchuria were the increasingly rare and valuable musk deer, small and hornless. The males had needle-like fangs—eyeteeth prolonged—with which they struck when fighting. A gland under their bellies near their genitals contained the dark viscous musk which formed the basis for many perfumes. Its scent was supposed to be more penetrating than that of any other known substance.

These were the great days of specimen collecting by museums and zoos and one of our leading collectors was a slim, soft-spoken Englishman born in China of missionary parents. Arthur Sowerby had been educated in England and made his way back to China via Canada where he'd worked as a cowboy, which gave us something of a common background. During his expedition with Clark through Shensi and Kansu, he'd seen the large burial mounds near Sian including a very large one said to be the tomb of the Yellow Emperor but none exactly resembling the pyramids I'd seen. Later he became prominent as founder and editor of the *China Journal of Science and Arts* and wrote several books.

Now, using Kalgan as his base, Sowerby was field-collecting for the British and Smithsonian Museums.

Together we went down into the mountains toward Kuei-hua-cheng for argali, the largest of all the wild sheep, and got one head with horns that measured twenty inches around at the butt and forty-eight on the curve. (When rams like that fought during the mating season you could hear the sound of their collisions for several miles on a still day and their necks were nearly devoid of hair as result of such impacts.) We went up into the Imperial Forest below Lama Miao for the high-flying Reeves pheasant which has a tail four to six feet long but is only half the size of the common ringneck, and we made several trips out along the Chinese Eastern and Trans-Siberian railways after bear, boar, and tiger, and into central and western China for the gray goral and golden takin. But the rarest specimen we hunted was the milu or Père David's deer. The legendary, semi-sacred milu or "*ssu-pu-hsiang*" (four-in-one), had the horns of a deer, the beard of a goat, the feet of an ox, and the tail of an ass. Milus were depicted in cave drawings and ancient tapestries and in popular story telling. Until 1900 several were alive in the Imperial Zoological Gardens in Peking, where they had been propagated for many years. During the looting and burning which accompanied the Boxer uprising they disappeared. After peace was restored a search was made so that the species might not be lost, but none had been found.

Sowerby and I were continuing that search. A milu dead or alive would be a collector's triumph and extremely valuable.

Beginning with the marshy areas of north China which they were supposed to have inhabited, we traveled hundreds of miles tracking down reports, talking to people in various parts of the country who claimed to have seen milus (always many years ago) but we never found one and neither did anyone else and the species passed into extinction.

Another creature, stranger even than the milu, was constantly in our minds when we went to the Far West. He was the humanoid "hairy wild man" or "wild bandit" (*jen-huza*, the Mongols called him) of Mongolia and northern Tibet, perhaps a northern cousin of the *yeti* we have heard so much about in recent years. He was said to be covered with hair or dressed in animal skins worn with hair side out. Supposedly he lived in caves far above snowline or in the loneliest parts of the deserts. He subsisted on berries, grass seeds, marmots, rabbits, the markhor (or elusive wild goat with the high, spiraled horns), wild sheep, wild camel (bands of wild camel still roamed the northern Tibetan highlands), wild ass, or yak. From time to time villagers found a domesticated yak with head smashed in and body ripped to pieces, evidence of the *jen-huzas'* ferocity and strength, and sometimes lonely herdsmen disappeared or their bloody remains were found.

Reports differed as to whether the wild bandits possessed weapons. Some claimed they used bone-tipped spears and arrows and bows of bone. Others insisted they were simply large apes that might have been seen with a stick or rock in hand. Opinions differed, too, as to whether they possessed fire but all agreed they could be lethal when provoked and should be strictly avoided.

While retaining my ties with B.A.T., I became increasingly an independent trader, buying and selling for other firms— skins and furs mostly, mostly for Wilson & Company of Tientsin, some of whose principals I'd met years earlier in London. I also guided representatives of U.S. firms on prospecting trips, men like G. T. Bridgman, field representative for the Guggenheim brothers (Daniel, Isaac, Murray, Simon, Solomon, founders and owners of the American Smelting and Refining Company which had acquired the Big Bonanza before I left it) and Harry Putnam, representing U.S. Steel, which had its eye on China's resources as did many big American corporations. These field trips took me from the Siberian to the Indochina borders and to the interior province of Hunan, where the ever-industrious ever-ingenious Chinese piped natural gas into their homes for heat and light entirely by bamboo pipes. The giant bamboo threaded easily and may be said to have been the forerunner of our non-metallic pipes of today. With similar ingenuity they produced high quality antimony. They heated crude ore in open clay pots to drive off the volatile components containing the antimony which was condensed on wires strung above the pots in large sheds and easily collected. Every first-rate miner, incidentally, made his own powder, just as every professional hunter did. Tom didn't use Harry's and Dick didn't use Jim's. They were very particular about it. The secret of making it was handed down from father to son. And the other fellow's was always considered inferior. It was coarse black powder but they used it with extraordinary skill.

In Manchuria again, I was looking over iron ore prospects north and east of Mukden in dense hardwood-forest country when I ran across fresh tracks of a wild pig herd. The pigs were after hazelnuts and ginseng root, the ginseng with its low broad leaves still being found in natural state despite its great value and consequent intensive harvesting for drug use. A so-called "perfect" root in the shape of "the little man"—that is, forked with arms and legs—could bring you $400 an ounce at Canton, the drug center of the Orient. The three-to-four-inch-long roots were also cultivated secretly, harvested late in the fall, macerated for several days in fresh water, then dried until hard and translucent. Ground up and added to tea, they were highly prized as a general tonic and aphrodisiac.

Following the pigs, I was careful to stay down wind. Once they wind you, silence falls and they disappear, and all that you hear is the blue whiskey jacks jeering from a nearby limb. If you hear a pig squeal, better choose your tree, because here, likely, comes the whole herd and they will mean business.

Manchurian pig herds produced the finest commercial bristles for brushes and also some very large boars weighing up to 500 pounds. When I noticed a track that could have been made by a yearling calf, my expectations began to rise. I could hear the pigs talking to each other a few yards ahead of me and smelled the pungent odor of freshly uprooted earth. Engrossed in my hunt, I reached a clearing overgrown with hazelnut bushes, exactly the kind of place where a boar might linger at the rear of a herd. I edged out into it, rifle ready—but not ready for what happened.

There was a flash of orange from what seemed almost under my feet as an enormous tiger jumped up and trotted off with stiff-legged strides. I was too astonished to react until he'd almost reached the trees. My snap shot had no visible effect and I felt sure I'd missed him completely.

The Siberian or Manchurian tiger is the largest of the big cats. He outweighs the African lion and is nearly twice the weight of his Chinese and Indian and Borneo cousins. He is more vividly marked than any of his relatives and his hair is much longer. He was little known to the western world until the construction of the Trans-Siberian Railroad through his territory in the 1880s and '90s, when his depredations became so severe that Russian troops were assigned to protect Chinese construction workers. It's one of the few cases when a nation's troops were deployed against wild animals. The tigers just seemed to resent human encroachment into their habitat. Or maybe because of their large population they welcomed the arrival of a new food supply. But I seriously think that animals are much more sensi-

tive to invasions of their territory than we realize. At Tsavo in
British East Africa lions staged regular attacks on railway workers on the Mombasa-Nairobi line and actually brought construction to a halt. And in our part of California in early days,
mountain lions became so depredacious that when Indian
women went down to the creeks to wash clothes, men with rifles
accompanied them. The atmosphere of the times may have had
something to do with it. Our back country was still wild. It still
belonged primarily to wild creatures. Man was an intruder. And
the animals knew it. The same may have been true at Tsavo and
along the Trans-Siberian Railway in the 1890s.

By the early 1900s the Siberian was one of the most sought
after big game trophies, and Sowerby and I had looked in vain
for one out along the Trans-Siberian as far as Lake Baikal, the
western limit of his range. Now one could have had me for
breakfast. There was no guarantee, of course, that he was a
maneater, but in that country you never knew.

My chance to get even came, or was thrust upon me, a few
months later. With Bridgman I was fifty miles north of the Amur
River in Russian territory looking for gold prospects. Entering
Siberia was no problem then. You simply went to the nearest
Russian ministry or consulate, had your passport stamped, got a
letter of introduction and went in.

The country north of the Amur was rolling grassland interspersed with patches of forest and an occasional rimrock, like
parts of Arizona. We'd pitched camp late one afternoon by a
spring near the base of a rocky bluff. While the boys turned the
stock out to graze and got things ready for supper and Bridgman
relaxed on his bedroll, I picked up my geologist's hammer and
strolled over to see what minerals the nearby bluff contained. I
didn't think of taking a gun. I was going only about 150 yards
from camp.

I'd knocked off a piece of rock and was sitting on a small
boulder at the base of the bluff examining it through my magnifying glass when I heard a pebble fall from above. Turning my
head carefully, I looked up. There in full sunlight on a ledge
twenty-five feet above me were the head and shoulders of an
enormous tiger. The light set off his vivid markings and his
extraordinarily long hair so that he seemed absolutely monstr-

ous. I was terrified half out of my wits until I realized he wasn't looking at me but at the camp. The activities there—pans rattling, boys calling to one another—were engaging his attention. A slight change in the wind, however, even a chance glance down, might make him aware of me, although I was fortunately in the shadow which had begun to accumulate at the base of the bluff. I didn't dare breathe deeply or even look directly at him again for fear of giving myself away, and remained absolutely motionless, rock in one hand, magnifying glass in the other, watching him out of the corner of my eyes while waiting further developments.

They weren't encouraging. The head and shoulders of a second tiger, slightly smaller, had appeared beside the first. It was probably his mate. Her attention also had been attracted by the activities of the camp. I wondered if they were reconnoitering for an attack on it as the tigers along the railroad had attacked construction camps in earlier days. Heightening my wonderment, a third tiger appeared. He was considerably smaller than the first two, probably last year's cub. Two more followed, much smaller, this year's kittens. Then I had five Siberian tigers hanging over me, and I was caught quite literally between a rock and a hard place.

Should I stay still and hope they didn't come any closer? Should I jump up and shout in hopes of frightening them off? Should I run for camp?

Without warning the big fellow vanished. The others followed suit in order of their appearance. I broke all records for the 150-yard dash. Long before reaching camp I was shouting at the *mafoos* to bring the horses because we were going to chase tigers.

We galloped after them for two or three miles across the rolling grassland but caught a clear view only once, all five loping along in the last light of the sun, before they entered some trees and disappeared.

Tigers behave in strange ways. Most cats hate water but tigers don't mind it. I've known them to swim the Amur when it was choked with blocks of floating ice. Near Hong Kong they swam regularly between the mainland and offshore islands;

from time to time fishermen killed them a mile or more at sea. They will live in close proximity to humans and never harm them. One had kittens in the Shwe Dagon Pagoda in Rangoon when a friend of mine was there. Yet they took our U.S. soldiers from guarded camps during the Korean War. So they carry on an unpredictable relationship with Homo sapiens.

In 1916 I was in Manchuria on business again and was thinking of the tigers that had bested me every time I'd encountered them so far. Accordingly I talked to Charles K. Moser, our U.S. consul at Harbin. Moser, always helpful in business matters and a sportsman besides, suggested I talk to the district manager of the Chinese Eastern Railway, a Russian who was also a tiger hunter. He in turn informed me that the tigers were moving south because of a cholera epidemic which had decimated the pig herds, their chief food supply, and recommended that I try the Korean border area. He furnished me a letter of introduction and a courtesy pass and I rode the Russian train with my two boys through beautiful hardwood forests of oak and walnut down toward the Korean line. They were burning that hardwood in their locomotives though there was plenty of coal in the country.

At a point where a narrow gauge joined the main line we got off and took the narrow gauge back into the forest to a camp where coolies were cutting and cording walnut and oak under direction of a burly young Russian superintendent. Before our first bottle of vodka was empty he was telling me about the opium outlaws who lived deep in the woods and played hide-and-seek with the tigers. He would send out inquiries; within a few days one of them would bring us word. And meanwhile here was some more vodka.

A day or two later a ragged emaciated Chinese appeared in camp. He wore a frayed bit of blue cloth, his head and feet were bare and his hair was pieced out with string to comply with the old law requiring every man to wear a pigtail. News of the revolution and the law's repeal hadn't apparently penetrated to these parts; or if it had, like many others he preferred to keep his pigtail, having worn it all his adult life. Our conversation went like this.

"Master, a tiger was in my poppy patch last night!"
"Where is he now?"

"Not far. He killed a rascally pig that was uprooting my poppies and dragged it into the underbrush. I think he's still there!"

"How far from here?"

"Six *li*."

"Do you know this tiger?"

"Oh, yes! At night when he prowls outside I sit in my house and pull strings to rattle the noisemakers in my poppy patch, and I light firecrackers to frighten him, but he does not go away. He's a *day-yan* [a bad one]. He eats the Long Pig [man]!"

"Have you friends who can help us?" Beaters might be needed.

"They are eagerly waiting!"

He led me and my boys through thick woods to a clearing where his log-sod hovel stood and his opium poppies were blooming. Though the production and use of opium were banned throughout China it was in such demand that its illegal cultivation was widespread, and since Manchurian or black opium brought the highest price, our friend could make a nice living if he didn't consume too much of his product himself, which, judging from his gaunt yellow look, he was in danger of doing; or if the *yamen* runners didn't catch him. The runners might reduce his ankle bones to pulp by repeated tappings with their sticks, so that he could never walk again except to hobble. Or they might put him in the stocks, standing on a pile of boards, and remove one board each day until he almost but not quite hung by his wrists and neck and almost, but not quite, choked or died of thirst or starvation. The Chinese principle of justice was simple. It was always to make the punishment a little worse than the crime. For serious infractions The Punishment of the Thousand Cuts was still in use. Your body was encased in a metal jacket resembling a jacket of mail. The jacket was tightened by a key until your flesh protruded through the meshed links. The flesh was sliced off flush with the metal by a razor or sharp knife. Then you were released. No doctor could treat you or friend help you without risking death, because you bore the official taboo of The Punishment. You soon died, your body a mass of suppurating sores.

His opium poppies were a beautiful sight against the background of green woods. They were predominantly red, blue, and white, waist high. Every day during the harvest season in late June, a few weeks hence, he would make a spiral incision in each poppy pod which allowed a drop of milky fluid to collect at its bottom, and every day he would go around with a bottle and collect that drop of opium. He would sell it to blackmarket dealers who would see that it reached the ten to fifteen million Chinese addicted to the drug. The authorities had been trying for years to control the use of opium. Just when they were on the point of succeeding, the British, in one of the most unconscionable acts the British ever committed, in my opinion, forced them to accept a huge quantity of Indian opium. It was the kind of thing that started the infamous Opium War of the mid-nineteenth century which resulted in China's ceding Hong Kong to the British and in the whole sorry system of foreign encroachment on Chinese sovereignty—and in the addiction of millions of people.

The swath the tiger had made through the poppies while dragging the pig away was plain. We followed it until it entered the trees. There two more opium outlaws were waiting. They resembled our guide in appearance and were armed with stick rattles and tin cans containing rocks for noise-making. They assured me in hushed tones that the tiger was nearby but that with their expert assistance we should have no trouble killing him. His carcass would be a rich reward for them. They could sell it to the apothecaries who would convert it—flesh, blood, bone—into valuable medicine. The Chinese believed in sympathetic therapy. A potion containing powdered tiger bone or dried tiger blood was supposed to give you the courage of a tiger, just as one containing crushed wapiti horns was supposed to make you more virile.

By now it was nearly noon and hot. There was no wind to speak of, only treacherously veering air currents that came from no particular direction. The light, too, was deceptive. When the leaves stirred, they cast a shifting pattern on the undergrowth. It was the kind of light in which a tiger's coat makes ideal camouflage.

The flies were thick but I was glad of that. Flies can be helpful when you are stalking a tiger by daylight.

After a few yards his trail disappeared into a large patch of brush containing a few scattered trees. Taking my .450 double-barreled express, I started around it, leaving the others where they were, and after making a circle of half a mile or more and finding no outgoing sign, I decided he must be in that brush patch. When a tiger has eaten he usually sleeps. With luck I might surprise him.

I'd hunted tigers successfully in south China and in the central and southwestern provinces, and once during a visit to Indochina and knew something of their habits, but I'd had such poor luck with the big northern variety that I was a little nervous.

I moved quietly to a spot which gave me the advantage of what wind there was, posted Way-bar, my gun-bearer, and my faithful Lu at fifteen-to-twenty-yard intervals to my right and the three outlaws at similar intervals to my left, with instructions to try and turn him back my way if he came out, and then started in after him. My youthful training under Yaqui Tom stood me in good stead on occasions like this, and I was wearing lightweight canvas sneakers that were the nearest things available to the moccasins I'd worn as a boy.

I went carefully a step at a time, parting the grass and twigs with the toe of my shoe before bringing my weight down, keeping eyes peeled. Strange as it may seem I wasn't looking for a tiger but for a swarm of flies. They would mark the place where he lay with his kill. If they hovered steadily it would mean he was asleep. If they rose and fell from time to time it would mean he was awake and swatting at them occasionally with his paw.

Suddenly I came under attack from an unexpected quarter. Small black flies resembling our American deer flies had been bothering me for some time. Now with what seemed unerring instinct they focused their attacks on my unprotected hands, face, neck, and the backs of my knees where my trousers tucked into my puttees, as if knowing perfectly well that under the circumstances I couldn't risk taking a slap at them. They fed to their hearts' content while I helplessly suffered.

I'd gone perhaps a hundred yards and had used up maybe an hour doing so, when I saw something that made me forget my painful predicament.

Thirty yards to my right was the fly swarm I'd been looking for. It was in the shadow of a tree and I'd nearly missed it and put myself upwind from a tiger. I watched it intently for perhaps half an hour. It hovered steadily. That meant he was asleep. I watched for another twenty minutes to be sure.

So far so good. But the treacherous wind was unfavorable. Should I backtrack and come around with it more in my face, or should I risk tackling him from where I stood? *My* flies decided me—they were literally eating me up. I couldn't stand the thought of another hour's exposure to their torture.

So I moved toward him a step at a time, keeping my eyes on *his* flies. After ten steps, they still hovered undisturbed. Ten more steps would put me practically in bed with him—if in fact he was still there. The thought ran through my mind that perhaps they were hovering over nothing but a dead pig. Perhaps he'd slipped away. Perhaps he was stalking me. I had to resist a temptation to look behind me. It was a good thing I did.

A tiger's head and shoulders had shot up in profile amid the fly swarm. Again I was looking at close range at those very orange, very black, very white markings.

I didn't contemplate them for long. His nose was up. He'd had news of me but couldn't tell just where it was coming from.

I could see the point of his shoulder as he crouched sidewise to me. As my bullet hit he went straight into the air clawing and squalling, came down and began doing backward somersaults. I had to step aside to give him room. But from the way he'd been sitting, I knew my bullet would have penetrated his heart and lungs and that he would for all practical purposes be dead before he left the ground.

He measured an inch over eleven feet from tip of nose to tip of tail. We judged his weight at 550 pounds. His skin became one of the most admired decorations of our Kalgan bungalow.

# 12.  The Death of Malunga

Violence or the threat of it underlay our border life, as I believe it underlies human experience everywhere. How we meet it may be the central challenge of our existence. We can ignore it, run from it, face it, but the questions it presents are inescapable and, in the end, personal. What does a man do, for example, when one of his friends murders another?

I first met George Grant when he was introduced to me at the Peking Club by John Fenton of the China Mutual Life Insurance Company.

I first met Malunga during a stand-off outside a border village gate.

The two were as different as my friendship for them. Grant, a British subject, civilized, urbane, was Assistant Superintendent of Communications for the Chinese Government. Malunga was a renegade Mongol priest and bandit who preyed on border caravans.

Grant leased a residence from an old Chinese family in the fashionable quarter between the south and east gates of Peking. There I heard him describe the construction of the newly completed telegraph line linking China to Mongolia which traversed the 900 miles of grassland and desert between Kalgan and Urga. Besides being something of an engineering feat, it had met with a good deal of popular resistance. The grass that fed their flocks and herds was sacred to the Mongols. They considered it sacrilegious to break the surface of the soil even to set the poles for a telegraph line.

Resentment against things emanating from China, as the line did, was strong too.

Chinese settlers pushing outward from the Outer Wall at

[177]

the rate of eight or ten miles a year were steadily bringing Mongolia under the plow. Their mud-walled villages might be devastated by Mongol raids but rose again as tenaciously as life itself. Finally the Mongols would give in to the extent that they merely levied tribute on the villagers or robbed them at regular intervals instead of trying to annihilate them or drive them back behind the Wall. Chinese encroachment went forward inexorably.

Grant had of course secured approval for his project from the authorities at Urga, but though the lama hierarchs were officially against the violence that threatened the line, in practice they did little to control it. Time and again, down came wires and poles. Rank-and-file Mongols enjoyed tying a rope to a pole and watching the line topple over. It wasn't hard to do. The tops of the poles were only nine or ten feet above ground and you could reach them by standing in your saddle.

For fun we used to tap the wires and send humorous messages to Kalgan or Urga and we sent some serious ones too.

Reports of increased vandalism against the line had reached me before I left on a business trip to the west. I was out near the Yellow River when I heard the grim news.

Grant had sent word to Malunga, a leader in the vandalism, that he could have all the poles and wire he wanted if he would let the line alone. Malunga had no great need for poles or wire. No Mongol did. They built no fences. Such walled compounds as they occasionally used at established camps along the Chinese border, or at Urga—never on the open plains or desert—were built for them by Chinese workers because Mongols disdained to engage in such menial labor. They were horsemen, not workmen. And they just didn't like the telegraph line. Grant finally decided to go and talk to Malunga.

The bandit camp was located within sight of the caravan trail in the region of the Seven Lakes where salt was mined for shipment to Kalgan in oxcarts.

Grant rode out along the trail with a party of maintenance men until he came opposite Malunga's camp. Leaving the rest of the party, he took a personal boy and rode toward the tents while the others watched. Malunga emerged from his yurta accompanied by several of his leaders. Grant dismounted. He and Malunga talked for a while and apparently reached an understanding. Grant turned and walked toward his horse which his boy was holding. Malunga pulled a pistol and fired. Grant fell forward. Then they killed the boy too. The repairmen waiting on the trail hurried to Kalgan and spread the alarm.

This was the news that reached me. Besides horrifying and amazing me it raised certain questions about my own future.

I'd first met Malunga in front of one of those devastated and rebuilt Chinese villages outside the Outer Wall. Jim Brodie and I were approaching it horseback at the head of a train of two-wheeled carts loaded with merchandise to be sold or traded, when a band of about twenty armed men rode over a nearby hill and headed toward us.

Removing our rifles from their scabbards and placing them across our saddlebows with muzzles pointing in the general direction of the approaching strangers, Brodie and I turned to face them, while our carts trundled on toward the village gate.

Descending the hill, the strangers disappeared into a water-cut three hundred yards from us and did not reappear. This put us in the position of having to retreat, deploy and get ready to fight, or stand our ground. We chose to stand, and after a few minutes a mounted man appeared on our side of the cut and rode slowly toward us.

He was powerfully built, his manner calm and confident. He carried a rifle slung across his back and a pistol in a belt holster. When he'd approached to within a respectful distance, he drew rein and inquired politely if we were trading at this village.

"Yes, we are trading here. And you and your friends—what is your destination?"

He grinned audaciously. "We trade at this village too!"

"No," I said firmly, though I admired his nerve and even sympathized with his desire to make the Chinese pay for their encroachment on Mongol soil, "you are not going to trade at this village. You are going to trade at that one, down the road there," indicating the direction from which we had come. "Your friends watching from the watercut will see your signal. They will meet you down the road. Not here. This is our village."

His smile grew broader while he said nothing for a moment or two. "Very well. Perhaps we shall meet again under different circumstances." He bade us goodbye and rode off down the road in leisurely fashion. His friends met him. That was Malunga.

We didn't meet again for nearly a year. Then, outward bound with a caravan for Urga, I stopped one afternoon near the Seven Lakes. From time to time we'd seen armed men on the promontories and knew bandits were watching us but there had been no attack. Our caravans were manned mostly by Outer Mongols, as tough fighting men as there are. Our rule-of-thumb was: one Inner Mongol equals ten Chinese; one Outer Mongol equals five Inner. As further deterrent we were flying the British flag as usual. Malunga, if it was his band, should know better than to attack his northern cousins in addition to the Union Jack.

Toward sundown his messenger rode into camp. After customary salutations the man handed me a calling card, a strip of red paper bearing three black characters arranged vertically, spelling "Ma-lun-ga." Then he invited me to dine that evening with his master.

I took a boy as Grant was to do later and rode to the camp in the hollow. As I approached through the gathering dusk, Malunga's people assembled to stare at me. He emerged from his tent in company with several of his headmen and greeted me cordially with a "God be with you!" which I returned. Following him inside, I left my whip at the door as custom also dictated. Had I carried rifle or pistol I would have left them too, and if I hadn't returned for a month I would probably have found them exactly as I'd left them, such was the sanctity of Mongol hospitality.

He led the way around the left-hand side of the circular tent, the male side, toward a low wooden bench where, after much discussion as to who should sit first, we both sat at the same time.

Malunga's wife had put on her elaborate jeweled headdress for the occasion. It was fan-shaped, about twenty inches high, of gold and silver filigree inlaid with precious stones, a crown that made those of most European princesses look paltry. Dignified by it, she served us hot rice wine from a flask kept warm in a brazier of burning camel's dung. And when we had drunk and she had drunk and the headmen and relatives who had crowded into the tent behind us had drunk, we played cards—fan-tan, and the poker the Mongols had learned from us foreign devils (played with the narrow Chinese deck whose face cards had Chinese faces)—and we ate boiled mutton by the light of the argol stoves, and played again and I took care to lose.

He said slyly at last: "You were as good as dead that day we met in front of the village gate!"

"So were you!" I rejoined. We had a good laugh. We understood each other.

On a later occasion he came to my camp, drank my whiskey and smoked my cigarettes, we played cards and I won back most of what I'd lost before. He never troubled my caravans.

Now, however, if he could kill Grant he could kill me. He must be punished for what he had done and for its implications. To survive in hostile surroundings among a population vastly outnumbering us, we foreigners on the border had to maintain the illusion of our invincibility or be swept away.

On returning to Kalgan I made inquiries. Malunga had vanished. Chinese soldiers were said to be scouring the countryside for him. His persecutions of the Chinese had given him prestige among Mongols while to the Chinese he was Public Enemy Number One. He was death and destruction to their caravans. His spies informed him, he struck, and there was little left for the wolves and wild dogs. I guessed that the soldiers scouring the countryside weren't scouring too hard, having small taste for the medicine Malunga's band administered. They numbered about forty fighting men. Though not so numerous as some bandit bands, they were an elite group. A lama led them. Once a lama always a lama, the Mongols believed. And perhaps the gods looked favorably upon one who had served their altars and still had the power to do so.

What changed Malunga from priest to renegade I never learned. Even now I could sympathize with his attitude toward the telegraph line. Had it not been for Grant's murder, I would have sympathized more. When I first came to Mongolia you could ride 3,000 miles from Manchuria to Turkestan, as far as across the United States, and never see a piece of plowed ground. Grassland, mountains, deserts lay undisturbed as in the beginning. Grant changed this. He was the forerunner of many such changes. Some premonition may have moved Malunga to raise his hand against Grant. Or perhaps it was pure deviltry. Perhaps elements of racial and religious animosity entered the picture.

I talked to the Chinese police. No word of Malunga from north, south, east, or west. My Mongols, who had their own sources of information, confirmed this. I decided that if he were nowhere else he might be right under our noses in the hundred-mile stretch of mountains lying along the border between Kalgan and Kuei-hua-cheng. But first it was necessary to find Grant's body to provide the evidence of death that would enable his mother back in Scotland to cash his policy with the China Mutual.

Taking one of my best Mongols, Jaw-tor, I rode out the caravan trail toward the Seven Lakes. On the hill beyond Malunga's abandoned campsite was a burial ground. The Mongols did not break soil even for burial. They exposed their dead. Wolves, eagles, vultures, and feral dogs disposed of the remains in short order. Jaw-tor was too superstitious to climb the hill to the cemetery so I went up alone. Its top was strewn with bones, the campsite below having been used since time immemorial. Most of the bones were old. Among the fresh ones I found a skull with gold fillings in its teeth and a bullet hole at its back. No dentist had ever practiced in Mongolia to my knowledge, and when I came across a piece of whipcord trouser bearing the mark of a Peking tailor, I felt I'd found what I was after.

Back in Kalgan we wired the British Ministry that the remains would reach Peking by rail next day, arranged the bones as best we could in a cigarette case, bored holes and fitted rope handles at its ends, covered the box with crepe and made a double bow of black chiffon. In company with Larson and other friends, we put the box on the train and said goodbye to Grant.

Then I turned my attention to Malunga. I took Jaw-tor who would go with me anywhere except into a graveyard. Wearing native sheepskins, he could if need be mingle with the local population, gather information, summon help. Like most Mongols he had exceptional eyesight and could see as well or better than I. He carried a .303 British Winchester, as I did, and his .38 Colt Army. In addition I carried my two .45s from California days, bone-handled, their triggers honed to a quarter-pound pull, and a pair of eight-powered Zeiss field glasses and a sixty-power telescope.

We made up saddle packs of dried antelope, biscuits, bully beef, and some American canned tomatoes. Then we selected two tough ponies and started up the pass into the barren mountains where I guessed Malunga might be hiding. For three weeks we wandered, searching out the land, traveling mostly by night, lying up and watching by day.

We looked for signs of men or stock and smelled for camp smoke that would hang long in those still valleys. A camp of two hundred persons is hard to hide. Counting women, children, and old men, Malunga had what amounted to a village, complete with flocks of sheep and herds of cattle and horses, possibly camels, certainly dogs. What we were searching for would look like a regular Mongol encampment. Or they might see us first and that might end the hunt. There was no question of my coming to pay a social call. Of course they could hold me for ransom, a recognized business practiced by a number of professional bandits.

One morning while scanning a distant peak through my field glasses I saw a black dot among some boulders. It was a man.

With the aid of my telescope I distinguished two more. They were a long way off—five or six miles—and on a ridge higher than ours, but I could see their rifles and bandoliers.

Jaw-tor and I lay still all day and watched. We discovered another lookout post on the same ridge three or four miles beyond the first. At sundown the guards changed. That meant their camp was close by, probably just over the ridge.

I selected a low spot on the ridge midway between the two lookouts, a spot I thought would be hidden from both and yet give us command of the country beyond, and now our really cautious moving began.

Riding was out of the question. Leading a horse enables you to feel your way in the dark and avoid the rocks and falls. A snort or a sneeze could be a major hazard but there was not much danger of our animals neighing unless they saw other stock. During the day we picketed them with a rope tied from halter to foreleg and remained in a secluded canyon in the shelter of some large boulders near a small spring. When night came we started afoot up the slope toward the low spot on the ridge between the two lookouts. At dawn we lay on the crest.

The first light showed us what we hoped to see—a faint haze of smoke, the smoke made by burning dung when the braziers are first lighted in the morning. At other times dung fires are practically smokeless. Below us lay a hidden valley shaped like a crooked squash. Its neck opened toward the grassland of the Mongolian Plateau. Its wider part was concealed by foothills and cupped by the mountains to form a natural hideaway. A stream ran through it. Stock grazed in it. Fifteen or twenty tents were pitched beside the stream and the only place you could see it readily was from above as we were doing.

We watched the women go down to the creek for water and the children playing with the dogs. Then the women went with some of the older children and milked the cows and mares before the herds were turned out to graze for the day. The horses were mostly adult stock that could readily be used or sold. Probably most of them had been stolen.

I focused my telescope on what I thought was Malunga's tent. After a while he emerged and greeted three or four boys who were bringing some ponies to water before taking them onto the plain.

Whether he performed priestly duties among his people I never learned. He didn't wear red robe or sacred medallions, just the ordinary padded sheepskin trousers, coat, and peaked wool hat.

Two groups of horsemen rode off in opposite directions. We guessed they were reliefs for the lookouts. Sure enough, after an hour or so, two similar groups came back.

Malunga talked with his men as they stood watching their women work, smoking their long-stemmed pipes with small brass bowls and a bone mouthpiece resembling those I'd first seen at Indian Point. Some repaired saddles or cleaned rifles, ran foot races or wrestled. Toward noon a fat-tailed sheep was killed for common use and after lunch there was a siesta. Riders came and went—spies perhaps, or messengers.

We studied the lay of the land and the habits of the camp. I sketched a map in my notebook. We took turns sleeping and watching, alert for unusual signs such as a lark rising without singing or a raven swooping low to look at something.

Toward sundown the herds were brought in and the women milked again before dark. The guards on the peaks changed at sunset.

After dark Jaw-tor and I climbed cautiously down to our camp, watered our horses, fed them a handful of grain and changed their picket ground. Then we ate cold dried antelope and canned tomatoes, wrapped ourselves in sheepskins and curled up behind rocks to sleep. At dawn we were at our observation post again. Another day's watching confirmed what I'd suspected. The camp was vulnerable to attack from the plain and to a properly led party crossing the ridge at the spot where we lay.

We left the country as cautiously as we'd come into it. I decided not to inform the Chinese authorities. They were too unreliable. This was a job for Mongols. I telegraphed Urga. Within a few days a detachment of troops met Jaw-tor and me at the first relay station on the telegraph line.

I briefed the lieutenant in charge. He divided his men into two groups, about thirty in each, he to lead one, I the other. Five mornings later we would attack the camp, he from the plains side, I from the mountain. I would guide my party along the route Jaw-tor and I had followed. Under cover of darkness, we would slip across the ridge between the lookouts. The signal to attack would be a coat waved from the crest of the small hill concealing the camp from the plain, at such time as it was light enough to shoot.

At dawn when the animals are beginning to stir and the smoke is starting to rise from the tents, I lay with my men against the bank of the creek about 200 yards from Malunga's camp. We'd crept as close as we dared. Even now the dogs might scent us. Daylight was growing. Soon the herd boys would be coming for the stock and the relief guards saddle up and leave for the lookouts.

I kept my eyes on the crest of the hill beyond camp. Malunga should have put a guard there but evidently felt safe from that side, his Mongol side. In a few minutes I saw the figure of a man rise in silhouette upon the hill and wave a coat. We stood up and walked toward the tents, firing as we went, hearing the simultaneous shots from the hill and seeing the muzzle flashes.

At first there had been no answering fire but now the lead was beginning to sing around us. They nearly equaled us in number and after the first surprise fought back hard. But Malunga's tent remained quiet.

Less than a hundred yards separated us when he emerged from his doorway. He held his rifle in his hands as I did mine. We saw each other at approximately the same time. He must have realized then who was after him. We started walking toward each other. I watched his hands. If you're too far away to see their eyes, watch their hands. When his started to move, I fired from the ready. He hesitated, then pitched forward on his face. He tried to raise his rifle but couldn't.

When I bent over him I saw my bullet had gone through his belly and a pool of blood was beginning to form under him and soak into the ground. He looked up at me, defiant, but unable to speak. If there was a reason deeper than deviltry for his sabotage of the telegraph line and his wanton destruction of so many Chinese caravans and his murder of Grant, the time was past for his telling it, just as the time was past for my saying I was sorry for what I had done to him. Of all the men I was obliged to deal with violently, none moved me so much as Malunga.

When the lieutenant and his men realized he wasn't going to die immediately, the question of what to do with him arose. He was their official prisoner but they didn't want to be troubled by doctoring him or hauling him all the way to Urga for punishment, assuming he lived till then. But they dared not put an end to him. He was a priest and to touch him with hostile intent would be to incur the wrath of the gods. So they caught a wild horse from his herd, tied him to its tail with some of the wire he'd taken from Grant's telegraph line, and Malunga was dragged to his death.

My life resumed its former channels. The border became a safer place for caravans. Chinese settlement of Inner Mongolia proceeded steadily, despite sporadic Mongol resistance. And the deaths of Grant and Malunga were soon overshadowed by larger and more violent events whose focus was elsewhere but which affected us all.

Kumbum Lamasary. (*The Bodley Head, Ltd.*)

The Tashi Lama. (*The Bodley Head, Ltd.*)

The Hutukhtu of Urga. (*F.A. Larson*)

The Hutukhtu's bodyguards.

My colleague Oscar Mamen and some of the bales of licorice we brought back by caravan from the far west of China. Mamen, a noted adventurer, led Mongol guerrillas against Japanese invaders of Mongolia during World War II.

My "Black Horse Troop" of Mongols patrolled the China-Mongolia border against bandits and freebooters. I'm on the gray at left.

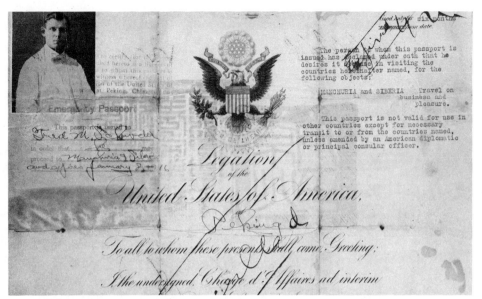

This passport enabled me to collect animal and bird specimens in Manchuria and Siberia for the British and Smithsonian Museums. Unfolded, it was about the size of a small saddle blanket.

J. W. G. Brodie and I (right) pose with some of the participants in the Chinese-Mongolian war of 1912-1915.

# 13. A Boy Emperor

Early in 1917 at the instigation of the International Red Cross, our American minister in Peking, Dr. Paul S. Reinsch, made arrangements with Prince Koudacheff, the Russian minister, for me to take a thousand-camel caravan to Siberia loaded with relief supplies for German and Austrian prisoners of war held by the Russians. Until now my contacts with World War I had been indirect. I knew that the Central Powers and the Allies were pressuring China to enter the war on their respective sides and were also trying (among the Allies, this was especially true of the Japanese) to enlarge their spheres of influence in China. But the U.S. by choice had no spheres of influence or special concessions and, like China, was not yet involved in the war. Events in France seemed remote and I could view with detachment some war-related incidents occurring close at hand.

The ornate lounge of the Hotel Wagons-Lits in Peking had become a center for international intrigue. At cocktail hour it resembled a scene from an old-fashioned spy movie: crowded with attachés, munitions salesmen, concession hunters, soldiers, tourists, journalists, a minister or two, gamblers, remittance men, gun smugglers, opium runners, beautiful Mata Haris, sycophants, and truly influential figures like Roy Anderson of Standard Oil. Roy—huge, fat, imperturbable, weighing nearly 300 pounds—was perhaps the most influential individual in all the Far East. Like Sowerby he'd been born in China of American missionary parents and knew the country and its people intimately. In his hotel room, surrounded by whiskey bottles, poker chips, and tobacco smoke, he held court like a mandarin. He was the only foreigner I knew who could outtalk an Oriental, and

I've seen him sit for the better part of two days surrounded by shouting Chinese, each suggesting how, when, and where things ought to be done, while Roy slowly and certainly consumed one bottle of whiskey after another, and talked right back, and at the end of two days the whiskey was gone, the Chinamen were silent, but Roy was still talking. Hutchison liked to tell how he sat in a poker game with Roy and three high-ranking officials in a room at the Wagons-Lits and watched one of the officials gracefully lose $200,000 Mex. to the other two. Next day the loser was proclaimed head of the Peking octroi.

How you did it mattered as much or more than what you did. Form, face, were vitally important.

Roy was edging China toward the Allied side, the side of Standard Oil, Democracy, and the U.S.A.

Because of my German name and the fact I could speak their language, and because I had certain contacts, the Germans regarded me as someone who might be useful to them and went out of their way to cultivate me. Earlier they'd invited me to visit their naval base at Tsingtao and after a bibulous weekend had presented me with a tiny white piglet as a souvenir. I took her home to Kalgan, christened her "Miss Bacon," raised her on brandy and condensed milk (there were no cows to speak of and consequently no fresh milk in China, cows being too costly to feed, and even the Mongols preferring mare's milk), and when she'd grown to weigh 200 pounds she would still come to the verandah at tea time for her lump of sugar.

Now I was taken by a well-known German *bon vivant,* a familiar figure at the bars of the Wagons-Lits and Peking Club, said to be the illegitimate son of the Kaiser, to an interview at the German Legation with their minister, Admiral von Hintze. An adventurer as well as a statesman, Hintze was famous locally for having reached China disguised as a stoker on a Swedish freighter, thus evading Allied naval ships during the long voyage from Germany. After cigars and a drink or two and a polite reference to my numerous trips into Mongolia, he asked if I'd heard anything about a small caravan reported to have left one of the foreign trading compounds at Kalgan a month or two earlier bound for Urga. I guessed what he was driving at and told him frankly what I had heard.

Late one night a small caravan of twenty or thirty camels left the compound of our neighboring, German-owned, trading firm, Arnhold, Karburg & Company, and took the usual route up the pass into Mongolia. Its cargo, however, was rather unusual. Instead of bricks of tea and bales of cloth it carried kegs of powder and sticks of dynamite. You couldn't keep a cargo like that secret. Long before the caravan reached wherever it may have intended to go, it was seized by a band of heavily armed Mongols. They arranged its powder kegs in a circle, stacked dynamite around the bottom of each keg and set a bound captive on top, connected everything to a single fuze, and blew the whole business to kingdom come.

"O-o-o-h!" was all Hintze said, very softly.

So ended the German attempt to blow up the Lake Baikal tunnels on the Trans-Siberian Railroad. If successful it might have blocked the line for a considerable period (there were a number of tunnels bordering the lake) and significantly disrupted the movement of men and supplies from eastern Siberia and the rest of the Far East—Japanese materiel, especially—to the Eastern European battlefront where Russians and Germans were fighting.

Thanks to better advance arrangements, my caravan trip across Mongolia and into Siberia with Red Cross supplies went off without difficulty, and I delivered my cargo of clothing and food stuffs at Troitzkosavsk, Verkne-Udinsk Park, Verkne-Udinsk Beresofka, and Irkutsk for distribution to prisoner-of-war camps in those areas and returned by rail to Peking.

Peking was increasingly a center for intrigue. Since the death of President Yuan Shih-kai in the summer of 1916, China's political situation had deteriorated rapidly. On the one hand were liberals pushing for a more democratic government, on the other conservatives who'd backed Yuan, quite rightly it seemed to me, as the one man able to bring order out of impending chaos. Now that Yuan was dead the conservatives were talking about restoring the monarchy in the person of the boy Pu-Yi, the last Manchu emperor, who'd been deposed by the Revolution of 1911. Meanwhile, with a do-nothing parliament and an ineffective president, the country was drifting into warlordism and outright civil war.

I was at Kalgan when I got a telegram which implied that

something interesting was afoot. It came from W. R. (Billy) Giles, special correspondent for the Peking and Tientsin *Times* and for several American and British newspapers. He shared rent with me on a house near the Legation Quarter. Billy wanted to know if I could come to Peking immediately. I took the next train and reached our house on the Mao-chung Hutung late the afternoon of June 30, 1917. Billy was busy in his office off the living room with an interpreter and a secretary, so I poured myself a whiskey and soda and settled onto the ottoman to relax and read the latest news. In a few minutes Billy finished his work, dismissed his help, poured himself a drink and began giving me the lowdown.

He spoke seriously; this was heavyweight stuff. Russia, tottering along under the Kerensky regime, was about to collapse. The Allies were preoccupied by the war in Europe. The Japanese were preparing to take advantage of the situation by seizing control of China. They'd stepped up their aggression a year or two before by presenting their infamous Twenty-One Demands and seizing all of Shantung Province which had been under German control. The Allies, preoccupied then as now and anxious to keep them in the war as an ally, had let them get away with it, and so had a weakened and intimidated China. Now the Japs were planning to extend their influence. They might even seize Peking on some pretext or other. They maintained a large contingent of troops at Tientsin and could easily move them up and take the capital from the corrupt and feeble government.

"President Li Huan-hung is definitely their man," Billy asserted. "If someone doesn't stop them, they'll soon have the whole country. That's what the meeting is about tonight."

The meeting that night of June 30 was held at the residence of a prominent merchant between the south and east gates. Fifty or sixty military, political, and business leaders were present. Dominant among them were the pigtailed, mustachioed old war dog Chang Hsun, who had served the Dowager Empress and been intimate with Yuan Shih-kai; and the liberal senior statesman Kang Yu-Wei, who had nearly persuaded the Imperial Government to accept reforms in pre-revolutionary days. Also present were a number of foreigners sympathetic to the republican cause, although some of them had supported Yuan Shih-kai as the only viable leader under the circumstances.

Chang Hsun harangued us. He'd moved a detachment of troops into the city secretly and was prepared to seize power now, tonight, and restore the Manchus to the Dragon Throne in order to establish political stability and prevent China from falling into Japanese hands. The restoration would be accompanied by creation of a constitutional monarchy patterned on England's. A national plebiscite would be held to permit the Chinese people to approve or disapprove it.

Chang proposed that, backed by his troops, we go at once to the presidential residence in the Imperial City and demand the resignation of Li Huan-hung, whom he characterized as a Japanese puppet, and then to the Winter Palace where the boy Pu-Yi, the last of the duly constituted Manchu emperors, had been held captive since the age of four when he'd been deposed, and there complete the coup d'état by restoring Pu-Yi to the throne. Chang's most compelling arguments were that speed and secrecy were essential, that faced with a *fait accompli* the Japanese would not dare intervene, and that most Chinese—he emphasized the "most"—being weary of political instability and foreign intervention would support a traditional symbol of authority such as the boy emperor.

When Chang's proposal was supported by Kang Yu-Wei and other respected leaders, the climate in the room became such that to oppose it seemed not only bad form but unpatriotic, and it was unanimously approved.

The meeting adjourned and Billy and I went with the others to the Imperial City. Peking was divided into four cities or districts: the Chinese, the Tartar, the Imperial contained within the Tartar City, and the Forbidden City with its Winter Palace contained within the Imperial City.

The gates in the high red walls of the Imperial City were guarded by Chang Hsun's troops so we had no difficulty gaining access. We proceeded directly to the Throne Room of the Winter Palace, learning later that President Li Huan-hung had thwarted Chang's plan to demand his resignation by fleeing and taking refuge in, appropriately, the Japanese Legation.

The Throne Room, or at least the room used for this occasion, was about forty feet by sixty, its walls covered with rich tapestries and its floor with a thick carpet of reddish ply. Electric bulbs had recently displaced the candles of the ornate chandeliers but there were still large candles in holders along the front of the dais at the end of the room where the throne or chair stood elevated, framed by gold filigree and lacquered woodwork.

It was two in the morning when Pu-Yi appeared at the door through which we had entered, surrounded by tutors, eunuchs, and other members of his personal staff. He was a little shaver, only eleven years old, and looked rather bewildered. He wore a cap of dark blue silk, a cloth-of-gold robe richly embroidered with jewels, and a gold neck-chain.

We all stood up. Chang Hsun accompanied by Kang Yu-Wei and one or two other leaders approached the boy, bowed low, and escorted him to the dais. Before seating him on the throne, Chang made him a flowery speech in which he said that events had decreed that the future of China be placed in firm and wise hands and so the gods had recalled the Manchus to their ancient power. Coached beforehand, the boy replied that, unworthy though he was, he humbly accepted the responsibility which necessity had thrust upon him. Then Chang led him onto the dais and seated him on the throne.

The Great Seal, a device resembling those ponderous hand-stamps our American printers used to print dodgers with, was brought and placed in his lap and he promised always to use it wisely. That was the heart of the ceremony. There was no crown, no prayer or other sacred rite. It was all over in a few minutes.

It had happened so quickly and smoothly that there seemed no reason to doubt its success—given the widespread support of the monarchical idea and the distrust of the present government and its close relationship with Japan.

Word of the coup d'état was sent immediately to the foreign legations. The influence of the foreign powers was such that no political regime was likely to succeed without their approval. They controlled about eighty percent of China's territory, most of her trade and finances including her internal customs, and their influence on her armed forces—through supplying munitions, training young officers, or bribing old ones—was enormous.

Billy went to send dispatches to his papers. I volunteered, in company with a number of other foreigners, to work with the new regime. It looked like the most interesting thing to do at the moment. Among my white colleagues was a gutty little Australian journalist named Smith who, for kicks, had climbed the outer wall of Peking with me one night when we were less sober than we should have been, wearing felt-soled Chinese shoes and wedging our fingers and toes between the cracks in the bricks to see how the smugglers did it. There was also Spurling the Sparrow. He was a former German Army officer, a large man, mechanically talented, who'd been captured by the Japanese when they seized the German base at Tsingtao and thrown into prison where he got so little to eat he said afterward he felt like a sparrow. Spurling means "sparrow" in German. Earlier he'd had charge of the Dowager Empress' gold-plated automobile and later of a small fleet of a dozen or so motor cars with which the Chinese government hoped to haul troops onto the plateau above Kalgan during the war against Mongolia. He'd also been mechanical superintendent of the "Chinese Air Corps," a handful of planes, mostly French made, located at the racetrack outside the walls of Peking where we raced our Mongol ponies and where Spurling helped us build a biplane out of piano wire, bamboo, and cloth, powered by a twelve-horsepower engine, which several of us flew until she came down one day on a sandbar below Kalgan and quit. Spurling was given responsibility for helping procure munitions and other supplies for the new government's troops. I was assigned to help my old general, Wong Shih-tai, organize internal security. I'd known Wong since revolutionary days when he had supported the republican cause and served for a time on the border. We posted guards at banks and pawnshops where looting was likely to start if it started, and dispatched small bodies of cavalry to patrol the streets with instructions to keep people moving and prevent disorder.

By 4:00 A.M. on July 1 the news was out: the Manchus were restored to the throne of China as an interim measure to preserve law and order pending the establishment of a constitutional monarchy and the holding of a national plebiscite in which the Chinese could choose between a republic and a limited monarchy. The lives and property of foreigners would be respected. Business would continue as usual.

Our headquarters was established in the War Ministry Building in the Imperial City. The Imperial City resembled the heart of Washington, D.C., in that it contained numerous administrative buildings housing various executive offices and bureaus of government. The buildings, however, were of modest size, two or three stories high at most—in fact most of Peking except for an occasional temple was composed of one-story buildings as consequence of the old law which forbade a Chinese to have a house higher than one story lest he presume to think of rising to the level of his Manchu overlords. All of this low-rise construction was set off by central tree-lined avenues and many beautiful private gardens whose foliage rose above their walls, and by the spacious Imperial City itself which was landscaped with parks, gardens, streams, lakes, and even an artificial mountain; so that, despite many narrow and tortuous byways, the general impression of Peking was one of spaciousness and beauty.

General Wang Shih-cheng, chief of staff in the former or yesterday's regime, became chief of staff in our new one. One of Wang's first acts was to send a message to young General Li Chin Hsi, a trusted partisan of the restoration movement, who commanded a large body of troops at the strategic railroad junction of Shih-kia-chwang, which I've mentioned, some 200 miles south of Peking. Wang asked Li to move his men to Peking immediately and bring his artillery. Our military situation was precarious. Chang Hsun's detachment, combined with the Peking garrison, which had come over to our side in its entirety, totaled only about 6,000 men. We had no artillery and there were several warlord armies in north China that might turn against us, depending on how payoffs went or power plays developed, not to mention the Japanese who might try to move up in force from Tientsin.

As word of the restoration spread throughout the city, yellow dragon flags, symbols of the Manchu regime, appeared on all sides as if by magic. Some of this was the usual Chinese obedience to whatever authority appeared strongest but much was genuine. Peking had always tended to support the imperial idea, as had most of north China.

Things went well throughout that first day of the coup. In the late afternoon, General Li detrained at the Chienmen Gate with the advance elements of his Shih-chia-chwang force and came in person to headquarters. He had moved with surprising speed. Like many of China's younger officers he'd been trained in Japan, Japan's victory in the Russo-Japanese War having given it much prestige in Eastern eyes. At the time of the 1911 Revolution, Li had commanded troops in the western provinces and had led them into the republican camp, thus establishing his credentials for the future. I hadn't seen him for several years. He still wore a mustache but had acquired several extra pounds. He struck me as a little more dapper, suave, and sophisticated than he should have been—much more so than the older military generation represented by the rough-cut Chang Hsun, Wang Shih-cheng, and my old Wong. However he outlined his plans with a precision which left us encouraged. Within two days he would have a protective cordon of men and artillery around the city strong enough, in all likelihood, to repel any attack.

Wang's final instructions to him were not to open fire without express orders from headquarters. It was essential to keep control of an unstable situation and avoid incidents that might lead to intervention by the foreign powers, particularly the Japanese.

All went well on July 2. No word had come from Reinsch or the other ministers as to their reaction to the coup but that was understandable. They would be contacting their respective governments for instructions and waiting to see what developed before declaring themselves. We still hoped for a personal interview with Reinsch. Chang Hsun had asked for it. The U.S. position in Chinese eyes was relatively strong because we'd demanded no extraterritorial rights or other special privileges, but instead fostered an open-door policy. Chang hoped that by gaining U.S. backing he could induce other nations to follow suit and at the same time increase his popular base of support.

Meanwhile the million inhabitants of Peking went about their business as if nothing unusual were happening and by nightfall a substantial percentage of Li's army and some artillery were in position around the city. For the first time in three torrid summer nights (Peking in summer can be very hot) I flopped on a cot in headquarters building and got some sleep.

I was wakened in broad daylight by the roar of a shell exploding in the grounds outside our building. It brought me to my feet with the instantaneous conviction that the Japanese had slipped up from Tientsin during the night and were attacking the city, a conviction shared at first by almost everyone else at headquarters. Everything was in confusion as two or three more shells exploded in quick succession. Then a telephone call to the main guardhouse at the Chienmen Gate (Western Electric Company had installed Peking's telephone system a few years earlier) told us the truth. Those were not Japanese shells. They were Li's. The Japs had gotten to him and he had sold us out.

I never learned exactly how it happened. Li may have been their man from the days of his early training in Japan. They used people that way, planning far ahead. It took the Chinese, for example, several centuries to weaken the warlike Mongols by fostering pacifistic Lamaism among them but it worked. Similarly Japanese plans for dominating China dated back into the 1800s but weren't fully implemented until the 1930s and '40s.

Wang sent Li a haughty message demanding to know the meaning of his shell fire. Li replied with an ultimatum: "Surrender or be destroyed." Wang retorted with an order to the traitor to lay down his arms or bear the consequences of his treason, and we got ready to fight. Our position if awkward was not hopeless. Though outnumbered ten to one and lacking artillery, we had a million people hemmed into the city with us and with their help and the assistance of friends elsewhere we might win out.

Li began by shelling the racetrack outside the walls which was held by our men. He set fire to its stables, and racehorses broke loose or were freed by their grooms and galloped wildly in all directions, adding to the confusion, while our men fell back, trading space for time, throwing up barricades, setting the pattern we would follow.

Chang Hsun had sent messages to army commanders north and south of Peking urging them to march to the aid of the government.

Next Li shelled the guardhouses over the gates, knocked them out quickly, and positioned his guns in the gates and in some cases on top of the city walls, while his men advanced along the streets. We replied as best we could with machine guns and rifles, making him pay and suffering some losses ourselves.

Civilians ducked in and out of the firing. Foreigners stood on the wall at the Legation Quarter, which backed up against the wall of the Tartar City, to observe the fighting and one or two were hit by stray bullets we learned later. Pu-Yi remained in seclusion in the recesses of the palace, issuing edicts prepared by others. Chang Hsun had been named premier of the new regime, Kang Yu-Wei secretary of state.

The foreign press was screaming about an imperialist coup d'état. Rumors flew that the Germans had staged it all in order to bring China into the war on their side. The Allies were hypersensitive on this point, being engaged as I've said in an intensive effort to get China and its manpower into the war on their side, and the fact that some of us had German names lent support to the rumors of a German plot.

The restoration got a bad press generally. Most of the reporters, Giles excepted, had little idea what was going on and wrote their dispatches as usual in the Wagons-Lits bar.

On the Fourth of July, riding past the entrance to the Foreign Quarter, I was tempted to turn my horse inside past the U.S. Marine guards, join the annual Independence Day Party (complete with bunting, champagne, and a military drill on the parade ground) at the U.S. Legation—and ask Dr. Reinsch to intervene on our behalf. Reinsch was an exceptionally able minister who really understood the situation in China. He'd been on the faculty at the University of Wisconsin before coming to the Far East and had a human touch as well as brains. I felt sure he realized the seriousness of the Japanese threat but perhaps misjudged our motives. However, Americans weren't supposed to be actively involved in the coup d'état and I decided I might harm our cause by making an appearance, and so rode on.

You may ask why I got myself involved in this troubled situation. The answer is that it was my nature to do so. I think that we are attracted to what we ourselves are: like seeks like. Frans August Larson lived a lifetime in Mongolia and once told me he had never had to kill a man or even use violence except on one or two occasions. Larson, though strong and virile, was a man of peace. He exuded peace. He created peace wherever he went. I was much the opposite. I was attracted to conflict. And perhaps created some of it wherever I went, without deliberately intending to or knowing that I did.

Bad news came. The armies north and south supposedly hurrying to our aid were barely moving. In the south a blown bridge halted Chang Hsun's main force. His troops detrained and started to march but their progress was hopelessly slow. In the north, General Feng Ling-ko, commander north of the Wall, rounded up most of the railroad cars in Manchuria to move men to our aid but somebody paid him off, or he got cold feet, or both. Many had cold feet to start with. Some sold out. No one came.

Our hopes of support from the foreign powers faded too. All of them except Japan maintained a hands-off policy, while the foreign press and most of the local English language papers shouted louder than ever about imperialists and reactionaries in league with German agents. They claimed we were overthrowing the legitimately constituted Chinese Republic and leading China into the war against the Allies. In the context of the times, it was effective propaganda. The repressive regimes of Manchus and Hohenzollerns could easily be linked in the public mind, and an attempt to restore the former could be made to appear an attempt to support the latter.

The Japs encouraged such false impressions and tried to persuade other powers to intervene with them against us. They failed but continued their behind-scenes efforts to undermine the restoration through bribery and intrigue.

When the coolness of the Allies became evident and no reinforcements reached us, our leaders began to disappear. Their instincts for self-preservation overcame any scruples they may have had about disloyalty to their colleagues or betrayal of our cause. It was easy to change allegiance. There were no fixed battle lines. All you had to do was cross the street and mingle with the crowd or slip out of the Forbidden City and not return. Chang Hsun took refuge in the Legation Quarter, as did Kang Yu-Wei.

Our troops, by contrast, remained loyal. They'd fought well although unpaid for several months. Now they were in a fix. As prisoners they would have little to look forward to but empty stomachs or a bullet in the back of the head. Their plight, plus a conviction that our cause was the right one, persuaded me to stay on a little longer in company with a few officers and politicians who felt similarly inclined, or had no other place to go.

Li split us into two groups. Six hundred including myself took refuge in the Forbidden City. Twenty-two hundred holed up in the Temple of Heaven a mile away. There was a lull in the fighting on the eighth and ninth of July while rumors flew and negotiations went on behind the scenes. On the tenth, a French-made biplane flew over the palace and dropped two bombs that did no damage to speak of but showed that superior force, including the latest military technology, lay with our adversaries. Nevertheless we had some good cards left.

Shortly before dawn on the morning of July 12 Li made a formal demand for our surrender.

When it was refused, he attacked the Forbidden City with artillery and small arms fire. There was a sharp skirmish at the main gate in which we lost twenty to thirty men killed and wounded. By noon his people were coming over the walls on scaling ladders, virtually unopposed because we were too few to defend them in strength. Further resistance seemed futile so we asked for a parley and half a dozen of us including myself and our finance minister, Chang Chen-fang, practically the only ranking official left, went out under a flag of truce in front of the gate to talk with Li, while our men kept their rifles on him and his aides, and his men kept us similarly covered.

Since we had asked for the parley, protocol required that we speak first. Without a word Chang handed him a paper stating our armistice terms. Our men were to be paid in full, by Li. They were to be allowed to keep their arms and ammunition and return to their homes unmolested. There were to be no reprisals. A national plebiscite was to be held to determine whether China preferred a limited monarchy or a republic. And in return Pu-Yi would step down from his throne and fighting would cease.

Li scanned the paper contemptuously, then asked why he should sign such an absurd document when we, not he, were the defeated party.

"So the Foreign Legations will know what you've agreed to!"

Chang replied. This caused him to glance at me.

"And if I do not choose to sign?" His voice was obnoxiously oily.

"Then you and your friends can come to power over the ruins of the palace. We won't leave one stone atop another. You can have what's left."

It was a bluff but one we could make good. We knew that destruction of the palace was the last thing he wanted. For generations it had been the focus for the ancestor worship of the entire nation. Despite the revolution, it remained dear to most Chinese. To come to power by destroying it would be a bad beginning indeed.

After much beating around the bush, including some remarks about our criminal insurgency and his praiseworthy desire to avoid further loss of life and property, Li signed the paper as though it was nothing. Actually it was rather remarkable. It represented one of the few instances where the victors not only agreed to pay the vanquished but allowed them to retain their arms. We based it on the belief that he and his Jap masters wanted us out of the way as quickly and quietly as possible. It could perhaps have happened only in the Alice-in-Wonderland world of Chinese politics where all things are possible.

"Now, if you'll clear the way," we told him summarily, "we'll march our men to the Temple of Heaven and you can pay our combined forces there." We never let him take the initiative, kept him constantly on the defensive—for having defeated us but not yet disposed of us! He was looking rather unhappy by this time, sensing himself in danger of losing face.

By prearrangement we left the boy emperor in the palace. The less he saw of us now the better. Later he would disclaim his involvement in the coup, saying we had coerced him.

We marched our men to the Temple of Heaven through a cordon of Li's troops. "Hold onto your arms," we instructed them. "When you've been paid, wait in the temple compound until every man has been paid. Then we'll all march out together. Be ready to fight if need be."

We didn't think Li would risk trying to kill us there at the heart of Peking with so much attention focused on him but we couldn't be sure.

The Temple of Heaven was an extraordinary structure and one of China's most sacred shrines. It was circular, three stories high, built of masonry and stone, with three tiers of blue-tile roofs, surrounded at ground level by marble balustrades and a compound. Every winter solstice, the emperor used to offer sacrifices there to the one god, Shang-ti. If anything the temple was a more sacred place than the palace. Its confines should never be defiled by violence, which was one reason our people had taken refuge there. Sharing the premises with them were a number of resident priests who officiated at the temple's shrines. They were friends of ours and had entered into our plans.

On arrival, we sent Li word that we were ready to meet him in the anteroom and implement the surrender agreement with his payoff of our troops. The anteroom was situated to one side of the temple's main entrance. It was often used by the priests to conduct business with the public. As Li and his party entered it through the main door, we did likewise through a side door opening into the compound. Again we showed our contempt by being a few steps late.

But this time when I saw him I lost my temper. The accumulated tensions and resentments of the past few days burst out. What triggered me was not so much Li as the three uniformed Japanese officers who were with him. He would be using their money to pay our men and they had come along to see he didn't cheat them. In the face of the sacrifices that had been made and the blood that had been shed, it was all so blatantly, disgustingly corrupt that next thing I knew I was confronting Li. What I said doesn't bear repeating. But everyone there heard it.

I watched him redden. "I'll have your head," he said quietly. His loss of face would be irreparable so long as I lived.

I laughed at him. I was wearing my pistols in open holsters and I think he realized I could use them before he or his men could stop me. He was also still uncertain as to what interests I represented and I guessed that this would help restrain him until he could find just the right moment to retaliate.

We sat down across the table from each other, among our respective groups, and my men began to file in from the temple compound while his clerks and our paymasters paid them—two dollars per man per month in the average case—and the

Japanese officers watched to see there was no cheating.

The payoff took most of the day and caused considerable unrest among Li's troops because they hadn't been paid. The Japs were investing all they could afford for the moment in us, not in his overdue bills. When the restlessness of his people became apparent we smiled and commented on it. That was the last straw. It really galled Li. "Your turn will come!" I could see him thinking when he glanced my way. Finally the last of our boys was being paid and I knew my turn had indeed come.

The ruse I'd decided to use was time-worn but seemed the best available. Keeping my eyes on him, I stood up, stretched my arms deliberately, and said I was going to go to the toilet, having been sitting at that table most of the day. Then I turned my back on him and began walking slowly toward the door which led from the anteroom into the main part of the temple. He could have stopped me. Perhaps he thought me trapped. His men filled the anteroom and compound outside. A mouse would have had a hard time getting through them unnoticed, let alone a white foreign devil. In any event he did nothing.

Quickening my pace I passed through the central shrine where the punk sticks were burning and the statues of the gods sat roundabout and descended a flight of steps that led to a corridor, glancing back now and then to see if I were being followed.

At the end of the corridor was a toilet room where the honey pots stood open in rows at either side, exuding their unforgettable aromas, and as I reached it I saw with intense relief that the wooden door at the far end of it was unbarred. Another moment and I was safe in the living quarters of the priests beyond.

I dropped the bar into place on that side, and it didn't take long to change my clothes. I kept my long-handled underwear and .45s as foundation garments. Outwardly I became a Buddhist priest wearing faded red robe, peaked wool cap, felt-soled shoes. Iodine added to the natural tan and dust and dirt of hands and face. Then I joined a religious procession that was forming. Carrying paper banners and intoning prayers, we priests marched up the ramp into the temple compound and out the gate, passing through Li's men and a number of my own, who weren't looking for me in such pious company.

A quarter of a mile into the city and four or five of us turned off along a side street to a small temple where a rickshaw was waiting. Usually it took an hour to cross Peking by rickshaw. It took me about thirty minutes. When one boy tired, another replaced him. They knew the shortcuts and shouted at the top of their lungs whenever traffic blocked our way. To onlookers I was simply a priest in a hurry.

At the North Gate ten or twelve of my Kalgan riflemen—soldiers who lived in Kalgan and who carried the rifles and ammunition with which they had left the Temple of Heaven despite orders to the contrary—were waiting for a train to take them home. The sight of them gave me an idea. A locomotive with steam up and a boxcar attached was standing on the track heading up the line. Whether it had been arranged for or not I didn't know but we didn't stop to ask. The engineer and fireman became cooperative. We uncoupled the car. I rode in the cab. My boys swarmed onto the tender.

From Kalgan I proceeded by horseback to the plateau. There I tapped the telegraph line and sent a message to Li, which he almost certainly never got, saying that if he would come alone to the top of the pass I would meet him there alone and we could settle our differences.

Within a few days, reports reached me that he'd placed a price on my head. To be on the safe side, I spent the next few months in Mongolia.

The restoration failed through lack of planning and good luck. It wasn't an unscrupulous power grab but a sincere attempt to save China from falling into Japanese hands. Chang Hsun was sincere. His chief error lay in acting too hastily and relying on supposed friends who failed him. With better preparation and judgment, the coup could have succeeded since popular support for it was unquestionably strong.

It was followed by what had preceded it: political chaos and Japanese encroachment. China entered World War I on the side of the Allies largely to secure herself a seat at the peace table from which she could and did protest Japan's aggression against her sovereignty. But her fragile political structure soon gave way. She was primarily a people, not a nation. She succumbed to warlordism complicated by Communism. Not till Chiang Kai-shek brought order in 1928 was there anything resembling peace. And that was soon broken by the Japanese conquest of Manchuria and Inner Mongolia in the 1930s and Japan's subsequent attempt to subjugate all China during World War II. Then came Chairman Mao.

Pu-Yi of course survived to become the puppet emperor of Japanese Manchuria ("Manchukuo") during the 1930s and '40s. He was captured by the Russians toward the end of World War II and held prisoner by them for a number of years. I felt sorry for him. The poor kid never had a chance. Puppet first to last.

In retrospect I'm convinced that as a price for Japan's continued participation in World War I, the Allies turned their backs on the restoration of Pu-Yi. Thus they lost a precious opportunity to stabilize China and help her become democratic. Instead, Japan's increasingly flagrant aggressions in the 1917-1920 period turned young Chinese students such as Mao Tse-tung and Chou En-lai into revolutionary Communists, thus decisively changing the course of history.

Perhaps the most revealing event of the restoration was what happened on the night of June 30 when President Li Huan-hung took refuge in the Japanese Legation. When a Chinese president takes refuge in a Japanese Legation, you can be sure there is something amiss.

As for General Li, he eventually fell from favor and lost his head. So far I still have mine.

# 14.  Finale

The rest is briefly told. When snowblindness incurred during a caravan trip permanently impaired my eyesight, I withdrew my savings from the Hong Kong-Shanghai Bank and headed for California. There I made two long-standing dreams come true. I married my red-headed woman from San Francisco. We had corresponded. Neither her former marriage nor my lack of one made any difference when we met again. We were both ready, approaching our sixties, to start life anew. We bought an orange ranch at Orland in the upper Sacramento Valley, in a frost free zone that constituted the northernmost citrus land in the state, and there Frances and I spent many happy days together, our satisfactions heightened by reunions with friends from former years.

Old China hands drifted into California, including Frans Larson, who reported Mamen last heard from leading Mongol guerillas against the Japanese invaders of World War II.

At a sourdough gathering at Seattle I met Mother Woods. Mother was into her eighties and nearly blind but still a handsome woman. I wasn't seeing too well myself, but we groped our way together back into the past and had a wonderful time.

And when Radio Station KFAR, Fairbanks, increased its power to 5,000 watts, several of us including Arthur Eaton and I had our voices broadcast via telephone from San Francisco over the Arctic wastes where we'd once yelled at our dog teams.

And then one day in the 1950s I revisited San Diego. As the plane descended low over the bay I felt my emotions rise. Three aircraft carriers lay where Billy and I once speared stingrays from our skiff. Skyscrapers loomed where I'd seen jackrabbits hopping through sagebrush. But beyond on the horizon the head and shoulders of Cuyamaca Peak loomed higher still, and it seemed I might still hear Jip up there with the Old Man and the grown dogs after a pig.

In town I found young mischiefmakers I'd chummed around with such as Hugh McKie and Frank Forward had become respected senior citizens. They'd provided the creative energy of which great communities are made. Hugh was a prosperous merchant, Frank a prominent banker.

A paved highway ran up to the ranch now. At either side of it, city-style houses and summer cottages and trailer homes made what amounted to a continuation of the city nearly all the way to the mountains.

Up at the ranch everything appeared to have changed. The main house was gone, burned to the ground (some said by the Old Man's enemies one night when he was away) and never rebuilt. All that remained of the bunkhouse, my youthful home, was a stone hearth and chimney. They looked pretty bleak and sepulchral, rising there in the early morning light. A white-painted cabin once occupied by Cap Hulburd, who succeeded to ownership of the grove, remained whole, as did a number of newer, tackier shanties built in the 1920s and '30s when "Hulburd's Grove" was a vacation and health resort. But all were silent now, all deserted. It seemed I'd come home to stand in a graveyard: my mother's, Yaqui Tom's, Indian Mary's, Jip's, the Old Man's (skeptical and disapproving for all eternity); and then, very faintly, I heard a familiar sound. For a moment I couldn't tell what it was and then I realized it was the Sweetwater River flowing clear and cold from the Peak. It said to me that nothing had changed, all was flowing on like a marvelous river, running a little dry in summer maybe, flooding a little high in winter, but always flowing on.

On my way down to it I noticed that the bumblebees were still making their nests in the wild grass of the meadow, where a boy and a dog might find them and taste that honey which is sweeter than any other on earth.

Looking back, there were some things I'd do differently but not many. I'd enjoyed myself and made a lot of friends. Maybe that's what matters most.

Arthur Sowerby (right) and I with some of our trophies.

I purchased a great many skins and furs at Hailar in Manchuria for Wilson & Company of Tientsin. Here I oversee the baling of several thousand of them, flanked at either hand by the local dealers from whom I purchased them.

At Peking in 1917, American volunteers, 115-strong, lined up for service in the war against Germany.

Dr. Paul S. Reinsch, American minister to China, 1913-1919, watches U.S. Marines march through the gate of the Legation Quarter, Peking.

Street scene, Peking, July 1917.

General Li's men scaled the wall of the Forbidden City to attack us during the fighting in Peking, 1917.

[214]

General Li betrayed the Restoration Movement that replaced Pu-Yi on the throne of China for twelve hectic days.

The Boy Emperor in ceremonial robes of the Ch'ing Dynasty at the time of his brief restoration.

Slightly squiffed, O. Mamen (left) and I celebrate after being awarded—and wearing—China's Order of the Golden Harvest, Second Class.

Fifty years after the Gold Rush when I (wearing vest and white shirt) was president of the San Francisco-Oakland Alaska-Yukon Sourdough Association and vice president of the Yukon Order of Pioneers, some of us posed for this photo during a reunion. Seated at my right are Charles Conroy who "came in" in 1883 and Mrs. Joe Matthews, 1888. At my left are F. E. Becker, 1894; S. S. (Skiff) Mitchell, 1886; E. Elvira Morrow, 1888; and E. L. Cedela Pole, 1889. Standing from left to right: Fred Chapman, 1895; Seth Ekstrom, 1893; Peter Bauman, 1892; Ross Moulton, 1895; Nettie E. Freu, 1894; J. N. Clarke, 1893; Anna B. Lewelyn, 1895; and R. L. Gillespie, 1893.

# NOTES

*Full titles, when not given, will be found in the bibliography.*

## I. GUNS ON THE MEXICAN BORDER

13, **Dr. F.D.C. Meyer:** a pioneer San Diego County rancher, was a native of Hanover, Germany, and at one time a resident of Charleston, South Carolina.

13, **Horse Thief Canyon:** or Robber's Roost, is a familiar landmark easily visible from U.S. Highway 80 (Interstate 8) near Descanso.

16, **arrow:** similar descriptions of arrow making, including the use of deer sinew moistened by chewing, are given in *History of San Diego County*, pp. 448-458, and in Theodora Kroeber's fascinating account of California's last Stone Age Indian, *Ishi*, pp. 100-101—although Ishi did not seem to realize that an arrow rotates in flight. Pope, p. 20.

17, **German Artillery Hall:** according to the South Carolina Historical Society, the "house next the Old German Artillery Hall" may have been the house next the German Friendly Society on Archdale Street, Charleston, a building once used by the German Fusiliers Society. However F.D.C. Kracke, grandson of "Uncle Kracke," remembered the German Artillery Hall as being on Wentworth Street near King.

18, **lynx:** "It is probable that I have kicked one hundred lynx out of trees to be killed by dogs. Sometimes, if you are climbing up directly under one, he may jump on you, but only after giving you warning by growling. I have seen one large lynx whip six dogs to a standstill, but that was because the dogs knew not how to kill a lynx. After he had done that, my little black-and-tan hound, although much smaller than the lynx, bravely walked in and had the lynx kicking his last within a minute of time." Powell, p. 273.

20, **burro:** the veteran California vaquero author, A.R. Rojas, pp. 12, 73, tells of jackasses and sometimes mules being pastured with mares and colts to protect them against lions.

25, **Yaquis:** persecuted Yaquis fled from Mexico to the U.S. beginning in the early 1800s and continuing into the 1930s. There is a substantial settlement of them near Tucson, Arizona.

26, **Homer:** Odysseus sat down when attacked by dogs. Rieu, p. 216.

26, **we roamed:** as recently as the 1960s, the memory of the roving Yaqui and his youthful protégé was still green in the minds of some San Diego County residents.

32, **draw:** today's fast-draw experts have been timed in 21/100 of a second during target practice. However, a few nineteenth-century stopwatches measured less than a fifth of a second and no timekeepers were present when so-called serious shooting was taking place.

32, **guns:** "Guns were again [c. 1888] carried openly in the streets and were still a necessity in the lonelier areas of the back country. Three persons died in one fight in a little, high-walled, well-watered valley isolated from the main courses of travel." Pourade, *The History of San Diego*, p. 204.

33, **Campo:** the so-called raid on Campo by a party of armed Mexicans took place on Dec. 4, 1875. Casualties on both sides were described as heavy. *San Diego Yesterdays*, p. 67; *Historical Landmarks of San Diego County*, pp. 19-20. A recent study puts the total killed and wounded at ten. Pourade pp. 127-128.

34, **General Cadwallader:** Sylvanus Cadwallader ("General" was an honorary localism) had been an outstanding war correspondent with the Union armies attached primarily to Grant's headquarters during the Civil War. His book *Three Years With Grant* is one of the most intimate and authoritative accounts of the war at high-command level. In the late 1880s and early 1890s he served as U.S. customs officer and government inspector at Campo. His "Line Riders" (forerunners of today's Border Patrol) were more properly known as the "Mounted Customs Inspectors." They had been established in 1853 by the U.S. Secretary of the Treasury to patrol the border against smugglers and illegal immigrants.

36, **Meyer's Grade:** construction of the first automobile road down the grade is described in *History of San Diego County*, p. 384,

36, **Apaches:** according to most authorities, Yumas rather than Apaches destroyed two Spanish settlements on the west bank of the Colorado, across from the modern city of Yuma, on July 17, 1781 and massacred their inhabitants. Chapman, pp. 330-342. The popular crossing place down-river from Yuma is discussed by Martin, p. 127.

36, **Kit Carson:** spent several days trapping near the mouth of the Colorado in 1830. Estergreen, p. 44.

## II. Gold on the Yukon

50, **coming out to Juneau:** "Thereafter [1880] from year to year miners . . . braved the dangers of the Dyea trail and the Chilkoot Pass, found 'bar diggins' on the Stewart and other tributaries of the Yukon, worked there in the summer season, crossed the pass to the sea in the fall and found employment at good wages at the Treadwell [Juneau] mines." Wickersham, pp. 9-10.

51, **bears:** "I have looked for anal plugs in a good many dens of both grizzly and blac! bears and have found only two," Dr. John J. Craighead, a leading authority on bears, writes from the Universtiy of Montana. "One of these was largely clay, and the other was densely compacted vegetation. This does not serve as a cap to previously eaten food but does serve as an anal plug; it is not digested. Just when the bear voids the anal plug is still undetermined. It probably occurs just before the bear emerges, but I suspect that many bears void the plug after moving away from the den, and I think it is quite possible that not all individuals form an anal plug."

[218]

52, **mosquitoes:** adult mosquitoes overwinter in the Yukon in protected places, according to James E. Morrow, head of the biological science department at the University of Alaska, Fairbanks, and emerge at the spring thaw to lay their eggs. Overwintering mosquitoes are larger and less aggressive than those hatched during the summer but they can and do bite.

53, **Leroy Napoleon (Jack) McQuesten:** his daughter Crystal wrote years later: "Dad and Fred Schroder were friends of long standing and he was always a welcome guest in our house."

56, **Circle City:** the strikes on Mastodon and Birch Creeks leading to the Circle City rush are usually credited to Pitka, Walaska (also spelled Sarosky and Cherosky), Jack Gregor, Pat Kennaley (Cornelli) and Jonathan Pemberton. Wharton pp. 151-158.

56, **mastodon:** stories about live Alaska-Yukon mammoths were so common and so widely believed that a tongue-in-cheek account of the killing of one and the donation of it to the Smithsonian Institution was published in *McClure's Magazine* for September, 1899. Lynch, pp. 328-329.

57, **breeding dogs to wolves:** by tying a bitch in heat to a tree near camp when wolves were about.

58, **whalers in Arctic Ocean:** since 1889. In fact the wintering ground at Herschel Island, "the world's last jumping-off place," had become notorious as a scene of drunken and sexual orgies staged by sailors and compliant Eskimo women. Phillips, pp.118-119; Stuck, pp. 320-321.

59, **Nigger Bill Ewing:** later (1906) appears to have operated a roadhouse on the Valdez-Fairbanks trail. Heller, p. 221.

60-61, **Oscar Ashby:** and his saloon-dance hall are mentioned at greater length by Adney, pp. 294-295, and Berton, *Klondike*, p. 66.

61, **Alaska in 1896:** a "civil and judicial district" from 1884 to 1912; became a territory in 1912.

61, **votes at Circle City:** for more about Circle City, "the Paris of Alaska," see Winslow p. 20; Walden p. 45; and Wickersham pp. 46, 122, 166. Berton says, *Klondike*, p. 29, it had a music hall, two theaters, eight dance halls and twenty-eight saloons, a school, a library which included the works of Huxley, Darwin, Carlyle, and Ruskin as well as the *Encyclopedia Britannica*; and a total population of around 1200. A list of Alaska-Yukon pioneers compiled by Andrew Baird of Dawson City contains the names of 274 white men known to have been in the Yukon watershed prior to 1897. Most of them plus some others can be assumed to have been at or near Circle City in the fall of 1896. See also Lung pp. 327 ff.

61, **Jack Carr:** read also Winslow pp. 20, 26; and Adney, pp. 224, 462.

63, **Dawson:** the name used by veteran "insiders" for the strike popularly known as Klondike. It was also applied to the town of Dawson or Dawson City, named in honor of Dr. George M. Dawson, director of the Canadian Geological Survey. "Klondike" was derived from the Indian name for the stream known to white men as "Deer Creek." It had little or no gold itself but its tributaries provided rich pay.

63, **George Carmack:** accounts of the famous strike vary in detail but are essentially the same as this one. Carmack, however, is said to have died in comparatively good financial circumstances after retiring to Vancouver. Berton, *Klondike*, p. 406. His use of a frying pan to wash the historic first ounces of gold is also mentioned in Sherwood, p. 355n.

64, **Dick Lowe:** accounts vary as to how Dick Lowe acquired his fraction but most agree it was probably the richest ground in the Klondike. Adney, pp. 309, 410-411; Wickersham, pp. 30-31; Berton, *Klondike*, pp. 73-74; Winslow, pp. 216-217. Lowe's official claim application states that his fraction was 86 feet long and was staked on March 1, 1897. Yukon Archives.

64, **Frank Manley:** real name was Hilliard B. Knowles. He was a Texan who'd got into trouble with the law and "gone north." After relatively unsuccessful mining ventures at Circle and Dawson, he struck it rich at Fairbanks, Iditarod, Shushanna, and elsewhere and became one of Alaska's most prominent figures. Manley Hot Springs near Fairbanks was named for him. After striking oil to the value of some $4 million near Bakersfield, he died at his home near Napa, California, in 1933. Orth, p. 619, and Sims, pp. 14-15, 58-61.

67, **Mother Woods:** is also mentioned by McKeown p. 172. She may have provided inspiration for one of Rex Beach's best stories, *The Thaw at Slisco's*.

69, **Fortymile:** so called because it was forty miles below old Fort Reliance.

70, **northern lights:** Morenus mentions the sound of northern lights, p. 47. The sound is believed caused by the action of high-energy solar particles.

71, **120 miles to Dawson:** is the correct distance. For a man to travel such a distance on foot at high speed, though remarkable, was not unique. According to Denison, p. 295, Mike Mahoney once covered 130 miles on foot in 20 hours. In 1910, John Johnston covered the 408 miles of the Nome-to-Candle dog-team race course in 74 hours. Carpenter, p. 199. The explorer, Commander Donald B. MacMillan, drove a team of dogs 100 miles in 18 hours. *The Complete Dog Book*, p. 148. Possibly Johnston and MacMillan "hitched" rides on their sleds but they would have traveled mostly on foot.

72, **Nicknames:** usually reflected an individual's personal characteristics, achievements, or non-achievements. For example: One-Eyed Riley, Up-Against-It-Bill, The Blowback Kid, Bull-Con Jack, Swiftwater Bill ( who avoided swift water), Roulette Joe, Piefaced Patsy. Wickersham, pp. 52-55, tells more about the strike and settlement on Seventymile Creek, as does Adney, p. 457.

73, **Skookum:** means "good" or "strong" in Siwash dialect. The restaurant is mentioned further by Sims, p.15.

73-74, **weight of gold:** a ball of gold the size of a basketball would weigh approximately one ton. The rates given are also given, with slight variation, by Winslow, p. 212 and Adney, p. 252.

74, **assayed:** a table of Dawson assay-office values varies slightly from this. Adney, p. 416.

75, **Frank P. Slavin:** the "Sydney Cornstalk," had beaten some outstanding fighters including Jake Kilrain and George Burke. Sullivan's refusal to meet him caused much unfavorable comment.

75, **Jack London:** Scearce, p. 88 and Bond, pp. 34-41 also give eyewitness accounts of Jack London in the Klondike, Bond finding him quiet, thoughtful, a good listener, but given to bursts of eloquent discourse on such subjects as soicalism. Scearce termed him a daydreamer and inveterate cigarette smoker who spent many hours lying in his bunk. Most witnesses including those quoted by his biographer Stone, pp. 83-87, agree that London bestirred himelf little and spent most of his time quietly observing the life around him—storing up capital for future fiction writing without really meaning to, according to his wife's account. Charmian London also says, pp. 241-242, that Jack lived in a cabin on lower Bonanza Creek part of the time during his stay at Dawson. London's own brief notes on his Klondike experience begin with the day he left Dawson by boat and deal with his uneventful trip down the Yukon to St. Michael, covering a period of about three weeks in June 1898.

76, **"Yellow Kid":** after a popular comic strip character who also had a front tooth missing. O'Connor, p. 216.

76, **Oregon Mare:** Lynch, p. 174, claimed he saw her spend $1,000 on roulette in a single hour.

76-77, **Queen's Birthday:** there was no newspaper in Dawson to record the Queen's Birthday Celebration of 1898, the first issue of the *Klondike Nugget* appearing three weeks later. The following year, hower, *The Nugget* reported the celebration in detail. Winning distances, heights, and times for sporting events were: shot put—33.7 feet, tossing caber—47, running high jump—4.10, foot race (100 yards)—11 $^2/^5$ seconds. Edward Ross won the Sword Dance and Bert Ford the Sack Race. *Klondike Nugget*, Saturday, May 27, 1899, p.1.

78, **Fred Burnham:** for his version of this journey see his *Scouting on Two Continents* pp. 268-269.

78, **Thatched House Club:** formerly the Thatched House Tavern, situated at 86 St. James's Street. Two successive buildings, both called the Thatched House Tavern, had stood on the site. The third, erected in 1865, opened as the Civil Service Club. It was modified in 1873 and changed its name to the Thatched House Club. For many years its members were recruited largely from the Civil Service but also included military men, explorers, and big game hunters. Around 1950, its name was changed to the Union Club.

78, **Arctic Brotherhood:** founded at Skagway in 1899 by Captain William A. Connell of the ship "City of Seattle." Local chapters were soon established in nearly every community in Alaska. A number of Canadians, mostly Klondikers, were included as members. In 1909, President William Howard Taft was initiated with the title of "Honorary Grand Arctic Chief." Colby, p. 183; Nichols, pp. 239, 329-332. The Prince of Wales, later King Edward VII, may have received a similar honorary membership but no record of it appears to have survived. However, many of the King's papers were destroyed after his death, according to the Royal Archives, Windsor Castle, "and it is quite possible that these included any records of his membership, if he was indeed a member of the Brotherhood."

**79, British Museum tiger:** labeled "Manchuria" but registered as from Mongolia, this specimen skin was purchased from Rowland Ward & Company, London taxidermists and natural history suppliers, in 1897, according to a Museum spokesman, and was mounted beside a tiger from Central India.

**80, Jimmy Carey:** sometimes spelled "Kerry." See Berton, *Klondike Fever*, pp. 389-392.

**81, beach claims:** said to be as small as 20 feet square. Gruening, p. 114. Henry W. Clark, p. 109, says that a million dollars was taken from the beach in two months, while Wharton, p. 267, states that eleven million ounces of gold were eventually taken from the Nome Beach sands, an amount equivalent to the entire output of the Klondike.

**83-86, John and Molly Dexter:** John is described by Rex Beach in *Appleton's Booklovers Magazine*, p. 5 as "a crippled trader and squaw man . . . as strong hearted a pioneer as ever blazed a trail." Dexter Creek near Nome was named for him. Sullivan, pp. 215-230, who lived at the mission on Golovin Bay and knew them both intimately, tells the story of John and Molly Dexter in greater detail.

The term "squaw man" was applied to whites who took Eskimo or Indian women as legal or de facto wives. According to Jed Jordan, p. 171, who was there, most resident white men in Arctic Alaska at the time of the Nome stampede had such wives or had sampled the charms of Eskimo women, they being regarded as highly satisfactory sex mates. Jordan, who knew them well, has a great deal to say about John and Molly Dexter. From his account and Mrs. Sullivan's, Dexter emerges as something less than the all-time sentimental favorite among northern traders but nevertheless a major figure who won the friendship and respect of natives and white men. Molly comes through as a remarkable person with genuinely heroic qualities.

**89, Wyatt Earp:** "I knew Wyatt Earp very well while he was in Nome," Frank R. Martin wrote during the 1960s. "He was a tame Duck because we had a few tough hombres here at the time and Earp kept his place at the Dexter Bar. . . . No, Earp was never connected with the fraudulent crowd. . . . I really don't see why people want to write up so much about that Bum, as he was Just a Fake to me. . . . The only thing he had here was a ½ interest in the Dexter Saloon here in Nome, in 1900, 1901. After 1902 he left Nome for good, by 1902 Nome was to [sic] slow for him so he pull [sic] stick and left. So be sure of that he had no connection whatsoever with any Peace Officers here, so anyone tells you he was a Officer here he is wrong."

Judge E. Coke Hill of Oakland, California, who knew Earp in Nome remembered him as a quiet man who went unobtrusively about his business.

A search of Nome newspapers reveals only the following mention of Wyatt Earp, an advertisement from the *Nome News* of Oct. 9, 1899:

THE DEXTER
Front Street
Hoxsie & Earp, Props.
The Finest and Largest Saloon North
of Seattle

**89, Arthur Eaton:** in the 1950s Fred Schroder was president of the San Francisco-Oakland Alaska-Yukon Sourdough Association, Arthur Eaton its vice president.

91, **H.M.H. Bolander:** his Chicago-based corporation was acquired by the American Tobacco Company in 1904.

92, **barter furs:** "They got their fur cheap, for if an Indian wanted a rifle, they stood it on the floor and the Indians stacked their skins to the top of the rifle. . . . Robbers, I say they were." Heller, p. 73.

92, **Indian Point:** the American name for the Russian and Eskimo settlement at Point Chaplin, Siberia, and for the promontory itself.

94-95, **sea otter:** the surround was a traditional method of hunting sea otter. Elliott, pp. 127-144.

95, **Winchesters:** the lever-action .40-65, along with the .40-82 and the .45-90 firing a 300-grain bullet, were popular game rifles of the 1880s, being displaced in the 1890s by the all-time Winchester favorite, the Model 94, or "Winchester .30-30"—priced at $18 in 1894. The Model 94 was followed by the versatile Model 95 chambered for the .303 British (which Schroder used in China) as well as for the U.S. Government .30 and the .30-40 Krag calibers.

The .40-65, or Model 86, was also made in calibers .45-70, .45-90, .40-70, and .50-100. Harold F. Williamson, *Winchester: The Gun that Won the West*, p. 62.

96, **London Fur Auction:** according to the Hudson's Bay Company, approximately 408 sea otter pelts were offered on the London market at the regular March sale of 1902. The average price per skin, all grades including pups, was £76.18.1 or around $385. However, by 1910, the last year in which otter hunting was legal, the price of a first-grade skin reached $2,500 to $3,000, believed to be an all-time high for an animal's skin.

97, **blue or glacier bear:** *(Euarctos americanus)* is a subspecies of the American black bear. A well-known specimen named Peter, captured at the head of Disenchantment Bay, resided at the National Zoological Park in Washington, D.C., from 1917 to 1941.

97, **Mrs. Havemayer:** wife of Henry Osborne Havemayer, who organized the American Sugar Refining Company in 1891 and was an officer and director of numerous banks and industrial corporations.

98, **Big Bonanza:** a contemporary account of the staking and development of the famous mine is given by Wickersham, pp. 426-427.

### III. Caravans in China and Mongolia

105, **Nine Banners:** more accurately eight, referring to the eight divisions of the Mongol (Manchu) army that conquered China in the seventeenth century and whose descendants maintained their identity as long as the Manchu Empire lasted. Anderson's *The Atrocious Crime of Being a Young Man* is a fascinating personal record of the China of this period.

106, **Tom Cobbs:** his pierhead privy enterprise is also described by Anderson, pp. 24-25, and Heller, pp. 147-148.

106, **British-American Tobacco Company:** today one of the world's largest multinational corporations. Under its new name of B.A.T. Industries Limited it is based in London, has 150,000 employees, revenues of more than 10 billion, deals in tobacco products, perfumes and cosmetics, and retailing including ownership of department stores.

106, **J.A. Thomas:** has given an account of his Chinese experiences in both his books.

111, **Frederick Townsend Ward (1831-1862):** commanded a mixed force of European and Philippine Spanish mercenaries employed by wealthy citizens of Shanghai to protect that city against the Taiping rebels. After he was killed in action against the rebellious Chinese, a young British officer named Charles George Gordon was named to command Ward's polyglot force. With the help of imperial Manchu troops, Gordon put down the rebellion, thus earning the nickname "Chinese."

111, **Pearl Buck:** see her *My Several Worlds* pp. 19-63, 108-109.

114, **Frans August Larson:** much has been written about the Kalgan of these days. One of the best accounts is in his own *Larson: Duke of Mongolia.*

114, **fossilized dinosaurs:** see also Larson, pp. 280-283, and Andrews' *On the Trail of Ancient Man,* pp. 16, 96-104.

115, **Peking:** Thomson, pp. 99-107, describes the turmoil in Peking at this period, when many observers felt another Boxer Uprising might be developing. See also Wright, p. 438.

115, **James Lafayette Hutchison:** later an executive of the J. Walter Thompson Advertising Agency and author of *China Hand.*

116, **transporting money:** as Carl Crow explains it in *Foreign Devils in the Flowery Kingdom,* pp. 54-60: "Thousands of [British-American Tobacco Company] retail dealers at regular intervals counted out their cash and carried it to the local city dealer in payment for the goods they had bought. The city dealers packed boxes of silver dollars, bank notes or subsidiary coins and delivered them to the nearest office of the B.A.T. Often the foreigner in charge of the office had to employ guards and personally escort the money through miles of bandit-infested territory."

118-119, **Boxer Rebellion:** for more about the origin of the Boxer Rebellion in the Pao-ting-fu area, see *The Boxer Uprising,* pp. 1-2; also Krausse, p. 159, and Clements pp. 82, 190. In the fall of 1976, following the death of Mao Tse-tung, Pao-ting-fu lived up to its reputation as a focal point for disturbance. It became a center for armed resistance against the ruling Chinese Communist regime headed by the new party chairman, Hua Kuo-feng.

119, **silver shoes:** may date from as early as the thirteenth century. Though usually of silver they were sometimes of gold. Bronze knife money dates from the seventh to the second century B.C. and probably originated in China. Yang, pp. 1-5, 46-47; Burns, p. 50; Rockhill, p. 3.

119, **cash:** older than shoes, the cash, or round money with the square hole in its center, dated from before the time of Christ. Its symbolism was "round as the [encompassing] sky and square as the earth." Burns, p. 51.

120, **beggars and thieves:** Thomas tells of enjoying similar protection, *Tobacco Merchant,* pp. 175-176.

120, **Standard Oil Company:** *Kong-lee hung-lung,* literally, "Universal profit and great prosperity company."

121-122, **Chinese Jews:** oral tradition dates their arrival in China as early as the first century A.D. Cordier, I, p. 347. According to the *Encylopedia Judaica,* V, pp. 467-468 the first authentic evidence of Jewish settlement in China dates from the 8th century A.D. An ancient Jewish community at Kaifeng, some distance south of Pao-ting-fu, originated in the 9th or 10th century. According to Solomon Grayzel, pp. 749-750, native Jews survived in China until the upheavals of World War II.

123, **Pao-ting-fu sacked:** see Thomson, pp. 99-107.

124, **B.A.T. funds:** William Ashley Anderson writes: "I first met Schroder in Tientsin in the fall of 1911 during the Chinese Revolution when all north China was in an uproar—cities being burned and looted. All of our men had been called in from the field to the safety of the Treaty Port, Schroder among them. He had currently distinguished himself by safeguarding the transport of a large quantity of silver dollars by train from Pao-ting-fu to Peking."

130, **pack camels:** in Chinese-operated caravans were usually tied eight to the string and led by a man on foot.

134, **wooden carts:** there is a drawing of one of these carts harnessed to a sheep in Tannahill, p.176.

134, **zigzagging:** Larson, pp. 224-226, gives his account of the border hostilities of this period and the hazards of caravanning through them, as does Bawden, pp. 188-205. See also Appendix II.

136, **bought and sold:** B.A.T. did business on a strictly cash basis. Money was deposited in Kalgan banks before goods left the warehouses there. Money dispatched from Urga usually came in the form of a draft through a Russian or Chinese correspondent bank in Tientsin.

136, **ceremonial headdress:** Ossendowski, p. 280, describes this or a similar headdress, likening it to a "royal crown."

136, **Hutukhtu of Urga:** Larson, who knew the Hutukhtu intimately over a period of many years, admired him greatly, terming him both childlike and sagacious. Larson, pp. 111-134. The *Encyclopedia Britannica,* Eleventh Edition, XXVII, p. 795, called him a drunken profligate.

136, **model "T" Ford:** Le Munyon's account of this is in the *National Geographic* for May, 1913, pp. 641-670.

137, **"Horse Gate":** more precisely, "morin-am" is Mongolian for "horse gateway."

137, **200,000 Chinese:** probably an exaggeration. Thomas, *Tobacco Merchant,* p. 183, puts the number at 45,000.

138, **Tashi Lama:** a rare reference to the Sixth Tashi Lama being at Kumbum earlier than 1923 when he visited there while fleeing from Tibet to China. Richardson, p. 127; Enders, pp. 218-220.

138, **Hutukhtu of Lama Miao:** William Ashley Anderson, who knew them both, tell of the Bogdo's intimacy with Schroder.

139, **Larson:** pp. 227-236, tells of his advisorship to both Chinese and Mongol governments.

139, **bandage cloth:** Enders, p. 138, and Ossendowski, p.110, also describe such wrapping.

139, **Lama Miao:** also called Dolon-Nor.

141-143, **Rubbens' Valley:** for more on the border settlement of the Belgian Catholic Fathers, see Appendix III.

143, **ungelded mules:** in the U.S. mules are usually gelded.

144, **Shensi province:** Nichols wrote at about this time, *Through Hidden Shensi*, p.1, "In the northwest corner of China is a province called Shensi. Its area is greater than that of England and Scotland combined. Its population is nearly eight millions. It is old and isolated; so old that no one in China knows the story of its beginning, and so isolated that the Pekingese speak of it as though it were a foreign country."

145, **collected information:** Enders, p. 230, discusses this kind of intelligence gathering by lamas.

146, **stone tablet:** according to the Metropolitan Museum of Art, N.Y., an exact replica of the Nestorian Stone (original still in Sian) was on loan in the museum from 1908 to 1916. In 1917 the replica was taken to Rome where it is now exhibited in the Lateran. There is a plaster cast of the stone at Yale University.

147-148, **pyramids:** the long known but little publicized pyramids and large burial mounds of the Sian region are probably imperial tombs. The oldest are believed by some authorities to date from the third century B.C. and perhaps earlier (see Appendix IV). Professors Charles D. Weber of the University of Southern California and James Cahill of the University of California at Berkeley, who visited the Sian area in 1973 at the invitation of the Chinese government, saw pyramids and burial mounds of enormous size. Dr. Laurence Sickman, director of the William Rockhill Nelson Gallery and Atkins Museum of Fine Arts, Kansas City, first heard of such a large pyramid as Schroder describes while with the U.S. Fourteenth Air Force in China during W. W. II.

148, **maps/Lanchow:** old maps show Tibet beginning about fifty miles west of Lanchow. Tibet was at the time a largely autonomous region. Lanchow is today a center for Chinese nuclear energy and arms production.

149, **licorice:** Thomas, *Tobacco Merchant*, pp. 76-77, says sixteen thousand tons were shipped.

149, **Kumbum Monastery:** "Kumbum means 'ten thousand images' and refers to the famous tree which, it is said, sprang from Tsong Khapa's hair and whose leaves thereafter were inscribed by Tibetan characters with religious significance." MacGregor, p. 235. Kumbum is also discussed by Shakabpa. The present Dalai Lama was born nearby. See also Huc and Gabet; Rockhill; David-Neel, *Magic and Mystery in Tibet.*

150, **hot bath:** Tibetan aversion to bathing was traditional. Enders, p. 126. In Mongolia a similar aversion was attributed to the superstition that anyone who bathed all over at one time would turn into a fish. Larson, p. 38. This superstition probably stemmed from the days of Jenghis Khan who supposedly forbade the use of water for bathing, in arid Mongolia, so that it could be conserved for people and domestic animals to drink.

151, **Tashi Lama:** his geniality and friendliness toward foreigners were noted by many observers. David-Neel *My Journey to Lhasa*, p. xiii; Enders, p. 248; Bell pp. 84-85.

151, **Tree of Faces:** a subject of much comment by foreign visitors who disagreed widely as to what its leaves supposedly or actually revealed. See Appendix V.

152, **ladders:** Huc, p. 76, says he and Gabet used them to climb to the roofs of houses to watch the Kumbum lamas pray.

152, **gold in Tibet:** Huc, p. 116, metions gold dust from the Kokonor (Kumbum) region being sent as tribute to Peking. Rockhill, p. 46, saw "large parties of gold washers" near Kumbum; he also mentions the "gold-roofed temple", p. 66. Enders, pp. 267-277, discusses Tibet's actual and potential gold production at about this period.

152-153, **Kumbum library:** Huc and Gabet, p. 62, give a similar description of it but say its copyists used "little sticks of bamboo cut in the form of a pen."

153, **clay discs:** Ossendowski, p. 277, saw similar clay tablets with hieroglyphic inscriptions at the monastery library at Urga a few years later.

154, **museum at Kumbum:** the Kumbum "treasure-house" contained "bowls of silver, ewers of gold, images of the gods in gold, silver, and bronze, pictures, beautifully illuminated manuscripts, carpets, satin hangings, cloisonne vases and incense-burners, enough for a museum!" Rockhill, pp. 68-69.

155, **metabolism:** the coolness of the yogi when yoga is complete is cited by Gopi, p. 163.

156, **clairvoyants:** Robert Ekvall, pp. 26, 41-42, explains the presence of what we call "magic" as an essential dimension of Tibetan life. Garma C. C. Chang explains how clairvoyance and out-of-body travel and perception can be achieved through the advanced practice of yoga, as does Yogi Ramacharaka, pp. 99-104, 189-205. W.Y. Evans-Wentz's *The Tibetan Book of the Dead* and *Tibetan Yoga and Secret Doctrines* are classics on the subject of Tibetan psychic phenomena. See especially the latter, pp. 22-25. David-Neel lived for a number of years in Tibet and studied its occult doctrines. In her *Magic and Mystery in Tibet*, p. 28, she describes the double or "ethereal self" that can "leave the material body" and while invisible can "accomplish various peregrinations." Ostrander and Schroeder discuss clairvoyance and out-of-body travel via the telepathic or "hypnotic" trance or "sleep," pp. 220, 305. "In this state of telepathic hypnosis, the subjects know about events happening at a great distance from themselves." And, p. 108, "as soon as the telepathic 'wake up' is sent, trance becomes less and less deep, full consciousness returning in twenty to thirty seconds."

Ossendowski, p. 278, quotes the Hutukhtu of Urga as saying (circa 1919) that lama clairvoyants had been numerous and widespread but were diminishing in number as faith and discipline declined.

157, **trance walking:** Evans-Wentz, in *Tibetan Yoga and Secret Doctrines,* pp. 22-25, and David-Neel in *Magic and Mystery in Tibet,* pp. 199-216, describe similar instances of gliding or "rapid walking" (trance walking).

157, **death of Old Man:** see Appendix VI.

158, **Herbert Hoover:** traveled by horseback to Urga where he found the Living God "riding a bicycle madly around an inner court in the great Tibetan Lamasery. He entertained us with a phonograph supplied with Russian records." *Memoirs,* I, p. 42. Hoover says nothing about a trans-Mongolian railroad but Larson, who talked with him in Kalgan, claims that Hoover surveyed the first or Peking-Kalgan section of such a road and that this section was later built by the Chinese government using data Hoover collected. Larson, pp. 253-254.

159-160, **polo:** Afghans play a similar game using a headless calf as "ball." Bronowski, pp. 82-86.

161, **Dwight Eisenhower:** served as executive officer in the Fifteenth Infantry during the early stages of World War II. For more on the regiment's earlier activities in China, see Thomson, p. 86, and Reinsch, p. 282.

162, **Tientsin:** see also Anderson, pp. 77-85, and Thomson, pp. 99-107.

162-164, **sing-song house:** Anderson, p. 79, gives his version of this episode.

164, **escapades:** Schroder's sprees were often memorable. "He almost got us both killed one night in Kalgan," recalls William Ashley Anderson, "when the town was full of sullen and mutinous soldiers. We know now how dangerous such soldiery can be. We knew they were dangerous then but that made no difference to Schroder. He and I had been looking forward to an exciting winter, and then he received orders to leave Kalgan and return to the routine of Peking. He was furious and in a mood to take it out on anything in sight. We went to a Chinese theater where we sat in the middle of the first balcony. The theater was packed with excited soldiers jumping up and down and shouting to one another. This jumping up and down interfered with Schroder's view of the stage. We always carried heavy walking sticks as a defense against dogs, etc., so having yelled once without getting satisfaction, Schroder stood up and began to strike at every head within reach. We had a hard time getting out of there. When finally we were out and in the broad dusty street, fearfully empty at this hour, Schroder remembered he had a revolver, so he proceeded to shoot at every lamp and light in sight. Then we must go to the sing-song houses and make his farewells. When this began to get rough, I managed to calm him down long enough to tell him he was pulling a damned dirty trick on me because he was leaving town next day but I would have to live with the mess he left behind; and I went back home to the bungalow. He followed me not more than fifteen minutes later, a bit maudlin but very apologetic for having got me on a spot. The joke was on him, because next day the orders were changed: I was called down to Peking; he had to stay in Kalgan."

While recalling his great sense of fun and absolute fearlessness, William B. Christian, a veteran of forty-five years in China, many of them with B.A.T. in Peking, found Schroder admirable in other respects. "We used him frequently for special projects. He was a man of infinite resources. He could make a saddle or talk to a viceroy."

Other B.A.T. veterans such as J. W. G. Brodie and Hunter Mann concurred with Christian's judgment, Brodie finding Schroder "Wholly reliable and agreeable" during several years' close association in B.A.T.'s "Frontier Division." But G.T. Bridgman, a mining engineer, who traveled with Schroder as guide in China and Siberia, did not like him much (the feeling was mutual) and said he stretched the truth at times, as did Oscar Mamen, Schroder's B.A.T. colleague in Mongolia. Anderson rebuts this by saying Schroder was capable of almost anything, including a good story. "He once successfully operated on one of his caravan crew members with a pocketknife, thus earning the nickname 'Doc' by which he was known to our border crowd. I saw him throw a champion Mongol wrestler nearly twice his size by use of a crotch hold learned from Frank Gotch in Dawson. One day in Kalgan he introduced me to the Grand Lama of Lama Miao, his close friend. He was not like the adventurers of the Adventurers Club who keep a careful record of their often too meager exploits. He lived for each passing hour, enjoyed it fully, and it was reward enough."

J. A. Thomas arranged a pension for him when he retired and apparently regarded him highly, as did Frans August Larson.

My own feeling is that although Schroder never let a good story down, he was on the whole truthful and extraordinarily perceptive. He was perhaps above all else an enhancer of life, one of those who form the center wherever people gather. He made unforgettable impressions. I've known few men more widely liked by both men and women.

165, **Peace in Urga and Peking:** see Larson, pp. 117-234.

165, **caravan:** originating at Suchow in far-western Kansu province, this caravan would have covered nearly fifteen hundred miles by the time it reached Kuei-hua-cheng, following the direct or desert route north of the Yellow River.

166, **Black grouse:** also found in western Europe.

166, **Arthur Sowerby:** see *Through Shen-Kan* by Clark and Sowerby, also Appendix VII.

167, **Père David's deer:** specimens had been sent to England and other countries prior to the Boxer Rebellion. Today *Elaphurus davidianus,* with its thick, shaggy, yellowish-brown coat, may be seen at zoos in the U.S. and elsewhere and has been reintroduced into its native China. Unlike other deer, it sheds its horns twice annually. Some experts, including Dr. James M. Dolan, Jr., Curator of the San Diego, California, Zoo, think the milu was propagated in captivity in China for an incredible three thousand years and thus represents a species long extinct in its wild state.

167, **hairy wild man:** U.S. Supreme Court Justice William O. Douglas reported, National Geographic, Mar. 1962, p. 315, that during a trip into the wilds of Outer Mongolia he saw a movement in the brush and asked his native guide what it was. "Maybe it's Almas," the guide replied, explaining that "Almas" was the "Snowman of the Gobi," similar to the Abominable Snowman of the Himalayas, "shorter in stature than a man, fur covered and elusive." Owen Lattimore, *The Desert Road to Turkestan,* pp. 185-186, and Rockhill, pp.150-151, tell of the *jen-hsiung,* or man-bear (Lattimore's term) of western China and northern Tibet, Lattimore quoting others who refer to the creatures as "hairy wild men" or possibly a bear; Rockhill quoting accounts describing them as "wild men . . . covered with long hair, standing erect, and making tracks like men's." Similar creatures have been reported as far west as the Pamirs. Heuvelmans, p. 180. Writing in a recent issue of *The Atlantic,* the zoologist Edward W. Cronin, Jr., positively identifies the *yeti* of the Himalayan region as a large hairy ape.

168-169, **ginseng:** The first trade between the U.S. and China was in ginseng. As Carl Crow tells it, *Foreign Devils,* pp. 17-18: "Less than three months after General Washington had watched the evacuation of the last British troops from New York, the frigate *Empress of China* sailed from that port on the long journey to Canton" with a cargo of Appalachian ginseng. The sailing was delayed so that it would occur on Washington's birthday, February 22, 1784. Around $210,000 was said to have been invested in the enterprise. Ginseng has continued to be prized for its energizing properties, especially in recent years. The Russians, for example, are reported to be giving it to their athletes and astronauts as a health tonic, and its use in the U.S. has skyrocketed, especially in California.

169-170, **Siberian tigers:** see also Digby, p. 195.

169-170, **lions in British East Africa:** brought construction of the Mombasa-Nairobi railroad to a halt and troops were employed against them. Patterson, pp. 90, 81.

170, **gold prospects:** a "Siberian Klondike" was discovered a few years later in 1922 north of the Amur River near Aldan in the Yakutsk Autonomous Republic.

171, **tigers:** at the mouth of the Ganges, Bengal tigers swam between mainland and offshore islands and raised their cubs by preference in the seclusion of one particular island, says Jennison, pp. 94-95. Numerous instances of tigers swimming in salt and fresh water are given by Burton and Digby.

172, **tigers killed U.S. soldiers during the Korean War:** as they did more recently in the Vietnam War.

174, **Indian opium:** British opium dealers pressured China into buying some 3,000 chests, each containing about 140 pounds of opium, at a cost of $20 million, says La Motte, p. 127.

176, **point of his shoulder:** stalking a sleeping tiger, and the deadly shot behind the shoulders, are also described by Burton, pp. 200-201.

176, **Siberian or Manchurian tigers:** adult males average 10 feet 4 inches from nose to tip of tail, according to the *Guinness Book of World Records,* 1976. They stand 39-42 inches at the shoulder and weigh about 585 pounds. The heaviest recorded specimen was killed near the Amur River in 1933. It weighed 770 pounds. In 1970, the total population of wild Siberian tigers was estimated at only 160 to 170 animals and they were under strict protection.

178, **Wire tapping:** Thomas, *Tobacco Merchant,* pp.186-187, describes this.

186, **murder of Grant:** since Thomas and Larson also claim credit for the recovery of Grant's remains, we may question the accuracy of Schroder's account of Grant's murder and Malunga's death. Quite possibly all three men were involved in the affair. Certainly Grant's murder was front page news in the Far East. Larson, pp. 226-227; Thomas, *Tobacco Merchant,* pp.183-185; *North-China Herald,* Sept. 20, 1913, p. 888.

192, **International Red Cross . . . thousand camel caravan:** see Appendix IX.

192, **Roy Anderson:** his influence was widely recognized. See for instance Reinsch, pp. 12-13, and Hutchison, p. 57.

193, **illegitimate son:** described as a "cousin" of the Kaiser, he was "a baron resembling the German Emperor in appearance," who had squandered his inheritance, then saved himself from ruin by marrying an American heiress. Finding life together incompatible, they reached an agreement whereby the baron received an income so long as he remained within a 100-mile radius of Peking. He wore a monocle in his left eye and a green Italian fedora cocked over his left ear. Hutchison, p. 57.

193, **Admiral Paul von Hintze:** earlier a naval attaché at St. Petersburg and Minister to Mexico, was later Germany's Secretary of State for Foreign Affairs and a key figure in the Kaiser's abdication. See also Baumont, p. 56, for his stoker's disguise.

194, **Baikal tunnels:** see Appendix VIII.

195, **June 30 meeting:** was held at the Kiangsu Guild Hall, according to Reinsch, p. 273.

197, **ceremony:** Pu-Yi in his autobiography, Paul Kramer, ed., pp. 88-93, mentions the Great Seal but no ceremony other than "an audience" with Chang Hsun. Reinsch, p. 274, states that a formal ceremony was conducted in the Throne Room.

198-99, **Manchu restoration:** for more see Appendix X.

199, **General Li Chin Hsi:** see also Thomson, p. 285.

199, **Shih-kia-chwang:** Keyte, pp. 184-185, tells of its strategic importance and describes the B.A.T. representative there.

199, **6,000 men:** an eyewitness puts the figure at 4,000 "ill-equipped troops." Weale, p. 204.

199, **Japanese intervention:** its possibility was openly discussed in news accounts of the restoration. See Appendix X.

199, **dragon flags:** the dragon symbolized the creative forces of the universe.

202, **Peking fighting:** Andersson, pp. 156-159, speaking as an eyewitness, describes how the walls were breached and cannon placed in the openings.

202, **Chang Hsun:** by Chang's account he was named regent. Johnston, p. 156.

202, **bad press:** Schroder may be correct. Contemporary press accounts emphasized the rumor that German agents had instigated and were participating in the restoration, and played up the allegedly reactionary nature of the coup, while playing down the sincere motivation of some of its leaders. See Appendix X.

202, **Reinsch:** gives his account of the restoration pp. 272-285.

202-203, **Kang Yu-Wei:** his role in the restoration is discussed at greater length by Jung-Pang Lo (q.v.) and by Johnston, p. 136.

204, **our adversaries:** many authorities credit the military intervention of General Tuan Ch'i-jui, based at Tientsin, as decisive in the failure of the restoration. Hsu, p. 575.

204, **armistice terms:** are reflected in contemporary newspaper accounts, Appendix X, also by Reinsch, Close, and others.

207, **payoff:** Close, p. 8, says that $70,000 was provided for the payoff. Reinsch, p. 285, says it came to $80 per man. Contemporary press accounts, *North-China Herald,* July 21, 1917, p. 131, speak of $80,000 borrowed from the Yokohama Specie Bank.

207, **disguise:** priestly or similar status-giving disguise was often used by foreigners—e.g. Hans Nordewin von Koerber crossing Central Asia from Siberia to India, David-Neel in Tibet, Van der Putte, Moorcroft, Nain Singh and others in China and Tibet. MacGregor, pp. 103,104, 251-252, 283.

208, **Manchu Restoration:** an authoritative account of the restoration is given by Johnston, later Pu-Yi's tutor, pp. 131-140, but Johnston was not personally a witness to it. Schroder's appears to be the only full account by a participant. See also Brackman, pp. 85-101, and Kramer, pp. 86-94.

209, **boy emperor:** in 1950 Pu-Yi was returned to China for trial as a war criminal, was pardoned by Chinese Communist authorities in 1959, and later worked for them as a historical researcher. He died in 1967.

209, **Japanese influence:** "To review the history of China's swift degeneration from the time of Yuan Shih-kai's death to the present would serve no purpose. . . . Suffice it to say that, with China in a satisfactory state of confusion and demoralization, Japan commenced to establish her own hold upon the Chinese government and the Chinese Army by actual purchase in 1917, and that, by the spring of 1920, she had invested approximately £20,000,000 on little or no security, and had gained absolute control of the recognized Government . . ." Gilbert, p. 253.

Reinsch observed prophetically: "The whole course of Japan in China during the Great War alarmed both Chinese and foreigners. The aims and methods of Japan's military policy in the Continent of Asia can bring good to no one, least of all to the Japanese people, notwithstanding any temporary gains . . ." Reinsch, pp. 333-335.

210, **Oscar Mamen:** survived to die in an auto accident in Kenya years later.

# APPENDIX

## I. Alaska-Yukon Pioneers.

According to records in the Yukon Archives at Whitehorse, the Yukon Order of Pioneers was founded December 1, 1894 at Fortymile. Its original officers were L.N. (Jack) McQuesten, president; F. Dinsmore, vice president; William McPhee, treasurer. At first membership was limited to persons entering the Yukon watershed prior to January 1, 1889. This limitation was later relaxed. Y.O.O.P. members shown in the photograph on page 100 taken at Fortymile in 1895 are among the sixty-eight charter members of the Fortymile Lodge. Lodges were established later at Circle City and Dawson, the latter remaining active today.

The following list of Alaska-Yukon pioneers, found among Fred Schroder's papers and revised with help from Crystal Morgan, Jack McQuesten's daughter, includes some who were not members of Y.O.O.P.

| Name | Date of Entry |
|------|---------------|
| 1. L.N. (Jack) McQuesten | 1873 |
| 2. Al Mayo | 1873 |
| 3. Andy Harper | 1873 |
| 4. Fred Hart | 1873 |
| 5. Gordon Bettles | 1888 (1887?) |
| 6. Andrew J. Maiden | 1886 |
| 7. George Friend | 1889 (1890?) |
| 8. F.A. Jones | 1894 |
| 9. K. Gilbert | ? |
| 10. George Carmack | 1886 |
| 11. Bob Henderson | 1893 |
| 12. Bill Hayes | 1888 (1883?) |
| 13. Johnny O'Donnell | 1887 |
| 14. Charley Anderson | 1888 (1897?) |
| 15. Joe McGuire | 1888 |
| 16. Billy Robinson | 1888 |
| 17. Gus Williams | 1888 |
| 18. Victor La Rue | 1887 |
| 19. Louie Cotey | 1886 |
| 20. Joe Ladue | 1886 |
| 21. Bob J. English | 1887 (1886?) |
| 22. Bill McPhee | 1885 (1888?) |
| 23. Fred Beauleau | 1890 (1885?) |
| 24. Felix Pedro | 1894 |
| 25. Manuel Gularte | 1894 |
| 26. Fred Schroder | 1894 |
| 27. Chilean Joe (Navarro?) | 1889 (1888?) |
| 28. Jim Lovett | 1885 |
| 29. George Matlock | 1889 (1887?) |
| 30. Sid Wilson | 1889 (1888) |

| 31. Floyd Wilson | 1894 |
| 32. Pete Wilson | 1894 |
| 33. Ned Gagnon | 1887 |
| 34. Dudley McKinney | 1892 |
| 35. Casper Ellinger | 1893 |
| 36. Jim B. Chronister | 1892 |
| 37. Frank (Fred H.?) Bowker | 1888 |
| 38. Frank Bennett | 1888 |
| 39. Nelson Picotte | 1888 (1886?) |
| 40. Tom O'Brien | 1888 (1886?) |
| 41. Jim O'Brien | 1892 (1890?) |
| 42. Fred Johnson | 1894 (1888?) |
| 43. Al Morenci (Morancy?) | 1888 (1889?) |
| 44. Charley Columbe (Columbia?) | 1888 (1889?) |
| 45. Hank Wright | 1890 |
| 46. Tom Young | 1888 (1894?) |
| 47. Jim O'Neil | 1890 |
| 48. John Nelson | 1886 |
| 49. Bill Lloyd | 1888 |
| 50. L. La Flem | ? |
| 51. H.H. Hart | 1886 |
| 52. Harry Rivers | 1895 |
| 53. Skiff Mitchell | 1886 |

## II. Correspondence Concerning the Mongol-Chinese War, 1912-1915.

Urga, Mongolia
January 8, 1913

W.A. Anderson, Esq.
B.A.T. Co.
Kalgan

Dear Mr. Anderson,

I have your letter of Dec. 7th also your wire and letter of Dec. 23rd for which I thank you. The cigarettes have not arrived yet, but I hope they will be here in due time as nothing has happened to caravans on that road as far as I know. If you have got candles for me in Kalgan, please forward same as soon as possible. The 500 cases candles, which arrived here on Dec. 25th, were sold out before sunset that day and now Urga is dark again. The road between Kalgan and Urga is reported to me as safe, but we know very little about the rest of the world here in Urga, so I can not guarantee anything in that line. I believe the time is not far off, when all transportation between Kalgan and Urga will be cut off because of a lot of my friends up here are preparing for a trip down to Kalgan and you will very likely see some gentlemen down there going about and knocking at peoples' doors with their Mauser pistols. We have had enough of these people here and shall be glad to get rid of them. Mr. Larson left Urga for Kalgan yesterday with a big cartload of dogs;* he will be in Kalgan in 20 days if he does not freeze too much in [the] Gobi. I am quite alone here now and do not see other people than Mongols, Burriats, Russians and other rot. What is

[234]

to become of our business here in the future, I really do not know. I have asked the Living God about the future but he did not know much more than anybody else. At present everything is peaceful here. My best wishes for a happy new year.

Very sincerely,

O. Mamen

[*possibly a code word for furs or silver]

*From William Ashley Anderson to William B. Christian, British-American Tobacco Co., Peking:*

Kalgan, January 12, 1913

Dear Chris,

You may put down any report of Russian troops being in Kalgan at the present time as false. That much I know; but as to any information of troops approaching from the north, I am afraid I cannot help you.

Strange to say, our knowledge of events in Mongolia is very slight, and the most we know is that the majority of reports in the Tientsin and Peking papers concerning affairs here are wrong. I think it probable that Cossacks have moved into Inner Mongolia, and certainly a great many Chinese soldiers have gone *out* of Kalgan, and up to the plateau, with mountain guns, automobile transports, and all munitions.

Larson, who is returning now from Urga across the Gobi, has written to Mrs. Larson here that war is apparently inevitable; and that the Mongols are reviving their ancient fanatic belief that they are predestined conquerors. Russian officers are drilling large bodies of Mongol troops in Urga; but recently, when some foreigners attempted to photograph them, all cameras and equipment were seized by the Russians and confiscated. As Mr. Larson is desirous of not having his name connected even remotely with Mongolian affairs, I hope you will not mention his name unnecessarily in this connection; but you may be sure that whatever he says on the subject is probably more authoritative than the opinion of any other foreigner in the East. I expect to get some more explicit information from him as soon as he arrives.

Several Chinese soldiers were recently executed here for highway robbery, and some of our dealers report that countrymen are not coming to town to purchase for fear of soldiers and fighting, but as far as I can ascertain everything is as quiet as can be expected.

No local preparations have been made for the defense of Kalgan, and if it becomes necessary to fight to keep it, the fighting will probably all be on the plateau around Hunorfsas . . .

Give my bestest to Ki . . .
Very Sincerely,

W.A. Anderson

## III. References to Belgian Catholic Priests in China.

The activities of Belgian Catholic priests in China are discussed by James A. Walsh in his *Observations in the Orient*, p. 143, and by Upton Close in his *In the Land of the Laughing Buddha*, p. 159. The central headquarters of the "Scheut Fathers" was at Brussels. They were also active in the Congo, the Philippines, and in various Central and South American countries. Their settlement on the China-Mongolia border is dealt with in *Bibliotheca Missionum*, vol. XIII, pp. 104-105, in Carlo van Melckebeke's *Service Social de L'eglise en Mongolie* (Brussels: 1969) p. 140, and there is a bibliographical note on Father (P. Edmundus) Rubbens in *Bibliotheca Missionum*, vol. XIV, p. 500, and in the *Bulletin Cath. de Pékin*, XVI (1929) pp. 501-502.

## IV. References to Pyramids and Tombs of Shensi Province.

An early twentieth-century traveler in the Sian region reported:

"The mounds were all pyramidal in shape. They were made of a kind of clay, apparently a different material from the loess of the plains. Their sides were covered with a verdure of coarse grass and low bushes. Although the action of time and the elements had partly obliterated the former angularity of the outline of the mounds, their original shape was still plainly discernible. They were all square pyramids about eighty feet in height . . . The four base lines of the pyramids are of equal length, usually about 300 feet. It seemed as though the intention were apparent in their construction to have the sides four square with the points of the compass. The road from Sian to San Yuan runs directly north, and as we passed a succession of mounds on on either side of it, I noticed that we were always confronted by the face of the pyramid, and never by one of its corners. The base lines of its northern and southern sides were invariably at right angles to the road. I found also that, although scattered over an area of ten square miles, the corresponding sides of any two of the pyramids always faced the same way. Although I did not test accurately their points of direction, I am strongly of the opinion that lines drawn at right angles with the four bases of the sides of any of the pyramids would lead directly north, east, south, and west.

" The mounds have always been held in great veneration by the people of the surrounding country. They are situated in the midst of a plain where until the famine every square foot of ground was in demand for cultivation, yet no crop was ever sown or reaped on the sides of the mounds.

" They were regarded as mysteries, and consequently it would be bad luck for any one to attempt to dig into them. The Sianese explain them by saying that they mark the burial-places either of some of the early emperors or of the great characters in Chinese history. It was formerly the custom when an emperor died to place his body in an immense tomb, in which his wives and several hundreds of his servants were buried with him in order that they might accompany him to the spirit-world. Over the whole structure was built an immense mound. These tombs of emperors

[236]

are found in various parts of China, usually near a city which was once the capital.

" But to my mind this theory does not satisfactorily explain the mounds of the plain of Sian. More than most nations the Chinese keep a careful record of their monuments. An accurate knowledge of the places where the great ones of antiquity are buried is part of the ancestor-worship of the country. If each of the Shensi mounds covered the tomb of an emperor the fact would be generally known, and a tablet recording the fact would be placed near it. But such is not the case. No inscription of any kind is found near the pyramids. Grimly silent, they rise from the plain as though guarding some secret of the past too sacred even for the Sons of Han. The shape of the mounds, too, is another objection to the idea that they are the burial-places of emperors. Over an emperor's tomb was usually piled a huge heap of earth of indiscriminate size and shape that in time assumed a rounding oval form, not unlike a natural hillock. But the pyramid, or anything like it, was never attempted. The pyramid is rare in Chinese architecture, although the tapering octagonal tower of the pagoda may be an evolution from it.

" A member of our party on the Han River was a scholar and teacher from Sian, who was exceptionally well informed on the history and monuments of China. In speaking one day of the mounds of the Sian plain, he said that they might have been the altars of the primitive religion that once prevailed over China . . . For several thousand years prior to the birth of Confucius, 551 BC, Shang Ti, the One and Supreme God, was worshipped in China. As the oldest province Shensi would naturally contain more evidences of the former faith that any other part of the Empire." Nichols, *Through Hidden Shensi,* pp. 234-246.

At about the time Nichols was writing, two other observers reported: "The following day, after crossing two more plateaux, and winding up and down several deep valleys, the party reached Chung-pu Hsien [northwest of Sian], close to which is situated a huge mound, supposed to be the grave of the great Huang Ti, or Yellow Emperor (BC 2700), one of the five mythical emperors of Chinese history. The mound was noticed certainly, but so great is it, that we actually took it for a hill. A large grove of cypress trees, planted near the town in memory of the same monarch, was also observed." Clark and Sowerby, *Through Shen-Kan,* pp. 36-37.

E.T.C. Werner in *Autumn Leaves,* pp. 250-253, describes pyramids in the Sian region visited in the 1920s and surveyed and plotted by Moore-Bennett. The dimensions of the most massive one examined, said to be the tomb of Emperor Shih-huang-ti, was situated near Lintung a few miles east of Sian. Its sides measured 1,320, 1,228, 1,295, and 1,365 feet at the base, with indications that their original widths had been more than 1,500 feet. Its height was 78 feet with indications of having been higher. It was made of alternate layers of debris (waste from tile furnaces, slag, broken tile, animal bones, small pieces of earthenware, etc.) and earth (loess) beaten and compressed.

The "rediscovery" of a large pyramid near Sian from the air in 1947 by an American flyer attracted considerable attention, as evidenced by the following excerpt from the *New York Times* (Mar. 28, 1947, p. 3):

## U.S. FLIER REPORTS HUGE
## CHINESE PYRAMID
## IN ISOLATED MOUNTAINS
## SOUTHWEST OF SIAN

SHANGHAI, March 27 (U.P.)—A giant pyramid in isolated mountains of Shensi Province in western China was reported today by Col. Maurice Sheahan, Far Eastern Director for Trans World Airline.

From the air, Colonel Sheahan said, the pyramid seems to dwarf those of Egypt. He estimated its height at 1,000 feet and its width at the base at 1,500 feet.

The pyramid, he said, is at the foot of the Tsinling Mountains, about forty miles southwest of Sian, capital of the province. A second pyramid, he continued, appears much smaller.

The pyramid, Colonel Sheahan went on, is at the far end of a long valley, in an inaccessible part. At the near end, he said, are hundreds of small burial mounds. These can be seen, he said, from the Lung-Hai railroad.

"When I first flew over it, I was impressed by its perfect pyramidal form and its great size," Colonel Sheahan said. "I did not give it thought during the war years partly because it seemed incredible that anything so large could be unknown to the world.

"From the air we could see only small footpaths leading to a village at the site of the pyramid."

Chinese said that because of the almost complete absence of communications, even trails, in some parts of the West China mountains it was not impossible that a huge pyramid might have been long forgotten.

Colonel Sheahan from Ontario, California, has spent nine years in lesser-known areas of western China. First he was transportation adviser to the Chinese Government. During the war, as an American Army colonel, he was forward supply director for the Flying Tigers.

Dr. James L. Clark of the American Museum of Natural History and Dr. Arthur Upham Pope of the Asia Institute last night characterized the reported discovery of the Chinese pyramid as of great scientific interest.

Dr. Clark called it a "very significant find." Dr. Pope said the presence of such a pyramid was "entirely consistent with the earliest known phases of the Chinese religion.

"From what we know of the religion it might be expected that such a pyramid be discovered," he said. "It is undoubtedly the burial mound—composed of tamped earth—of a high potentate."

Dr. Phyllis Ackerman of the School for Asiatic Studies, New York, suggested that the story behind the Shensi pyramids "goes back 7,000 or 8,000 or more likely some 14,000 years" to the primitive cult of North Star worship. Estimating the big pyramid observed by Sheahan to be about 2,500 years old, Ackerman described it as possibly a religious site, possibly an emperor's tomb. She said that human sacrifices probably took place on its summit or within its sacred precinct. (*Science Digest,* Vol. 22, pp. 82-84, October 1947.)

Accounts of Colonel Sheahan's observations of the Shensi pyramids were published in a number of U.S. newspapers, often in association with the photo of the large one reproduced on page 128 of this text. The pyramid was described as approximately 1,000 feet high and 1,500 feet wide at its base.

Professor Te-k'un Cheng of Cambridge University, author of the authoritative *Archaelogy in China,* identifies the large pyramid shown on page 128 as "one of the burial mounds of the Han 202BC—220 AD emperors to the northwest of Sian," but Professor Cheng says reports of its size have probably been exaggerated. "There are 10 or 11 mounds in the region," he writes, "and most of them have a flat top like the one in your photograph."

*Nagel's Encyclopedia-Guide: China* (1968, 1973) lists a number of imperial tombs and burial mounds in the Sian region. It identifies one of the largest and oldest as that of Shih-huang-ti, (d. 210 BC), founder of the Ch'in Dynasty and connector-builder of the Great Wall. His tomb is described as about 1,500 feet wide at its base and 260 feet high.

Joint Operations Map NI-49-51, Series 1501, Sheet NI 49-5, Edition 1, prepared by the U.S. Department of Defense and published by the U.S. Army Topographic Command in 1968 locates fifteen "pyramids" in the vicinity of Sian.

Since Schroder's time there, access to the Sian region by foreigners has been severely limited, first by the turmoil of civil wars, then by World War II, then by the struggle between Communists and Nationalists which followed, more recently by the restrictive policies of the Chinese government. However in 1973 a group of American archaeologists and art historians visited Sian under government auspices. They saw and photographed numerous pyramidal shaped burial mounds of enormous size. And in 1975 the Peking government announced the discovery of a burial pit associated with the tomb of China's first emperor Shih-huang-ti (see above) near Sian. The pit was said to cover an area of almost eight square miles. Among the first relics uncovered were 530 lifesize ceramic warrior figures and twenty-four horses arranged in military formation. The helmeted and armored figures carried real bows and arrows or held real swords, spears, and crossbows. Chariots were drawn by four lifesize horses. Spectro-analysis showed the double-edged bronze swords to consist mainly of copper-tin alloy plus thirteen other elements. They were shiny, unstained by time. In addition many iron farm tools, gold, jade and bone objects, as well as linen, silk fabrics, leather, and wooden vehicles were discovered. Excavations are continuing.

### V. References to Kumbum Lamasery and Its Tree of Faces.

The French priests Huc and Gabet saw the tree in the 1840s. Afterwards Huc wrote (*Travels in Tartary, Tibet, and China, 1844-1846,* II, pp.53-55): "At the foot of the mountains on which the Lamasery stands and not far from the principal Buddhist temple, is a great square enclosure formed by brick walls. Upon entering we were able to examine at leisure the marvelous tree, some of the branches of which had already manifested themselves above the wall. Our eyes were first directed with earnest curiosity to the leaves, and were filled with an absolute consternation of astonishment at finding that, in point of fact, there were upon each of the leaves well-formed Tibetan characters, all of a green colour, some darker, some lighter than the leaf itself."

After careful examination of several leaves and of the bark Huc and Gabet noted that the "characters all appeared to us portions of the leaf itself, equally with its veins and nerves . . . The bark of the tree and its branches, which resembled that of a plane [sycamore] tree, are also covered with these characters."

When they peeled away the outer bark, "the young bark under it exhibited indistinct outlines of characters in a germinating state."

Huc and Gabet began to perspire with astonishment but their careful examination revealed no explanation of the mystery and no evidence of fraud. The tree appeared to them very old. "Its trunk, so big around that three men joining hands would not have embraced it, was no more than eight feet high and its branches, instead of shooting up, spread out like bushy plumes or feathers . . . The wood which was reddish, had an exquisite odor like cinnamon. The lamas said that in summer it produced large red flowers and that no tree like it existed anywhere else and that many attempts to propagate it elsewhere from cuttings and seeds had all failed."

Rockhill, who saw the tree (or trees) in 1889 described them as follows (*Land of the Lamas,* pp. 66-68): "In front [of the temple] inclosed by a low wooden paling is one of the sacred 'white sandalwood trees' (*tsandan karpo*), but not the most sacred one which is in a special inclosure . . . " The special high-walled inclosure contained three trees about twenty-five feet high. "These are the famous trees of Kumbum, or rather tree, for to the central one only is great reverence shown, as on its leaves appear outline images of Tsong-k'apa. The trees are probably, as conjectured by Kreitner, lilacs (*Philadelphus coronarious*); the present ones are a second growth, the old stumps being still visible. There were unfortunately no leaves on the tree when I saw it; and on the bark, which in many places was curled up like birch or cherry bark, I could distinguish no impress of any sort, although Huc says that images (of Tibetan letters, not images of the god) were visible on it. The lamas sell the leaves, but those I bought were so much broken that nothing could be seen on them. I have it, however, from Mohammedans that on the green leaf these outline images are clearly discernible. It is noteworthy that whereas Huc found letters of the Tibetan alphabet on the leaves of this famous tree, there are now seen only images of Tsong-k'apa (or the Buddha?). It would be interesting to learn the cause of this change."

David-Neel, who saw the tree (or trees) in the early 1920s, says in her *Magic and Mystery in Tibet,* pp. 110-113, that she observed neither writing nor faces in its leaves but tells of others who had done so.

Writing in the 1940s a few years before travel restrictions and censorship were imposed by the Chinese Communists, Dr. Y.P. Mei of Yenching University reported a sacred tree alive and well at Kumbum. Like Schroder, Mei was skeptical of what he saw and heard and took some unauthorized liberties. "The holy of holies at Kumbum consists of the two gold-roofed chapels and the sacred tree. The tree is believed to have grown on the spot where Tsong-ka-pa's placenta was buried. Our lama guide insisted that each leaf was a likeness of the great master and that Providence had inscribed a holy script on the trunk of the tree. The Tibetan letters on the tree at first mystified us not a little. But, with a curious mind, I did the forbidden thing behind the back of our guides and tried out the blunt edge of my knife. Lo and behold, with a little practice I was able to produce any mark or character in any language I liked. But, since we were, after all, visitors enjoying the hospitality of our lama hosts, I did not wish to embarrass and offend them by calling the bluff." (*Asia,* December 1941, p. 678.)

## VI. Obituary of Dr. F.D.C. Meyer.

Dr. Fred D. C. Meyer, a pioneer stock raiser of the county and one of its earliest settlers, died in his little three-room cottage at Descanso shortly after noon yesterday. He was about 70 years of age. . . . At one time Dr. Meyer possessed large tracts of land in the vicinity of Descanso and was reckoned a wealthy man, but he lost all and at the time of his death was living in rented quarters. He came to California nearly 40 years ago, following the civil war. During the four years of the struggle between the north and the south he served as a Union soldier . . . As far as is known, the old pioneer had no living relatives in this country. He was a German by birth and came to the United States when a young man . . . " (*The San Diego Union,* Sept. 1, 1910.)

A more extensive account of Dr. Meyer's life, in which he is referred to as a "millionaire cattle man," appeared in company with his photograph in the *Union* for October 26, 1919, p. 9.

## VII. References to collecting specimens for the Smithsonian Museum

### AMERICAN CONSULAR SERVICE

Harbin, China, September 11, 1915.

TO WHOM IT MAY CONCERN:

This is to certify that the bearer, F.M. Schroder, is a citizen of the United States, known to and under the protection of this Consulate. He is assisting Mr. Arthur Sowerby in the collection of specimens of zoological and scientific interest for the Smithsonian Institute of the United States Government along the Chinese Eastern Railway, and in the lawful pursuit of his affairs I earnestly request for him the assistance and courtesy of all local officials, both Russian and Chinese, who may have relations with him.

C. K. Moser

Consul of the United States of America.

## VIII. References to German Attempt to Sabotage Trans-Siberian Railway, 1915.

In Hintze's report of the attempt to blow up the Baikal tunnels *(The German Foreign Ministry Archives, 1867-1920. World War I, No. 11m, Secret, Undertakings and Provocations against our enemies in Siberia, September 1914–December 31, 1916.* [Weltkrieg Nr. 11m, Geheim, Unternehumungen und Aufwiegelungen gegen unsere Feinde in Siberien, 9.14—31.12.16] Microfilm, Saint Antony's College, Oxford, *sa Reel 30,* National Archives, Washington, D.C.) he says he received his information from a "confidant" and that the bodies of the "murdered" party were "buried." In brief what happened was this: In the winter of 1914, the Imperial German government, concerned about the vast amount of war material (heavy guns, other weapons, ammunition) going from Japan via Mukden over the Trans-Siberian Railway to the Russian western front, ordered the German military attaché in Peking, Captain Rabe von Pappenheim, to interrupt this traffic permanently by destroying the Railway.

In late February 1915, therefore, the attaché outfitted a "hunting" and "scientific" expedition to go to Inner Mongolia. The expedition consisted of seven Europeans, a goodly number of Chinese and Mongols, twenty camels and a large stock of munitions. By mid-March it had reached Tsitsihar.

The British news agency monopoly in Asia, *Reuters,* picked up the information of the expedition and exposed it in the European press. Shortly thereafter, British official efforts to embarrass the German Legation by forcing the Chinese government to demand the recall of the German officials, failed.

At the end of April, *Reuters* reported that Pappenheim and party had been murdered. On May 7th the Danish envoy in Peking notified his government to this effect also. But later in the month, the German minister in Peking, Admiral von Hintze, wired Berlin that Pappenheim was still alive, had abandoned the project and was proceeding to Constantinople via Afghanistan. In July, Hintze wired Berlin again to ask if the attaché had reached Constantinople. By November 2nd, however, the murder was confirmed in a telegram of Hintze to Berlin: "The latest report of reliable confidant, Pappenheim and companions murdered in the night and his papers as proof delivered in Charbin [Harbin]. Pappenheim, while in Inner Mongolia near salt sea north of Dolomar, had hired more escorts who were from Outer Mongolia, in Russian pay, and did the murder."

## IX. References to International Red cross caravan carrying supplies to Siberian prisoner-of-war camps.

### LEGATION OF THE UNITED STATES OF AMERICA

Prince Koudacheff
    Russian Minister,
                                   Peking, January 26, 1917.

My dear Colleague:

May I make known to you and bespeak your assistance in behalf of Mr. Fred M. Schroder, an American citizen who is presenting himself at your Legation to request the visa of his passport, to enable him to proceed by caravan to Kiakhta and Verkne-Udinsk and thus back to China by the Trans-Siberian Railway. The local Committee of the American Red Cross, working under the supervision of this Legation, is endeavoring to make arrangements for the transport by caravan, via Urga and Kiakhta, for a quantity of relief supplies to be delivered to the camps of prisoners of war at Troitzkosavsk, Verkne-Udinsk Park and Verchne-Udinsk Beresofka (and possibly Irkutsk and Innokentievskaia, via Baikal Lake). The arrangements for this purpose are now under consideration between the Russian Government and our Embassy at Petrograd; and if these proposals are approved, Mr. Schroder will be in charge of the caravan carrying the relief supplies.

I remain, my dear Prince Koudacheff,

Very sincerely yours,

Paul S. Reinsch

[242]

## X. References to the Abortive Restoration of the Manchu Dynasty, 1917.*

*Pu-Yi's dynastic title as Manchu Emperor was Hsuan-Tung, sometimes spelled Hsun Tung.*

From *The New York Times,* 1917:

LONDON, July 2.—General Chang Hsun, says a Reuters dispatch from Peking, has informed President Li Yuan-Hung that he must retire, as the Manchu Emperor. Hsun Tung, as been restored to the throne.

Another Reuters dispatch from Peking says that Hsun Tung issued a mandate Saturday morning announcing his succession to the throne of China.

There appears to be no substantial evidence of Germany or any other foreign power backing the restoration (see Bibliography: Reinsch, Anderson, Brackman, Johnston, etc.), although Reinsch (p. 279) mentions "certain Germanic affiliations of Chang Hsun." Reinsch further states (pp. 275-276) that the successful opposition to the restoration was financed by Japan, also (p. 286) that by secret agreement with France, England, and Italy, Japan was given a free hand in China at the conclusion of World War I. While unsympathetic and believing the restoration doomed to failure, Reinsch as U. S. minister at Peking did not actively oppose it. He thought it might have succeeded under better leadership.

## PROOFS OF GERMAN HELP

*Peking, July 14.*

A number of incidents during the past few days substantiate the previous reports that Chang Hsun received help from the Austrians and Germans in the matter of the Restoration. In fact it is believed in some quarters that he was actually bought by Germany. This assertion appears to be borne out by the fact that just before the Restoration Chang Hsun circulated a telegram denouncing Liang Chi-chao and Tang Hua-lung for favouring the declaration of war against Germany, declaring that they had created numerous difficulties in China's foreign relations and had stirred up internal disturbances in the country for personal gain, and demanding that they be declared outlaws.

The rather theatrical rescue of Chang Hsun's family and the rescue of Chang Hsun himself were obviously prearranged. It is reliably reported that a foreigner remained with Chang Hsun on Wednesday evening and Thursday morning. This was probably the Austrian or German who brought Chang Hsun into the Legation quarter when things became too hot. The commandants of the Legation guards had resolved that no Chinese should be permitted to enter the Legation quarter without a special pass. Whether this regulation was complied with in the case of Chang Hsun cannot be verified as he "naturally" was brought in through the entrance guarded by the Austrian marines.

*The North-China Herald,* July 21, 1917.

# AUTHOR'S ACKNOWLEDGMENTS

I am indebted to William Ashley Anderson who provided the impetus for my first meeting with Schroder. Anderson's later assistance was invaluable. I'm also grateful to the publishers of the original *True: The Man's Magazine* and of *Outdoor Life* for permission to use material which appeared in their magazines in somewhat different form, and to Cleaver Jones Salbach for her faithful aid during many interviews and exchanges of letters with Schroder; also to Crystal McQuesten Morgan who generously provided recollections and historical material from Alaska-Yukon Gold Rush days.

It is impossible to name all who have helped but I thank especially: G. F. MacMullen of the San Diego Historical Society; E. L. Keithahn of the Alaska Historical Society and Museum; M. Healy of the Colonial Secretariat, Hong Kong; Professor R. C. Rudolph of the University of California at Los Angeles; Sybil E. Hamlet of the National Zoological Park; Linda Johnson of the Yukon Archives at Whitehorse; John Edwards Hill of the British Museum (Natural History); Mrs. J. Craig, Archivist, Hudson's Bay Company, London; Father Albert Raskin, Archivist General, Casa Generalizia C.I.C.M., Rome; Marise Johnson of the Metropolitan Museum of Art, New York; Commander Richard T. Speer, Department of the Navy, Historical Center, Washington; L. J. Rowinski, Director of the Museum, University of Alaska, College, Alaska; Professor William R. Hunt also at College, Alaska; Frans August Larson; the Bodley Head Ltd. (for permission to use the photographs of the Tashi Lama and the Monastery at Kumbum from Alexandra David-Neel's book, *With Magicians and Mystics in Tibet*); the librarians at the University of California Libraries at Berkeley and Santa Barbara, and at the Santa Barbara Public Library and at the City of Westminster Central Library, St. Martin's Street, London; also James B. Rhoads of The National Archives, Washington, D.C.; the South Carolina Historical Society; E. K. Wiley of Esso Eastern Inc.; Irving Lee Palmer of Escondido, California; Paul Ellerbe, William Richardson, Jack Schaefer, and Kenneth Millar of Santa Barbara.

Also Professor and Mrs. Henry Adams; Professor C. Y. Chen; Pao-k'ang Ma; Adelia Whitson; Strohm and Catherine Newell; Ynez Haase; Josephine Green; Sandra McDonald; Alice Kladnik; Ernestine Brown and Robert D. Monroe of the University of Washington Library; Marion L. Buckner and Rhoda Kruse, librarians at the California Room, San Diego Public Library; Rebecca C. Bush, Reference Librarian, Yuma City-County Library, Yuma, Arizona; William Siemens, Reference Librarian at Anchorage Community College; and Wilma E. Pfeifer at the University of Alaska Library, Fairbanks.

Also Professors Charles D. Weber of the University of Southern California, James Cahill of the University of California at Berkeley, Prudence R. Myer of University of California, Santa Barbara, Dr. Wilma Fairbank of Cambridge, Mass., and Waldo Ruess of Santa Barbara. These are among many to whom I'm indebted.

—R. E.

# INDEX

[247]

McQuesten, Jack, 53, 54, 55, 59, 61, 74, *100,* 219. *See also* Appendix I

Malunga, 177-187

Mamen, Oscar, 114, 135, 137, 139, 165, *190,* 210, *215,* 229, 232. *See also* Appendix II

Mammoth Creek, 56

Manchuria/Manchurian: hunting in, 166-167, 168-169, 172-176; opium, 172-174; tobacco culture, 107; tigers, 79, 169, 170-171, 172-176, 222, 230; wild pigs, 168-169

Manley, Frank 54-56, 62, 63, 64, 65, 72, 73, 77, 79, 97, 220

Mann, Hunter, 161, 229

Mao-tse Tung, 144, 209

Marron, Juan, 26

Mastodon, 56-57, 219

Mastodon Creek, 56

Mayo, Al, 77. *See also* Appendix I

Meadows, Arizona Charlie, 75

Merle, Annie, 60

Meteor in Mongolia, 133

Mexico/Mexican: cattle ranch, 37-41; gun fights in, 33, 42; money, 40; relations with Yaquis, 25, 26; rurales, 34; rustlers, 34

Meyer, Frederick David Conrad (the Old Man), 11-20, 22-27, 29-36, 38, *44,* 49, 55, 157, 211, 217

Meyer's Grade, 36, 218

Miller Creek, 50

Miller, Joaquin, 75

Miller, Johnny, 50

Milu. *See* Deer, Pére David's

Mitchell, Skiff, 50, *216. See also* Appendix I

Mizner, Wilson, 76, 221

Mohammedan Rebellion, 145

Mongolia/Mongolian: bathing, 227;Black Horse Troop, 165, *190;* dispatch riders, 139; hairy wild man, 167-168; horse and camel racing, 160; hunting, 166-167; Inner, 138, 180, 209; mules, 143-144;

Outer, 138, 180; people, *102,* 133; Plateau, 129-131, 139; polo, 159-160; prayer wheels, 132; railroad, 158; resentment against China, 177-178; revolt against China, 129-131, 134, 137-139, 151, 165. *See also* Appendix II

Montana Pete, 61

Moose, 73, 97

Moosehide Mountain, 66, 77, *99*

Moran, Casey, 61

Morenci, Al, 60, 61. *See also* Appendix I

Moser, Charles K., 172

Mosquitoes, 52, 87, 219

Mountain lion, 19-23, 170

Mounties, Canadian (North-west Mounted Police), 55, 76, 151

Mt. St. Elias, 51

Mulcahy, Charlie, 81

Mules, 61, 120, 143-144, 226

Mu-Yan, *126,* 132-133

Nanking, China, 107, 115

Nestorian Stone, 146, 226

Niukluk: Eskimos, 83-86; River, 83, 84

Nome, Alas., 67, 81-82, 86, 89, 222

North Carolina, 106-107

Northern lights, 70, 220

Northwest Passage, 57

Oakland, Calif., 82, 91

Ogilvie, William, 70

Ophir, Alas., 91

Opium, 109, 172-174

Opium War, 174, 230

Ordos Desert, 144-145

Oregon Mare, 76, 221

Palm Springs, Calif., 26

Panchen (Tashi) Lama, 138, 146, 151-156, *188,* 225, 227

Pantages, Alexander, 76

Pao-ting-fu, China, *101,* 113, 115-123, 225

Peking China, 115-116, 124, 160, 192-208, 224, 231

Pemberton, Jonathan, 219

Pennoyer, Bess, 55

# BIBLIOGRAPHY

## I. MANUSCRIPTS, DOCUMENTS AND NEWSPAPER FILES

Alaska Historical Society and Museum. Documents and newspaper files.

Anderson, William Ashley. Personal papers, notes, documents, correspondence. Unpublished manuscript entitled "Fred M. Schroder." Miscellaneous writings in *Everybody's, The Saturday Evening Post, Bluebook,* pertaining to Schroder.

City of Westminster Public Libraries, Central Reference Library, St. Martin's St., London W.C. 2. Documents and records.

National Archives, Washington, D.C. Department of State Record Group 43, pp. 78-84. American Legation in China Records, File 711.4, Documents Nos. 3526, 3546, 3548, 3560, etc.

——. Office of the Secretary of Interior Record Group 48.

——. German Foreign Ministry Archives, 1867-1920. *World War I, No. 11m, Secret, Undertakings and Provocations Against our Enemies in Siberia, September 1914-December 31, 1916.* (Weltkrieg Nr. 11m, Geheim, Unternehumungen und Aufwiegulungen gegen unsere Feinde in Siberien, 9.14-31.12.16) Microfilm, Saint Antony's College, Oxford, *SA Reel 30.*

Palmer, Irving Lee. Manuscripts, records, maps, correspondence pertaining to "The Hulburd Grove Property" formerly known in part as "Dr. Meyer's Ranch" San Diego County, California, and to F.D.C. Meyer, Justin Robinson and Wallace Hulburd.

Royal Archives, Windsor Castle, Berkshire, England. Records pertaining to King Edward VII.

San Diego Historical Society. Documents, manuscripts, newspaper files.

San Diego Public Library. California Collection and newspaper files.

Schroder, Fred Meyer. Personal papers, notes, documents, correspondence.

South Carolina Historical Society. Documents, manuscripts, newspaper files.

Title Insurance and Trust Company, San Diego, California. Documents and records.

United States Department of Justice, Office of the Attorney General, Executive Office for the U.S. Marshals, files.

University of Alaska, Fairbanks. Archives.

University of California, Berkeley. Newspaper collection.

University of California, Santa Barbara. *New York Times* microfilm file.

University of Washington Library. Newspaper files.

Whitson, Adelia. Correspondence and newspaper clippings on the subject of early-day San Diego County and Fred M. Schroder.

Yukon Archives, Whitehorse, Yukon Territory. Documents and files.

## II. BOOKS, ARTICLES, AND MISCELLANEOUS PRINTED MATERIALS

Adney, Tappan. *The Klondike Stampede.* New York and London: Harper and Brothers, 1900. Reprinted as: *The Klondike Stampede of 1897-1898.* Fairfield, Washington: Ye Galleon Press, 1968.

American Tobacco Company. *"Sold American!"—The First Fifty Years.* Privately printed, 1954.

Anderson, William Ashley. *The Atrocious Crime of Being a Young Man.* Philadelphia: Dorrance & Co., 1973.

Andersson, Johan Gunnar. *The Dragon and the Foreign Devils.* Boston: Little, Brown, 1928.

Andrews, Roy Chapman. *Camps & Trails in China.* New York: D. Appleton & Co., 1918.

——*On the Trail of Ancient Man.* New York: G. P. Putnam's Sons, 1926.

——. *This Amazing Planet.* New York: G. P. Putnam's Sons, copyright 1937, 1938, 1939, 1940.

_____. *This Business of Exploring*. New York: G. P. Putnam's Sons, 1935.

_____. *Under a Lucky Star*. New York: The Viking Press, 1943.

Baum, Allyn. "Auroral Display Linked to Noises," *The Polar Times*, 55 (December 1962): 6.

Baumont, Maurice. *The Fall of the Kaiser*. London: Allen & Unwin Ltd., 1931.

Bawden, Charles R. *The Modern History of Mongolia*. New York: Frederick A. Praeger, 1968.

Beach, Rex. *Personal Exposure*. New York: Harper & Brothers, 1940.

_____. *Pardners*. New York: Doubleday, Page & Company, 1910.

_____. *The Spoilers*. New York: Harper & Brothers, 1906.

_____. "The Looting of Alaska." *Appleton's Booklover's Magazine*, 7 (January 1906): 5.

Beattie, Kim. *Brother, Here's a Man*. New York: The Macmillan Company, 1940.

Bell, Charles. *Tibet Past & Present*. Oxford: The Clarendon Press, 1924.

Berton, Pierre. *The Klondike Fever*. New York: Alfred A. Knopf, 1958.

_____. *Klondike*. Toronto: McClleland & Stewart, Ltd., 1972.

Bond, Marshall, Jr. *Gold Hunter*. Albuquerque: University of New Mexico Press, 1969.

Brackman, Arnold C. *The Last Emperor*. New York: Charles Scribner's Sons, 1975.

Brockett, R. W. *A History of the Ranchos of San Diego County, California*. San Diego: Union Title and Trust Co., 1939.

Bronowski, Jacob. *The Ascent of Man*. Boston: Little, Brown and Co., 1973.

Buck, Pearl S. *My Several Worlds*. New York: John Day Co., 1954.

Burnham, Major Frederick Russell. *Scouting on Two Continents*. Garden City: Doubleday, Page & Company, 1926.

Burns, A. R. *Money and Monetary Policy in Early Times*. New York: Alfred A. Knopf, 1927.

Burton, R. G. *The Book of the Tiger*. Boston: Houghton Mifflin Co., 1933.

Cadwallader, Sylvanus. (Benjamin P. Thomas, ed.) *Three Years With Grant*. New York: Alfred A. Knopf, 1955.

Carpenter, Frank G. *Alaska, Our Northern Wonderland*. New York: Doubleday, Page & Co., 1926.

Chang, Garma C. C. *Teachings of Tibetan Yoga*. Hyde Park: University Books, 1963.

Chang, Kwang-chih. *The Archaelogy of Ancient China*. New Haven: Yale University Press, 1968.

Channing, Fairfax C. G. *Siberia's Untouched Treasure*. New York: G. P. Putnam's Sons, 1923.

Chapman, Charles E. *A History of California: The Spanish Period*. New York: The Macmillan Co., 1939.

Cheng, Te-k'un. *Archaelogy in China*. Toronto: University of Toronto Press, 3 vols., 1959-1963.

Childs, Marquis. *Eisenhower: Captive Hero*. New York: Harcourt, Brace, and Co., 1958.

Clark, Henry W. *History of Alaska*. New York: The Macmillan Co., 1930.

Clark, Robert Sterling and Sowerby, Arthur de C. *Through Shên-Kan: The Account of the Clark Expedition in North China, 1908-9*. London and Leipsic: T. Fisher Unwin, 1912.

Cleland, Robert Glass. *A History of California: The American Period*. New York: The Macmillan Co., 1939.

Clements, Paul H. *The Boxer Rebellion*. New York: AMS Press, Inc. 1967.

Close, Upton. *In the Land of the Laughing Buddha*. New York: G. P. Putnam's Sons, 1924.

Colby, Merle. *A Guide to Alaska: Last American Frontier*. New York: The Macmillan Co., 1945.

Cronin, Edward W., Jr. "The Yeti," *The Atlantic*, 236 (November 1975): 47-53.

Crow, Carl. *Foreign Devils in the Flowery Kingdom*. New York: Harper & Brothers, 1940.

_____. *Four Hundred Million Customers*. New York: Harper & Brothers, 1937.

David-Neel, Alexandra. *With Mystics and Magicians in Tibet*. London: John Lane, 1931.

_____. *Magic and Mystery in Tibet*. New York: Dover Publications, 1971.

_____. *My Journey to Lhasa*. New York: Harper and Brothers, 1927.

Davis, Mary Lee. *Sourdough Gold*. Boston: W. A. Wilde Co., copyright 1930.

Dennison, Merrill. *Klondike Mike.* New York: William Morrow & Co., 1943.

Digby, Bassett. *Tigers, Gold, and Witch-Doctors.* New York: Harcourt, Brace & Co., copyright 1928.

Dolan, James M., Jr. "Ssu-pu-hsiang," *Zoonooz,* 43 (December 1970): 12-17.

Douglas, William O. "Journey to Outer Mongolia," *National Geographic,* (March 1962): 315.

Ekvall, Robert K. *Religious Observances in Tibet: Patterns and Functions.* Chicago: University of Chicago Press, 1964.

Elliot, Henry W. *Our Arctic Province.* New York: Charles Scribner's Sons, 1887.

Enders, Gordon B. with Edward Anthony. *Nowhere Else in the World.* New York: Farrar & Rinehart, 1935.

Estergreen, M. Morgan. *Kit Carson: A Portrait in Courage.* Norman: University of Oklahoma Press, 1962.

Evans-Wentz, W. Y. *The Tibetan Book of the Dead.* New York and London: Oxford University Press, 1960.

——. (ed.). *Tibetan Yoga and Secret Doctrines.* New York and London: Oxford University Press, 1958.

Forman, Harrison. *Through Forbidden Tibet.* New York: Longmans, Green & Co., 1935.

Franck, Harry A. *Wandering in Northern China.* New York: The Century Co., 1923.

Gilbert, Rodney. *What's Wrong With China.* New York: Frederick A. Stokes Co., 1926.

Gopi, Krishna. *The Secret of Yoga.* New York: Harper & Row, Publishers, 1972.

Grayzel, Solomon. *A History of the Jews.* Philadelphia: The Jewish Publication Society of America, 1947.

Grow, Malcolm C. *Surgeon Grow: An American in the Russian Fighting.* New York: Frederic A. Stokes Co., 1918.

Gruening, Ernest. *The State of Alaska.* New York: Random House, 1954.

Heizer, R. F., and Whipple, M. A. (cplrs. and eds.). *The California Indians.* Berkeley and Los Angeles: University of California Press, 1970.

Heller, Herbert L. (ed.). *Sourdough Sagas.* Cleveland and New York: World Publishing Co., 1967.

Heuvelmans, Bernard. *On the Track of Unknown Animals.* New York: Hill and Wang, 1959.

*History of San Diego County.* San Diego: San Diego Press Club, 1936.

Homer. *The Odyssey.* Translated by E. V. Rieu. Baltimore: Penguin Books, 1946.

Hoover, Herbert. *The Memoirs of Herbert Hoover.* 3 vols. New York: The Macmillan Co., 1951.

Hsü, Immanuel C. Y. *The Rise of Modern China.* New York: Oxford University Press, 1970.

Huc and Gabet. *Travels in Tartary, Thibet, and China, 1844-1846.* New York: Harper & Brothers, 1928.

Hutchison, James Lafayette. *China Hand.* Boston: Lathrop, Lee and Shepard Co., 1936.

Jennison, George. *Noah's Cargo.* New York: The Macmillan Co., 1928.

Johnston, Reginald F. *Twilight in the Forbidden City.* New York: D. Appleton-Century Co., 1934.

Jordan, Jed. *Fool's Gold.* New York: The John Day Co., 1960.

Keyte, J. C. *The Passing of the Dragon.* London: Hodder and Stoughton, 1913.

Kramer, Paul (ed.). *The Last Manchu: The Autobiography of Henry Pu Yi, Last Emperor of China.* New York: G. P. Putnam's Sons, 1967.

Krausse, Alexis. *The Story of the Chinese Crisis.* London: Cassell and Co., Ltd., 1900.

Kroeber, Theodora. *Ishi.* Berkeley and Los Angeles: University of California Press, 1961.

Lake, Stuart N. *Wyatt Earp.* Boston: Houghton Mifflin Co., 1931.

LaMotte, Ellen N. *Peking Dust.* New York: The Century Co., 1919.

Larson, Frans August. *Larson, Duke of Mongolia.* Boston: Little Brown, and Co., 1930.

Le Munyon, Ethan C. "The Lama's Motor-Car," *National Geographic,* 24 (May 1913): 641-670.

Lo, Jung-Pang (ed.). *K'ang Yu-Wei: A Biography and a Symposium.* Tucson: University of Arizona Press, 1967.

London, Charmian. *The Book of Jack London.* 2 vols. New York: The Century Co., 1921.

Lung, Edward B. as told to Ella Lung Martinsen. *Black Sand and Gold.* New York: Vantage Press, 1956.

Lynch, Jeremiah. *Three Years in the Klondike,* ed. Dale L. Morgan. Chicago: R.R. Donnelley & Sons Co., 1967.

MacGregor, John. *Tibet: A Chronicle of Exploration.* London: Routledge and Kegan Paul, 1970.

McKeown, Martha Ferguson. *The Trail Led North.* New York: The Macmillan Co., 1949.

McWhirter, Norris and McWhirter, Ross. *Guinness Book of World Records.* New York: Sterling Publishing Co., 1974.

Maisel, Albert Q. "The Riddle of the 'Abominable Snowman'," *Reader's Digest,* 74 (May 1959): 55-60.

Martin, Douglas D. *Yuma Crossing.* Albuquerque: University of New Mexico Press, 1954.

Morenus, Richard. *Alaska Sourdough.* New York: Rand McNally & Company, 1956.

*Nagel's Encyclopedia-Guide: China.* Geneva: Nagel Publishers, 1968.

Nichols, Francis H. *Through Hidden Shensi.* New York: Charles Scribner's Sons, 1902.

Nichols, Jeannette Paddock. *Alaska.* Cleveland: The Arthur H. Clark Company, 1924.

O'Connor, Richard. *High Jinks on the Klondike.* New York: Bobbs-Merrill Company, 1954.

Orth, Donald J. *Dictionary of Alaska Place Names.* Washington, D.C., U.S. Government Printing Office, 1967 (Geological Survey Professional Paper 567).

Ossendowski, Ferdinand. *Beasts, Men and Gods.* New York: E. P. Dutton and Co., copyright 1922.

Ostrander, Sheila and Schroeder, Lynn. *Psychic Discoveries Behind the Iron Curtain.* New York: Bantam Books, 1971.

Patterson, J. H. *The Man-Eaters of Tsavo.* London: Macmillan and Co., Ltd., 1921.

Phillips, R. A. J. *Canada's North.* New York: St. Martin's Press, 1967.

Polo, Marco. *Travels of Marco Polo.* Translated and edited by Henry Yule, edited by Henri Cordier. 2 vols. London: John Murray, 1921.

Pope, Saxton. *Hunting with the Bow and Arrow.* San Francisco: James H. Barry, Co., 1923.

Pourade, Richard F. *The Explorers.* San Diego: The Union-Tribune Publishing Co., 1960.

_____. *The History of San Diego: The Glory Years.* San Diego: The Union-Tribune Publishing Co., 1964.

Powell, Addison M. *Trailing and Camping in Alaska.* New York: Wessels & Bissell, 1910.

Ramacharaka, Yogi. *Fourteen Lessons in Yogi Philosophy and Oriental Occultism.* Chicago: The Yogi Publication Society, 1909.

Rasmussen, A. H. *China Trader.* New York: Thomas Y. Crowell Company, 1954.

Reinsch, Paul S. *An American Diplomat in China.* Garden City: Doubleday, Page & Company, 1922.

Richardson, H. E. *A Short History of Tibet.* New York: E. P. Dutton & Co., Inc. 1962.

Rockhill, William Woodville. *The Land of the Lamas.* New York: The Century Co., 1891.

Roerich, Nicholas. *Heart of Asia.* New York: Roerich Museum Press, 1930.

____. *Trails to Inmost Asia.* New Haven: Yale University Press, 1931.

____. *Altai-Himalaya.* New York: Frederick A. Stokes Company, 1929.

Rojas, A. R. *Lore of the California Vaquero.* Fresno: Academy Library Guild, 1958.

Sanderson, Ivan T. *Abominable Snowman: Legend Come to Life.* Philadelphia: Chilton Co., 1961.

*San Diego Yesterdays.* San Diego: The Book Committee, San Diego Chapter, D.A.R., 1921.

Satterfield, Archie. *The Chilkoot Pass Then and Now.* Anchorage: Alaska Northwest Publishing Co., 1973.

Scearce, Stanley. *Northern Lights to Fields of Gold.* Caldwell: The Caxton Printers, Ltd., 1939.

Shakabpa, Tsepon W. D. *Tibet: A Political History.* New Haven: Yale University Press, 1967.

Sherwood, Morgan B. (ed.). *Alaska and Its History.* Seattle: University of Washington Press, 1967.

Sims, Virginia Crowe. "But His Name Wasn't Manley," *Alaska Sportsman,* (May 1965) 14-15, 58-61.

Smythe, William E. *History of San Diego, 1852-1908.* San Diego: The History Company, 1908.

Stone, Irving. *Jack London: Sailor on Horseback*. Garden City: Doubleday & Co., 1938.

Stuck, Hudson. *A Winter Circuit of Our Arctic Coast*. New York: Charles Scribner's Sons, 1920.

Sullivan, May Kellogg. *A Woman Who Went to Alaska*. Boston: James H. Earle & Co., 1903.

Tannahill, Reay. *Food in History*. New York: Stein and Day, 1974.

*The Boxer Uprising: A History of the Boxer Trouble in China*. New York: Paragon Book Reprint Corp., 1967.

*The Complete Dog Book*. New York: Garden City Books, copyright 1935, 1938, 1941, 1942, 1947, 1949, 1951, 1954 by The American Kennel Club.

Thomas, James A. *A Pioneer Tobacco Merchant in the Orient*. Durham: Duke University Press, 1928.

———. *Trailing Trade a Million Miles*. Durham: Duke University Press, 1931.

Thomson, John Stuart. *China Revolutionized*. Indianapolis: Bobbs-Merrill Company, 1913.

Walden, Arthur Treadwell. *A Dog-Puncher on the Yukon*. London: T. Werner Laurie Ltd., 1928.

Walker, Franklin. *Jack London and the Klondike: The Genesis of an American Writer*. San Marino: The Huntington Library, 1966.

Walsh, James A. *Observations in the Orient*. Ossining, New York: Catholic Foreign Missionary Society, 1919.

Warner, Langdon. *The Long Old Road in China*. Garden City: Doubleday, Page & Co., 1926.

Waters, Frank. *The Earp Brothers of Tombstone*. New York: Clarkson N. Potter, 1960.

Weale, B. L. Putnam. *The Vanished Empire*. London: Macmillan and Company, 1926.

———. *The Reshaping of the Far East*. New York: Macmillan and Company, 1905.

Werner, E. T. C. *Autumn Leaves*. Shanghai: Kelly and Walsh, Ltd., 1928.

Wharton, David B. *The Alaska Gold Rush*. Bloomington: University of Indiana Press, 1972.

Wickersham, James. *Old Yukon*. Washington: Washington Law Book Co., 1938.

Williamson, Harold F. *Winchester: The Gun that Won the West*. Washington: Combat Forces Press, 1952.

Winslow, Kathryn. *Big Pan-Out*. New York: W. W. Norton Co., 1951.

Wright, Mary C. (ed.). *China in Revolution: The First Phase, 1900-1913*. New Haven and London: Yale University Press, 1968.

Yang, Lien-sheng. *Money and Credit in China*. Cambridge: Harvard University Press, 1952.

III. PERSONAL CORRESPONDENCE AND/OR INTERVIEWS

Roy Chapman Andrews, Pierre Berton, J. W. G. Brodie, Professor James Cahill, Professor Ralph Chaney, Professor Kwang-chih Chang, Professor C. Y.. Chen, Professor Te-k'un Cheng, William B. Christian, Daniel A. Conforti, Professor John J. Craighead, Arthur Eaton, Robert S. Elegant, Lulu Fairbanks, Victoria A. B. Faulkner, Mrs. H. C. Frederick, Jr., Maurice H. Getty, Manuel Gularte, E. Coke Hill, Professor Hans Nordewin von Koerber, F. D. C. Kracke, Frans August Larson and family, Anjanette Gregory Little, Alfred Lobley, Mr. and Mrs. Hugh McKie, Mrs. Tom McKinnon, Carrie McLain, Oscar Mamen, Jr., Hunter Mann, Frank R. Martin, Mrs. Perry Martinsen, Crystal McQuesten Morgan, James E. Morrow, Barry J. Nova, Professor Kuo-Yi Pao, C. T. Pedersen, A. A. Polet, Dick Racine, Professor R. C. Rudolph, Waldo Ruess, Bess Pennoyer Rutherford, Charles Sivertsen, Colonel Harry Snyder, Henry Swanson, Professor Charles D. Weber.

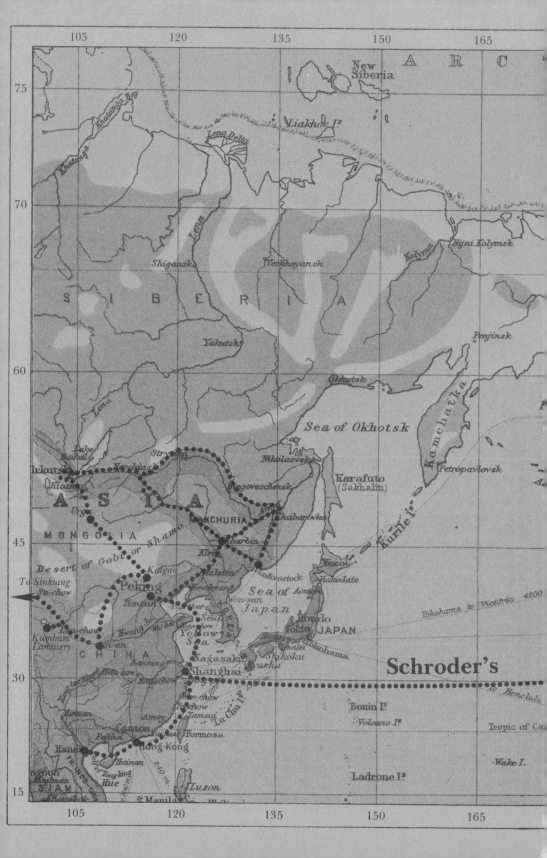